Dancehall In/Securities

This book focuses on how in/security works in and through Jamaican dancehall, and on the insights that Jamaican dancehall offers for the global study of in/security.

This collection draws together a multi-disciplinary range of key scholars in in/security and dancehall. Scholars from the University of the West Indies' Institute of Caribbean Studies and Reggae Studies Unit, as well as independent dancehall and dance practitioners from Kingston, and writers from the UK, US and continental Europe offer their differently situated perspectives on dancehall, its histories, spatial patterning, professional status and aesthetics.

The study brings together critical security studies with dancehall studies and will be of great interest to students, scholars and practitioners in theatre, dance and performance studies, sociology, cultural geography, anthropology, postcolonial studies, diaspora studies, musicology and gender studies.

Patricia Noxolo is a senior lecturer in the School of Geography, Earth and Environmental Sciences at the University of Birmingham, UK.

'H' Patten is an experienced choreographer, filmmaker, visual artist, storyteller and performer and has developed an international reputation in African and Caribbean arts for over 30 years.

Sonjah N. Stanley Niaah is a Jamaican cultural theorist, scholar-activist, author and an international speaker based at the University of the West Indies (UWI) at Mona, where she is a senior lecturer in cultural studies at the Institute of Caribbean Studies.

Routledge Advances in Theatre & Performance Studies

This series is our home for cutting-edge, upper-level scholarly studies and edited collections. Considering theatre and performance alongside topics such as religion, politics, gender, race, ecology, and the avant-garde, titles are characterized by dynamic interventions into established subjects and innovative studies on emerging topics.

ASHÉ
Ritual Poetics in African Diasporic
Paul Cater Harrison, Michael D. Harris, Pellom McDaniels

Dancehall In/Securities
Perspectives on Caribbean Expressive Life
Patricia Noxolo, 'H' Patten, and Sonjah N. Stanley Niaah

Circus and the Avant-Gardes
History, Imaginary, Innovation
Anna-Sophie Jürgens and Mirjam Hildbrand

Aesthetic Collectives
On the Nature of Collectivity in Cultural Performance
Andrew Wiskowski

Dance Data, Cognition and Multimodal Communication
Carla Fernandes, Vito Evola and Cláudia Ribeiro

Theatre and the Virtual
Genesis, Touch, Gesture
Zornitsa Dimitrova

For more information about this series, please visit: www.routledge.com/Routledge-Advances-in-Theatre – Performance-Studies/book-series/RATPS

Dancehall In/Securities
Perspectives on Caribbean Expressive Life

Edited by Patricia Noxolo, 'H' Patten and Sonjah N. Stanley Niaah

LONDON AND NEW YORK

First published 2022
by Routledge
4 Park Square, Milton Park, Abingdon, Oxon OX14 4RN

and by Routledge
605 Third Avenue, New York, NY 10158

Routledge is an imprint of the Taylor & Francis Group, an Informa business

© 2022 selection and editorial matter, Patricia Noxolo, 'H' Patten and Sonjah N. Stanley Niaah: individual chapters, the contributor

The right of Patricia Noxolo, 'H' Patten and Sonjah N. Stanley Niaah to be identified as the authors of the editorial material, and of the authors for their individual chapters, has been asserted in accordance with sections 77 and 78 of the Copyright, Designs and Patents Act 1988.

All rights reserved. No part of this book may be reprinted or reproduced or utilised in any form or by any electronic, mechanical, or other means, now known or hereafter invented, including photocopying and recording, or in any information storage or retrieval system, without permission in writing from the publishers.

Trademark notice: Product or corporate names may be trademarks or registered trademarks, and are used only for identification and explanation without intent to infringe.

British Library Cataloguing-in-Publication Data
A catalogue record for this book is available from the British Library

Library of Congress Cataloging-in-Publication Data
Names: Noxolo, Patricia, editor. | Patten, H., editor. | Stanley Niaah, Sonjah, 1970– editor.
Title: Dancehall in/securities: perspectives on Caribbean expressive life / edited by Patricia Noxolo, 'H' Patten and Sonjah Stanley Niaah.
Description: Abingdon, Oxon; New York, NY: Routledge, 2022. | Series: Routledge advances in theatre & perfromance | Includes bibliographical references and index.
Identifiers: LCCN 2021046966 (print) | LCCN 2021046967 (ebook) | ISBN 9781032071251 (hardback) | ISBN 9781032071268 (paperback) | ISBN 9781003205500 (ebook)
Subjects: LCSH: Dance—Social aspects—Jamaica. | Dance halls—Social aspects—Jamaica. | Poor—Jamaica—Social conditions. | Security (Psychology)—Jamaica. | Jamaica—Social life and customs.
Classification: LCC GV1632.J25 D36 2022 (print) | LCC GV1632.J25 (ebook) | DDC 306.4/84—dc23/eng/20211025
LC record available at https://lccn.loc.gov/2021046966
LC ebook record available at https://lccn.loc.gov/2021046967

ISBN: 978-1-032-07125-1 (hbk)
ISBN: 978-1-032-07126-8 (pbk)
ISBN: 978-1-003-20550-0 (ebk)

DOI: 10.4324/9781003205500

Typeset in Bembo
by Apex CoVantage, LLC

For all our families and friends, and all those who live, dance and work in dancehall spaces.

Contents

Notes on contributors	ix
Foreword – 'pull up!': confronting dancehall in/security	xiii
CAROLYN COOPER	
Preface	xvi
PATRICIA NOXOLO	
Notes on style	xviii
Introduction	1
PATRICIA NOXOLO, 'H' PATTEN AND SONJAH N. STANLEY NIAAH	

1 **Corporeal in/securities in the dancehall space**   14
  PATRICIA NOXOLO

2 **Practice, vision, security**   27
  ORVILLE 'XPRESSIONZ' HALL

3 **Me badi a fe me BMW (my body is my BMW): engaging the badi (body) to interrogate the shifting in/securities within the co-culture daaance'all**   36
  L'ANTOINETTE STINES

4 **Interrogating in/securities in the recording studios of Kingston**   55
  DENNIS HOWARD

5 **The mask for survival: a discourse in dancehall regalia**   66
  MONIKA LAWRENCE

viii *Contents*

6 **Dancehall dancing bodies: the performance of embodied in/security**   78
'H' PATTEN

7 **An in/secure life in dance; thoughts on dancehall's in/secure lives**   101
PATSY RICKETTS

8 **The warrior wine – the rotation of Caribbean masculinity**   107
THOMAS "TALAWA" PRESTO

9 **'Sounding' out the system: noise, in/security and the politics of citizenship**   130
SONJAH N. STANLEY NIAAH

Index   150

Notes on contributors

Carolyn Cooper

Carolyn Cooper is Emerita Professor at the University of the West Indies (UWI). She conceived the Reggae Studies Unit at the UWI, Mona, which was established in 1994 and has hosted numerous public lectures and symposiums featuring reggae/dancehall artists and other practitioners in the music industry in Jamaica and internationally. Professor Cooper founded the Annual Bob Marley Lecture in 1997. The Reggae Studies Unit has also convened academic conferences, including the annual Global Reggae Conference, the plenary papers for the first of which are collected in *Global Reggae* (2012), edited by Cooper and published by the University of the West Indies Press. With Dr Eleanor Wint, Cooper co-edited *Bob Marley: The Man and His Music* (2003). Cooper is also internationally recognised for the innovative books *Noises in the Blood: Orality, Gender and the 'Vulgar' Body of Jamaican Popular Culture* (1993) and *Sound Clash: Jamaican Dancehall Culture at Large* (2004).

Orville 'Xpressionz' Hall

Orville 'Xpressionz' Hall – known as the Dancehall Professor – is one of the best-known names in dance and dancehall in Jamaica. He is the artistic director for Theatre Xpressionz, which is a professional company that operates the popular dance group Dance Xpressionz and Xpressive Moves dance workshops. Orville is also the resident and chief judge for Jamaica's premier dance programme 'Dancing Dynamite'. Orville holds an associate degree in performing arts with a double major in dance and drama. Together with Patsy Ricketts and Kenny Salmon, Orville also wrote the first institutional dancehall course in the Caribbean. Today Orville 'Xpressionz' Hall is one of the chief choreographers of music videos and corporate functions in Jamaica.

Dennis Howard

Dennis Howard has worked in the creative industry for almost 30 years. Howard has a PhD in cultural studies and ethnomusicology from the University of the West Indies. He is the managing director of the Institute of Cultural Policy and Innovation. His research has been presented in the United States, Brazil, the United Kingdom, Mexico, South Africa and several Caribbean Islands. He is a member of the Jamaica Association of Composers, Authors, and Publishers, the Jamaica Music Society and the International Association for the Study of Popular Music. Howard has written numerous articles and books, including *The Creative Echo Chamber: Contemporary Music Phenomenon* and *Rantin From Inside the Dancehall*.

MoniKa Lawrence

Dr. MoniKa Lawrence holds a PhD in Cultural Studies from the University of the West Indies. She has also studied in the USA, South Africa and Israel. Dr. Lawrence is an Associate Professor and Artistic Director of the Performing Arts at The University College of the Cayman Islands. She brings a wealth of experience in teaching, performing and artistry in the development and introduction of courses in dance, cultural studies and related areas. Prior to joining University College of the Cayman Islands, Dr. Lawrence taught as an Adjunct Lecturer and Artistic Director for the Centre of the Performing Arts at University of Technology in Jamaica. She has also worked extensively with the Government of Jamaica in developing creative concepts, choreography, creative consultant, and costume designer and management for most major Government functions in Jamaica. Dr. Lawrence is founder and Artistic Director of The Stella Maris Dance Ensemble of Jamaica, which was founded in 1994 and is renowned for its innovative presentations both internationally and locally in Jamaica.

Sonjah N. Stanley Niaah

Former Director of the Institute of Caribbean Studies at the UWI at Mona, and the inaugural Rhodes Trust Rex Nettleford Fellow in Cultural Studies (2005), Sonjah N. Stanley Niaah is Senior Lecturer in cultural studies at the UWI, Mona Campus. She is a leading author, teacher and researcher on Black Atlantic performance geographies, popular culture and the sacred, and Caribbean cultural studies more broadly. Stanley Niaah is the author of Reggae Pilgrims: Festivals and the Movement of Jah People (forthcoming Rowman and Littlefield), Dancehall: From Slave Ship to Ghetto (2010, University of Ottawa Press), and editor of Dancehall: A Reader on Jamaican Music and Culture and 'I'm broader than Broadway: Caribbean perspectives on producing celebrity' (Wadabagei, Vol. 12: 2, 2009). Dr Stanley Niaah has served as Vice Chair of the International Association for Cultural Studies for which she coordinated the first conference held in the Global South at the UWI (2008). Stanley Niaah has and currently serves on the boards and editorial collectives of numerous academic associations, institutions, and journals including Cultural Studies, The Black Scholar and DanceCult.

Patricia Noxolo

Patricia Noxolo is Senior Lecturer at the University of Birmingham, UK. Her research brings together the study of international development, culture and in/security, and uses postcolonial, discursive and literary approaches to explore the spatialities of a range of Caribbean and British cultural practices. Her recent work has focused on: re-theorising Caribbean in/securities, theorisations of space in Caribbean literature, Caribbean laughter and materialities, re-thinking the decolonial city, and African-Caribbean dance as embodied mapping. Patricia Noxolo is a lead researcher on the Caribbean In/Securities and Creativity (CARISCC) research network, funded by the Leverhulme Trust, and on Creative Approaches to Race and In/Security in the Caribbean and the UK (CARICUK), funded by the Arts and Humanities Research Council. She is a former chair of the Society for Caribbean Studies, co-editor of Transactions of the Institute of British Geographers, and secretary of the RACE group of the Royal Geographical Society. She is also the author and editor of a number of books and articles, including a collection on Caribbean In/Securities in Small Axe, 2018, 22, 3.

'H' Patten

'H' Patten is an experienced choreographer, filmmaker, visual artist, storyteller, performer and University lecturer, with a PhD degree from Canterbury Christ Church University. The founder and Artistic Director of Koromanti Arts he has developed an international reputation in African and Caribbean arts for over 30 years. 'H' has worked with the Jamaica School of Dance, the Jamaica National Dance Company (NDTC), L'Acadco, the University of Technology (UTECH) and the African Caribbean Institute of Jamaica (ACIJ). The recipient of several awards including the Jamaican High Commission 50th Anniversary Award for services in Arts, Culture and Entertainment (2012), 'H' has choreographed for Stella Maris Dance Ensemble (Jamaica), and the National Dance Companies of Ghana, Nigeria, Sierra Leone, Malawi and Zambia, as well as UK companies: Adzido Pan African Dance Ensemble, Kokuma Performing Arts, and Irie! dance theatre, in addition to high-profile projects such as the British Council's Queen's Golden Jubilee project (West Africa). Having authored multiple articles and chapters, including 'Feel De Riddim, Feel De Vibes: dance as a transcendent act of survival and upliftment' (2016) Adair, C. and Burt, R. (eds.) *British Dance: Black Routes*, Routledge, Oxon, New York, 'H' is currently completing his own book, *'Reading Religion and Spirituality in Jamaican Reggae Dancehall Dance: Spirit Bodies Moving'* (2022) for Routledge publishing. He is presently an Independent Social Research Foundation (ISRF) Independent Scholarship Fellow, hosted by Goldsmiths University.

Thomas 'Talawa' Prestø

Thomas 'Talawa' Prestø is an internationally renowned lecturer, instructor, choreographer and performer. Thomas is the founder and Artistic Director of Tabanka Dance Ensemble and creator of the Talawa Technique™. He holds a Master Degree in Choreography from the Oslo National Academy of the Arts and is currently doing a doctorate in decolonial dance performance at Østfold University. His doctoral project is called Anansi's Web and particularly looks at 'Dancing in the pressure cooker' and marginalised Africana peoples use of Dance as resistance. Thomas has toured 28 countries with Tabanka Dance Ensemble and has held masterclasses in the Talawa Technique™ in 44 countries to date. Having successfully branded and profiled Africana dance technique and aesthetics Thomas is internationally sought after as a lecturer and consultant on audience development strategies. Talawa Technique™ structures elements of African and Caribbean practices uniquely designed to facilitate poly-centrism, multiple movement qualities, grounding and poly-rhythm. Prestø is intimate and initiated into indigenous Caribbean and African Spiritual practices in Haiti, Trinidad, Cuba, Jamaica, The Congo, Benin and Nigeria respectively. He therefore pulls strongly from these sources in his theoretical, practical and artistic work.

L'Antoinette Stines

L'Antoinette Stines is a dancer, choreographer, actress, teacher/lecturer, administrator, author and visionary, with a PhD degree from the UWI. Creator of L'Antech, a modern contemporary Caribbean dance technique, Stines continues to impact the direction and future of Caribbean dance as founder and creative director of L'Acadco, a contemporary dance company. Dr Stines has a long and varied performing history, which ranges from classical ballet to Yoruba 'Orisha' dance. Her dance career began in Jamaica with Alma Mok Yen (1961–71), continued to the Martha Graham School and finally to Pepsi Bethel Authentic Jazz Dance Company (1975–77) and the Alvin Ailey American Dance Theater (1977–78). Widely regarded as an expert in popular, folkloric Jamaican dance and the development of contemporary dance, Dr Stines has lectured in Africa, the Caribbean, Europe, and North and South Americas. She is also the author of numerous articles and books, including *Soul Casings: A Journey from Classical Ballet to the CARIMOD Daaance Technique L'Antech* (2014: Zight/L'Antoinette Stines Publishing).

Foreword – 'pull up!': confronting dancehall in/security

Grounded in the theory and practice of critical security studies, this compelling volume conceptualises dancehall culture as a primal site of contestation of the fundamental precarity institutionalised in Jamaican society. Down-market dancehall culture is routinely vilified by the elite as a violation of conventional norms of respectability. Rigid hierarchies of race, class, gender and sexual orientation often demarcate the spaces through which subaltern bodies can move without surveillance. Policing of dancehall events is designed to confine revellers within prescribed spatial and social boundaries that limit both verbal and corporeal freedom of expression. Conversely, the contributors to this book all acknowledge the therapeutic power of dance and, more broadly, dancehall culture as an emancipatory practice. The dancing body becomes a signifier of resistance against the crippling constraints of a supposedly 'post-colonial' society in which the lingering trauma of dehumanisation is manifested in a constant struggle for survival.

The ritual DJ command to 'pull up' – to pause and 'rewind' an on-stage performance – can be extended as a trope of interruption of conventional scholarship on dancehall culture. The reflexive and reflective pull-up and rewind challenge academics to rethink the ways in which we define disciplinary boundaries in general; and, more specifically, how we conceive the appropriate disciplinary perspectives from which to engage with dancehall culture. Much of the scholarship on dancehall has been located primarily in the intersecting fields of cultural studies and literary criticism. Originally rooted in the single discipline of literature, cultural studies has flourished into a trans-discipline, seemingly liberated from the regime of compulsory textual analysis. But textuality itself constantly assumes new forms, as is evident in the shapeshifting corpus of 'texts' that now constitutes the field of cultural studies.

Security studies provides a new perspective from which to view the substantial body of dancehall scholarship that has been consolidated over the last three decades. In November 1989, *Jamaica Journal* published the first academic paper on dancehall culture in the 1980s, "Slackness Hiding from Culture: Erotic Play in the Dancehall." The title was taken from the 1987 tune, "Culture a Lick" [Culture Is in Vogue], by dancehall DJ Josey Wales. I wrote that paper, appropriating the DJ's trope to investigate 'slackness', in its invariant coupling with 'culture,' as a politics of subversion. I argued that slackness is not mere sexual looseness – though it certainly is that. Slackness is an embodied revolt against repressive law and order; an undermining of consensual standards of decency.

"Slackness Done", also by Josey Wales, confirms the pressure felt by some DJs to self-protectively submit to the demands of respectability. The opening frame of the song, with its militaristic motif, defines the terms of the DJ's heroic and presumably suicidal mission – cleaning up the dance-hall:

> 'Colonel Joses Wales!'
> 'Yes, Commissioner.
> 'I would like yu to go into di dance-hall an clean up
> All dose slack DJ who is spoilin di kids of today'.

The DJ, faced with two mutually hostile orders of responsibility – that of the massive who require out-of-order lyrics, and that of the Commissioner of Police, the voice of official morality and social order – simply bows to the censorial authority of state power. Or so it seems. Ironically, the DJ's assumption of the persona of 'Colonel' itself confirms the mutability of dancehall culture. It becomes a domain to which the Commissioner must turn for assistance in policing slackness. Self-regulation by dancehall DJs becomes a potentially subversive practice.

That early essay evolved into the book *Sound Clash: Jamaican Dancehall Culture at Large* (2004). The sub-title signified both the global reach of dancehall and its constant evasion of restrictive policing practices. Self-protectively on the run! Marginalised bodies, both male and female, become victimised and their security is compromised. I explored the ways in which the "high/low" cultural divide that is endemic to Jamaican society is (re)produced in the hierarchical relations of gender and sexuality that pervade the dancehall. My critique of dancehall culture, from the perspective of literary studies, focused on the testimonies of dancehall DJs that are inscribed and recorded in their lyrics. Foregrounding the vulnerability of hard-core dancehall performers and fans in an increasingly militarised state, my textual analysis of dancehall lyrics anticipated the engagement with in/security that is the central preoccupation of the present volume.

Norman Stolzoff's *Wake the Town and Tell the People: Dancehall Culture in Jamaica* (2000), written from the disciplinary perspective of anthropology, a variant of cultural studies, methodically explores the ways in which the body becomes a site of creative expression: music, dance, poetry, fashion, film, graphic design – a whole array of aesthetic practices. Stolzoff also acknowledges the criminalisation of dancehall culture and the clash of values it engenders. Furthermore, he locates the genesis of contemporary dancehall politics in plantation slavery, thus delimiting the originary in/security at the very root of modern Jamaican society. Resistance to enslavement was manifested in a variety of cultural practices of African origin, particularly religion, dance and music that continuously reproduce themselves in new forms. A classic example is the re-emergence of Revival music in the riddims of the dancehall. The polarisation of the sacred and the secular in Western epistemology is contested in holistic Jamaican folk culture.

Donna Hope's *Inna Di Dancehall: Popular Culture and the Politics of Identity in Jamaica* (2006), located in cultural studies, offers a comprehensive taxonomy of dancehall culture. Examining the power dynamics in Jamaican society, Hope delineates the multiple insecurities that participants in dancehall culture must negotiate in order to sustain themselves and the culture. In *Man Vibes: Masculinities in the Jamaican Dancehall* (2010), she elaborates a typology of dancehall masculinity in which promiscuity, homophobia, violence, consumerism and, ultimately, insecurity are defining characteristics. From the perspectives of cultural geography, performance studies and cultural studies, Sonjah N. Stanley Niaah's *DanceHall: From Slave Ship to Ghetto* (2010) traces an even longer genealogy of dancehall culture than Stolzoff's. She excavates a history of in/security that extends back over centuries to the Middle Passage.

From the fringes of academia, dancehall scholarship has bubbled and wined to centre stage like a dancehall queen preening in the video light. From a variety of disciplinary perspectives, scholars have paid rigorous attention to a broad range of contentious issues: constructions of masculinity and femininity, the slackness versus culture binary, the politics of location, sound as a weapon of resistance against systemic brutalisation by state power, and dance as liberation. Furthermore, global networks of dis/empowerment and in/security compel citizens of economically impoverished societies like Jamaica to engage in predatory behaviour beyond purely individual volition. Critical security studies, as evidenced in this wide-ranging volume, explicitly engage and thus make the contestations about personhood that have recurred in the study of dancehall culture over the last three decades more visible.

Carolyn Cooper

Preface

This collection is the outcome of a workshop that was part of the Leverhulme-funded CARISCC interdisciplinary international network. The CARISCC network consists of seven academics – Dr Patricia Noxolo (University of Birmingham, UK), Dr Anyaa Anim-Addo (University of Leeds, UK), Dr Susan Mains (University of Dundee, UK), Dr Kevon Rhiney (Rutgers, The State University of New Jersey, USA), Dr David Featherstone (University of Glasgow, UK), Dr Rivke Jaffe (University of Amsterdam, the Netherlands) and Dr Ronald Cummings (Brock University, Canada). The network was funded to organise a series of international meetings and creative encounters over a three-year period (January 2016 to December 2018) to consider the relationships between security, insecurity and creativity, with a focus on how these concepts work together in the Caribbean region.

One of the international meetings, in February 2017, was focused on dancehall in/securities, and that was the foundation for this book. The meeting was organised on the Mona campus of the UWI in Kingston, Jamaica, in partnership with Dr 'H' Patten (Canterbury University, UK), and in collaboration with Dr Stanley Niaah and Professor Emerita Cooper of the UWI. From the outset, the aim of the workshop was to bring together not only the world-famous academics who have been researching dancehall in the Reggae Studies Unit (Dr Sonjah N. Stanley Niaah, Carolyn Cooper, and Donna Hope), but also the wealth of Kingston's notable dancehall academics who are also influential dance and music practitioners (Dr Dennis Howard, Dr L'Antoinette Stines, Dr MoniKa Lawrence, Dr Maria Smith), as well as dance practitioners who have been key to the development of dancehall and dance culture in the city (Orville 'Xpressionz' Hall, Shelley Expressionz, Patsy Ricketts). The presentations, dance demonstrations and fertile discussion coming out of that workshop laid the groundwork for the development of the concept of creative in/security that was one of the main outcomes of the CARISCC network. *Dancehall In/Securities* exists to continue this in-depth exploration of how in/security is negotiated in dancehall spaces.

We are very grateful for the hospitality of the Reggae Studies Unit of the UWI, without which this book could never have come to fruition. The workshop was timed to coincide with the fourth Global Reggae Conference, and we very much appreciated all the thoughtful and inspiring papers and conversations that the event engendered. We are also profoundly grateful to all those who opened up their homes and hearts to us at and around the February 2017 event: the names are too numerous to mention, but we can never repay your kindness. And this is an important point that we want you to bear in mind as you begin to read this collection – we have created a book called *Dancehall In/Securities* and we're very proud of it. But the point of this book is not to reinforce the all-too-common discourses that circumscribe Kingston as a violent and insecure place. In fact, one of the important contributions that *Dancehall In/Securities* makes is to give due consideration to the active everyday negotiation of a much wider range of securities and insecurities – for example, environmental, climatic and, in particular, livelihood in/securities – and to give full appreciation to the everyday agency and creativity that people in dancehall spaces display in walking all the lines between them.

Patricia Noxolo

Notes on style

The editors would like to draw attention to the distinctive range of voices and perspectives that feature in *Dancehall In/Securities*. The negotiation between security and insecurity is located and relational, but it is above all perspectival – what makes one person feel secure will make another person insecure, and the resources available to negotiate in/security are not the same for everyone. For this reason, *Dancehall In/Securities* takes pains to bring together a range of perspectives on Jamaican dancehall, including academics who research and theorise dancehall, dance practitioners who participate directly in dancehall, people who have been influential in dancehall through dance practice and dance education in Jamaica, and people who contribute to the music industry and legislative frameworks on which dancehall relies. Each of the contributors is theorising in/security in dancehall from their own standpoint, drawing on their own research and experience. Many chapters are very explicit about this; at some point in their chapters, they each state their relationship with dancehall, which is often one of many years of research, through both theory and practice. Unavoidably, given that dancehall is a set of practices firmly centred on Kingston, albeit with a global reach, many contributors are familiar with each other's work and with each other's lives; they have worked together, danced together, disagreed with each other, and influenced each other's work and perspectives. When read in dialogue, these relationships and contestations are often visible in the chapters. Moreover, for most contributors, there is something personally at stake in the study of dancehall and its in/securities – for example, Pestø speaks of the physical danger involved in his embodied position as a wining man, whilst Stines speaks of her resistance as a choreographer to the marginalisation of Jamaican dancehall artists in favour of foreign choreographers. In all these senses, *Dancehall In/Securities* is not a disinterested or detached collection of essays, nor does it aim to be.

The range of perspectives in *Dancehall In/Securities* has resulted in a range of different kinds of contributions. Some contributions are short interventions, whilst others are much longer reflections. Similarly, the chapters differ in their writing style: some pieces are written in a dense, academic style that varies in relation to the disciplinary base of their author (geography, theology or dance studies, for example); others are written in a looser, more autobiographical style. As an editorial team, we have recognised that editorial decisions are also negotiations, and we have made decisions not to smooth out these differences. To make the collection more accessible for an international audience, we have cut down on repetitions that are common in Jamaican forms of oral English, and we have standardised many, but not all, spellings. However, our decision to respect the range of writing styles is a decision to respect and present dancehall as a polyvocal, and intrinsically Jamaican, expressive space. We hope that you will enjoy your negotiation with its in/securities.

Introduction

*Patricia Noxolo, 'H' Patten and
Sonjah N. Stanley Niaah*

Jamaica is a small island with a big global impact. Apart from the sunshine that tourists flock to and its wide range of diasporic and geopolitical connections, Jamaica regularly hits the global headlines for the profound and diffuse creativity of its music and dance, particularly reggae and dancehall, but also for the violence and insecurity that have plagued the downtown area of Kingston. This book brings both of these persistent global impacts together, focusing on how in/security works in and through Jamaican dancehall, and on the insights that Jamaican dancehall offers for the global study of in/security.

This book draws together a multi-disciplinary range of key scholars in in/security and dancehall. Scholars from the University of the West Indies' Institute of Caribbean Studies and Reggae Studies Unit, independent dancehall and dance practitioners from Kingston, as well as writers from the UK and continental Europe offer their differently situated perspectives on dancehall (its histories, spatial patterning and aesthetics), and each chapter relates these various aspects to an active theorisation of in/security.

This introductory chapter briefly characterises the key concepts and contexts in which the book is located and then draws them together – in/security, reggae/dancehall culture, and then dancehall and in/security. Then, after a brief summary of each of the chapters in the collection, the chapter ends by exploring their intersections and linked themes.

In/security

Security is a global preoccupation of the twenty-first century. However, academic interest has moved in the last 20 years away from a sole focus on war and terrorism (in which governments define levels of security threat) towards more diffuse and banal existential threats, such as threats from climate change, poverty and global inequality (Roberts, 2010).

The concept of in/security draws on critical security studies (Huysmans, 2009; Noxolo and Huysmans, 2009), which, with the expansion of arenas of security, has expanded from political studies into other disciplines, including geography (Philo, 2012; Fluri, 2011; Aradau, 2008; Rhiney, 2018). In/security reconceptualises the lived experience of security and insecurity as an everyday negotiation between the

DOI: 10.4324/9781003205500-1

two. In other words, security and insecurity are understood as relational terms, rather than as polar oppositions. Most people, particularly those who are most vulnerable, walk a tightrope between security and insecurity in everyday life: they never find complete security (see Noxolo, 2017).

Violent in/security is an ongoing issue around the world, but in/security can also be understood in terms of wider precarity and uncertainties, such as livelihood in/securities, environmental in/securities and creative risk. The Leverhulme-funded CARISCC, and its Arts and Humanities Research Council funded the successor CARICUK,[1] focuses, in particular, on how in/security is negotiated in and through creative arenas such as literature, music and dance (see Noxolo, 2018).

Reggae/dancehall culture

The term 'dancehall' originates from the dance hall spaces and venues where people congregate and dance in celebration of the major birth-to-death lifecycle events. It provides a space in which individuals entertain themselves, release tensions, negotiate identity and gain profile. Above all, dancehall facilitates dancing, singing and music-making as an important survival mechanism for many disenfranchised and marginalised individuals. Conversely, 'dancehall' is also the discrete music and dance genre that emerged out of reggae from the late 1970s to the present. It is therefore both a phenomenon and a historical space that incorporates Jamaica's long genealogical trajectory of cultural expression from the present, going back through the quarters of enslaved Africans, beyond the Trans-Atlantic 'middle passage' slave-ship decks and dungeons, to multiple continental African rituals, spaces and events (see Stanley Niaah, 2010; Patten, 2016, 2022).

Dancehall is frequently characterised by its digital beats, developed from the embrace of new technology by Jamaican artists and technicians from the 1940s through the height of the 'sound system' era in the 1980s,[2] to the present. Sound systems, 'sounds' or 'sets' comprise powerful heavy wattage amplifiers and turntables connected to a number of multi-storey banks of speaker boxes, which were 'sometimes called house of joy' as Clinton Hutton (2007, p. 17) rightly expounds. These portable sets enable disenfranchised and marginalised people at the lower socio-economic end of society to entertain themselves and experience joy, whilst "striving for survival", to quote Bob Marley (Robert Nesta Marley) and the Wailers, one of Jamaica's best-known musical icons, taken from their 'Buffalo Soldier' (1983) anthem. Prince Buster, as a recording industry pioneer in boldly naming his sound, 'the Voice of the People' and describing sound systems as 'the people's radio station' (in Bradley, 2000, p. xv), aptly conveyed the importance of cultural expression as a survival strategy.

Sound systems continue to challenge hegemonic value systems by playing the music the Jamaican masses wish to hear and highlighting the issues that concern them through the voice and persona of the deejay (DJ). The DJs are modern-day Griots/orators/recording artists, from Count Machuki to Beenie

Man, through to the emerging young generation such as Grammy Award-winning Koffee, amongst numerous others. Their controversial lyrics foreground the plight of the poor, celebrate individual and group achievements, uplift and memorialise national and local heroes and heroines both past and present, as well as deliver slackness and violence to channel and release tensions. Thus, in/security has always been a part of dancehall dance and music culture.

As technology replaced live music bands (see White, 1984), it forced innovative developments within sound system culture, facilitating the growth of its participants. Dancehall participants consist of both practitioners and adherents. Practitioners include deejays, dancers, selectors, dancehall queens (DHQ), modellers/divas/flossers[3] and soundmen/women, who are also encompassed under the term participants, which further includes the audience, also termed the dancehall 'massive' or adherents, alongside the informal workers (food vendors, peanut sellers, stylists, barbers, hairdressers, dressmakers, tailors etc.). Dancehall has developed an increasingly informal economy. Consequently, it is now recognised as: a cultural identity, an informal and creative economy, a venue, music and dance, a language, fashion, an aesthetic, a geographical space, a community, a ritual, an attitude, a cultural and ideological phenomenon, and a technical and creative industry (Cooper, 1993; Stolzoff, 2000; Bakare-Yusuf, 2006; Hope, 2010; Stanley Niaah, 2010; Henriques, 2011; Howard, 2016; Patten, 2016; Fullerton, 2017).

Dancehall and in/security

The history of Jamaica and the Caribbean region is built upon the dichotomous relationship between security and insecurity in relation to place and space, socio-politico-economic issues and cultural expression (Abrahams and Szwed, 1983; Nettleford, 2003; Johnson and Soeters, 2008; Rediker, 2008; Charles, 2009). Many reggae/dancehall participants negotiate the obvious physical and ideological in/security of place and space on a daily basis. In attending dancehall events, numerous participants are forced to cross the insecure borders between home and alien neighbourhoods, frequently navigating dangerous and hostile gang-affiliated garrison territories (Stolzoff, 2000; Charles, 2002). In relation to the reggae/dancehall genre, in/security facilitates a redefinition of the lived experiences of security and insecurity within the 'livity' (daily lifestyle) of dancehall participants. Thereby, within an environment where the performance and performativity (the learnt or constructed behavioural actions) of dancehall practitioners frequently clash with that of 'normative' Jamaican hegemonic society, what secures one individual can often create insecurity for another.

Security and insecurity are relational. Dancehall may be perceived as being insecure because it emerges out of Jamaica, which being located within the Caribbean may epitomise for some, a geographically insecure region where hurricanes, tropical storms and health risks such as dengue fever and the Zika virus remain constant threats. Others are more concerned by its supposed "geopolitical significance as the USA's 'backyard' [which] has made it a recurring focus for western anxieties" (Noxolo and Featherstone, 2014, p. 604). A number of scholars have highlighted the historical convergence between Jamaican popular cultural expression, changing party politics and outside governmental influences on Jamaica's social and economic development (Campbell, 1987; Stolzoff, 2000; Hope, 2006; Howard, 2016). Against this backdrop dancehall participants may appear especially insecure as many live in underdeveloped and under-resourced volatile areas, facing varying levels of poverty, political tensions, real and ideological violence, whilst continually being marginalised and oppressed by the hegemonic structures that govern their society (Stolzoff, 2000; Hope, 2006). In/security in this study is therefore employed to move beyond normative notions of being secure. Focusing on the agency of those individuals who attempt to secure their lives through dancehall culture, which in turn often takes place in real and perceived insecure locations, this book explores how due to both its glocal and global appeal dancehall furnishes growing opportunities for many to gain security.

Chapter summaries

Chapter 1 sets out the concept of in/security in greater detail. Drawing on her experience with the CARISCC network, rather than as a dancehall practitioner or researcher, Patricia Noxolo offers a critical review of the work of some of the key theorists of dancehall – Sonjah N. Stanley Niaah, Carolyn Cooper, Donna Hope and Julian Henriques. Her chapter theorises corporeal negotiation of in/security and then applies this theorisation to dancehall spaces. She delineates the negotiative agency of dancehall bodies, in terms of their sonic, affective and visual meanings, with a view to mapping out a field of enquiry around embodied in/security in the dancehall space.

In Chapter 2, Orville 'Xpressionz' Hall reflects on his own experience as one of the foremost dancehall dancers. He takes us through the 1980s and 1990s, when both dancehall spaces and dancehall dances were shaped by the political violence that plagued downtown Kingston at that time, through to the early twenty-first century, when dancehall has become a truly global art form. From his own position as a key dancehall practitioner and teacher, Hall reflects on the impact of US dancehall parties and European dancehall tourism, and he raises profound issues around cultural in/security in relation to the appropriation and formalisation of dancehall moves, as well as describing successful initiatives to deploy dancehall as a means of securing livelihoods for people living in downtown Kingston.

In Chapter 3, L'Antoinette Stines draws on her extensive experience and research in what she terms 'daaance'all', to consider the security that is carried in bodies that live in garrison spaces. Reflecting on plantation histories and on encounters that she has witnessed on movie sets, where Jamaican dancers encounter foreign dancers, she notes the embodied security of 'warrior women' (p. 43) whose bodies show the marks of their struggles and whose effortless dancing shows they have nothing to prove. Compared to these women,

Introduction 5

those who seek to appropriate daaance'all are, Stines argues, the ones who are insecure.

Dennis O. Howard, in Chapter 4, provides an enlightened ethnographic insider view of Jamaican popular culture through the lens of the recording industry and the in/secure gatekeeping practices that both promote and restrict the development and emergence of creative talent in Kingston's music studios. His sociological approach highlights some key issues within Jamaica's recording industry which negate the established creative class and creative city theoretical frameworks wherein "a peaceful and conflict-free environment are prerequisites for their sustainability" (p. 64). Howard demonstrates the resilience of Jamaican cultural and creative expression through those individuals who negotiate the in/secure line between visibility and invisibility, success and failure, production and acceptance. Howard ultimately lays bare a range of threats to the growth and development of both Jamaican artists and the country's hit-making machinery on the global market scene and explains how these threats are managed.

In Chapter 5, MoniKa Lawrence applies her analysis of masquerade to material from extensive interviews with dancehall queen Carlene, dancehall artist Danielle and dancehall aficionado Orville 'Xpressionz' Hall. Her reflection on sartorial negotiations of in/security considers how, in dancehall's revealing and rapidly changing style and fashion, aspects of the self are both masked and revealed. Despite the insecurities of an empty fridge and unpaid bills, the secure sense of 'inner space' that dancehall adherents put on along with their outrageous and expensive clothing contrasts with the insecure mask of outrage worn by Kingston's middle classes, in response to what they dismiss as slackness.

Chapter 6 approaches dancehall both corporeally and spiritually. 'H' Patten's chapter foregrounds in/security through dancehall dance culture, as dancehall tourism provides a 'safely vulnerable' (p. 79) exploration of Jamaican inner-city lifestyles, in which the normative boundaries of femininity and masculinity are expanded in their construction. He explores dancehall's embedded African/neo-African spiritual dance vocabulary and codes as continuities, which serve to secure and strengthen, whilst opening and expanding dancehall's gendered performance and performative roles. Patten proposes that through corporeal dancing bodies and the spot-light (ideological or physical), the dancehall space represents a signifying practice, which establishes the crossroads between the material and spiritual realm as a survival strategy providing temporary physical and psychological liberation.

Chapter 7 gives a rare insight into a dance practitioner and teacher who has been enormously influential to the lives and practice of dancehall dancers in Kingston. Ricketts offers an autobiographical account of her own training and travels in contemporary dance, which has culminated in pivotal roles training dancers at Kingston's Excelsior High School and Community College. This account, along with her philosophy on dance and her insights into dancehall culture, presents an invaluable archive of an influential teacher – Ricketts reveals the lived in/securities that characterise life in dance and reflects on the in/securities that characterise the lives of dancehall adherents.

6 *Patricia Noxolo et al.*

Thomas 'Talawa' Prestø's contribution focuses on the in/security of the hip wine in relation to the male body within the dancehall space. In Chapter 8, Prestø explores the security that hip wining[4] engenders within most African and Caribbean traditional and popular practices such as Voudun, Shango, Kumina, SoCa, Merengue, Kwasa, amongst others. He therefore questions how the male wining hip in dancehall culture became a signifier of femininity and homosexuality. Prestø argues that this is a Western influence emerging from the brutalising subjection of enslaved African men and women to traumatic public rapes, castration and other dehumanising punishments meted out by European enslavers. He subverts this insecure narrative by presenting the anti-clockwise wining action as a secure spiritually renewing rejection of "the genocide of healthy black male sensuality" (p. 128) in the liberation of male and female wining hips.

In Chapter 9, Sonjah N. Stanley Niaah considers dancehall in relation to its legislative context in Jamaica, in particular in relation to the implementation of the Noise Abatement Act 1997, and its historical antecedents. Routing her argument through larger concepts of 'sounding' (which is often contrasted to 'noise'), Stanley Niaah discusses the 'moral silence' to which black bodies are often subjected and locates the heavy policing of dancehall within a wider politics of citizenship, not only within Jamaica but also globally, wherever dancehall travels to.

Interconnections and linked themes

The main contribution of *Dancehall In/Securities* is to rethink both dancehall and in/security in relation to each other. This concluding section of the introduction unpacks that contribution. The concept of in/security considers security and insecurity as relational terms, negotiated one with another within particular located contexts. Drawing on insights from critical security studies (see, for example Huysmans, 2009; Noxolo and Huysmans, 2009; Bigo, 2014), in/security moves beyond the more popular understanding of insecurity (for example the threat of terrorism) as the defining problem of the twenty-first century. This dominant concept views security as a destination that can be attained through various security measures, for example, through the military presence or heightened surveillance. Instead, in/security is understood as the everyday reality for the majority of people in the world, who walk a tightrope between feeling secure and feeling insecure, as well as between a range of different insecurities – the insecurity of fearing violence, but also the threats produced by precarious employment or by the environmental or climatic crisis (Noxolo and Featherstone, 2014; Noxolo, 2017). Beginning by considering what in/security perspectives do to dancehall, and then moving on to think about what dancehall does for in/security perspectives, this section draws together the insights that *Dancehall In/Securities* offers everyday negotiative practices around security and insecurity within dancehall spaces.

Dancehall has an established Jamaican and transnational scholarship (for example Stanley Niaah, 2020, 2010, 2009; Cooper, 1993, 2004; Henriques,

2011; Hope, 2010, 2006), on which many of the chapters draw. This scholarship reveals that dancehall is not just a space in which people dance and play music, but also a culture or lifestyle, and a set of complex spatially and temporally located practices that are nonetheless contested. As an addition to this scholarship, using in/security as a lens focuses attention specifically on diverse sites of negotiation between security and insecurity, and the diverse kinds of negotiative agency that each engenders, within a wide assemblage of dancehall practices and spaces. A primary focus of *Dancehall In/Securities* is dance (Patten, Prestø, Hall, Ricketts and Stines), revealing the body as a sophisticated terrain for corporeal negotiation between a wide range of different forms of security and insecurity. These include existential in/securities: for example, the pelvis is a primary symbolic site for the negotiation between life and death, and wining is a spectacular form of negotiative agency (Patten, Ricketts, Stines, Lawrence, Prestø). It is iconic within the dancehall space as it invokes the capacity of the body to create new life even when the dancehall space, and the garrison communities that often surround it, have been disproportionately afflicted by violent death (Bogues, 2007; Thomas, 2011). As Patten puts it, in this volume (p. 91): "As the pelvis replaces the life that death removes, through dance the pelvis constantly signals its centrality as the life-giving force." The potency of wining is powerfully reinforced by Prestø's (p. 115) repetition and explanation of Charles-Harris' warning that "the stilling of the black man's hip is a genocide" (p. 125): the living body, both male and female, must be free to graphically display its everyday negotiation between the ultimate in/security of life and death.

The body also negotiates creative and spiritual in/securities: for example, the 'bashment gal' is a 'rhythmatician' (Henriques, 2014) whose bumper grinding supplements and articulates the beats in the music. She moves seamlessly between the security of practised dance technique and the insecurity of possession by a creative spirit that can mean the bashment gal herself is no longer in control of what her body is doing (Noxolo). Through what some contributors (Ricketts, Prestø, Patten) describe as spirit possession, the dancehall body is a lively resource for reconnecting with the domain of spirits and spirituality (Prestø) and also with the collective memory stored within the flesh (Patten). Moreover, the visuality of the body (Noxolo) is paramount in relation to style and fashion as a terrain of corporeal negotiation in the dancehall space (Lawrence, Stines, Hall, Patten). Lawrence, for example, recognises the tensions and contradictions of the nakedness of the dancehall queen Carlene as a mask that covers a lack of confidence that comes from not being fully accepted either in the dancehall (because of her light skin) or in middle-class Jamaican society (because of her association with dancehall). Moreover Stines, in dressing Carlene for a fashion show, recognises that Carlene's 'near-nakedness' (like a mask, flesh-coloured clothing gives the *impression* of nakedness without revealing any flesh) is not a cover but a genuine acceptance of her own body, a way to push beyond her own bodily insecurities towards an even more glamorous and open dancehall space. Stines (p. 44) notes that in dancehall women are secure in the beauty of the marks of their struggle to survive, "posturing their stretch marks, called beauty spots, as this is her proof of fertility". In contrast to this security in the skin and flesh of the body, Lawrence notes that in the dancehall space expensive clothing can be a mask that presents an acceptable face of secure affluence whilst the woman wearing it has such an insecure livelihood that she has nothing to give her children at home; as Rickets (p. 106) notes, "The only thing she can do is go to the dancehall. She gets away – it's her moment." Stanley Niaah sums this ethos of dancehall up as a 'culture of celebration', one that she notes is often "banned and regulated in deadly ways" (p. 136), as the visual 'loudness' of the Black dancehall body is seen as disrupting the 'moral silence' (p. 136) of the Jamaican city.

Dancehall In/Securities therefore focuses on bodies in motion in the dancehall space (Hall, Patten, Lawrence), but it also reveals diverse forms of negotiative agency in a range of spaces that contribute to defining dancehall, for example, film sets (Stines), music studios (Howard), dance workshops (Ricketts) and tourist hostels (Hall). Taken in dialogue with one another, the chapters in the collection undertake complex spatio-temporal mappings of dancehall in/securities. In some chapters, the temporalities of dancehall are traced as linear genealogies and evolutions of dance forms. Dance and music practitioners in the collection (Stines, Ricketts, Patten, Hall, Prestø) use their knowledge of traditional African and Caribbean dance forms to connect dancehall dance with its genealogical roots: in a wide range of antecedent dance styles and histories – for example, Kwasa Kwasa, Lizombi, Kumina, Bruckins, Limbo, the set girls – dancehall is located as a securely rooted branch of the ongoing and multiform dance history of Jamaica, the wider Caribbean and the African continent. In discussing dancehall's external geographies – the ways in which dancehall has travelled, first to the UK and the US, then to Europe, then increasingly in social media and online spaces – Hall, in particular, draws lines forward to sustainable futures for dancehall embedded in genre formalisation, community tourism and skilful negotiation, between the livelihood security that can come from being the source of a cultural resource with global recognition and the insecurities that can come from appropriation and marginalisation of a culture that defines one's own identity. By contrast, Howard (p. 56), though in alignment with Hall in his concern about cultural appropriation, makes the startling claim that "dancehall in terms of a musical expression with a particular signature and musical identity has not been practised for the last ten years": the unstoppable creativity of music production in the Caribbean may mean that every musical genre, including dancehall, is always under threat of imminent erasure and replacement.

In her own temporal mapping of fashion in the dancehall space, Lawrence (p. 71) notes that in the African diaspora, including in Jamaica, culturally embedded views of temporality can be more cyclical than linear, turning uncertain futures from insecurities to recurrences of what we have already survived: "the future is not only ahead of us, it is behind us". Lawrence proposes this cyclical temporality as the context for the apparent irresponsibility of dancehall proponents who spend so much on looking affluent and financially secure at night when they may not have any money to pay their bills in the day. In line with existing literature (see Stanley Niaah), the spatial patterns and divides that surround dancehall are similarly distinctive. For example, several contributors note that dancehall was born directly out of the cultures and experiences of downtown Kingston, particularly the violence of the 1980s. However, contributors also note that increasingly uptown Kingstonians, distinguished not only by higher incomes but also (as a legacy of the racialisation that comes from colonialism and enslavement) by lighter skins, are organising their own dancehall events, investing large amounts of money and attracting paying audiences. Nonetheless, spatial divides are not just policed but are also crossed. In music production, Howard notes that even a prominent performer like Garnett Silk had to start outside Kingston, performing in a bus shelter in Mandeville, before being invited to Kingston and performing in the studio yard, before being granted access to the studio, where he could make the relationships that would enable him to record a big hit. This is a socio-spatial journey, negotiated across a range of divides, from the margins to the centre of musical production. Stanley Niaah notes the globalisation of sound systems and sound clash culture, celebrated for its 'coolness' across the Americas and Europe. But she also recognises that, in the hegemonic marketing and performance of dancehall by companies such as Red Bull, Jamaica itself (even though it is the originary source of dancehall and sound system culture) is often excluded or pushed into the background. Such spatio-temporal mappings of dancehall in/securities reveal dancehall as a variegated and uneven terrain, filled with different kinds of cultural agency, but also multiform in its times, spaces, roles and relationships, and constructed within a thick mesh of competing viewpoints.

Another contribution of *Dancehall In/Securities* is to deploy dancehall in order to further develop the relatively new concept of in/security. In the introduction to a special issue in Small Axe, Noxolo (2018) unpacks in/security in terms of the ongoing relation, or negotiation, between security and insecurity, but also as "deeply located and historically grounded" (p. 38). In/security is a negotiation that plays out in many different ways, depending on where and when it takes place. Reflecting on the era of enslavement, Cummings (2018), for example, speaks of the Maroon in/securities, which relates to Maroon military strategies of resistance, balanced against land and food insecurities. Focused on the post-emancipation era, Anim-Addo (2018) explores the historical strategies of small-scale market traders (higglers) who negotiate their livelihood in/securities through their constant mobility between rural producers and urban markets. By contrast, in an analysis of testimonies of the West Kingston Commission following the notorious 2010 Tivoli Gardens Incursion, Harriott and Jaffe (2018, p. 82) note the strategic "mobilizing [of] embodied and discursive performances of citizenship" by mothers who do all they can to protect their loved ones from the violence of security forces. Among these diverse times and situations, creative arenas are particularly fertile locations for the study of in/security: they provide case studies of a range of resources that offer a range of affordances (within specific limits) in the negotiation between security and insecurity. For example, Noxolo (2018) locates the negotiation of in/security in Erna Brodber's literary treatment of gender-based violence, noting how the novel is able to focus on the multiplicity and slipperiness of language and naming in Jamaican communities to explore how debates about gender-based violence are articulated. Similarly, Mains (2018, p. 94) locates the negotiation of in/security within the cinematic affordances of Stephanie Black's 2001 film *Life and Debt*. She notes how the editing together of "the film's evocative musical soundtrack . . . face-to-face interviews, and archival and television news footage" sets up complex conversations around in/security that effectively resist simplistic ideas about inequality, globalisation and the effects of Jamaica's heavy debt burden. Dancehall, like literature and film, offers its own affordances and limits in understanding the located negotiation of in/security.

One of the striking things about *Dancehall In/Securities*, given the preoccupations of some scholarship about dancehall (see Patten), is that contributors are so little preoccupied with histories of violence within dancehall and in the garrison communities to which it is connected. The contributors do mention several different forms of violence. For example, Prestø begins his chapter with an almost casual mention of his own experience of being beaten with a baseball bat in Jamaica in connection with male wining. Ricketts speaks of her concerns over the hopeless violence of dancehall song lyrics, which she contrasts with reggae lyrics that she feels offer more hopeful solutions. Howard (p. 60), too, critiques the violent urban environment within which major music studios have been situated, stating that, despite the fact that their status as music stars could often be some protection "Creative personnel have regularly been the victims of crimes ranging from robbery, assault, fraud, kidnapping and murder." So contributors do not deny that dancehall has real connections with violent practices, ideas and environments. However, the pervasive idea that dancehall is violently insecure is not the focus of these contributions: instead, the focus is on a range of other in/securities.

One reason that violent insecurity is not a central focus is perhaps that, despite ongoing outbreaks of violence (Thomas, 2011), times have changed: both Hall and Howard locate the height of the violence that tends to be associated with dancehall in the very specific conditions of the 1980s and 1990s. Hall in particular links the violence of the 1980s with rival political factions, rather than with dancehall itself. Instead, he specifies the *effects* of the violence on dancehall culture: men, in particular, had to join parties uptown, where there was less threat of violence so that they could relax and dance, rather than having to stand with their backs to the wall in the downtown spaces, so that they could look out for trouble. Beyond these logistical negotiations, Hall points out dancehall's creative responses to violence, in particular the creation of classic dance moves such as 'gulley creeper', inspired by having to crouch down and walk quietly to hide from assailants. In relation to the negotiation of violent in/securities, the dancehall space, as Hall, Stine and Ricketts all suggest, has been a space for release from the pressure of living with violence, but also a space of creative recuperation around the everyday experience of violence.

One of the most important affordances of dancehall then, in relation to the study of in/security, is the way it opens out negotiation to a range of creative practices – corporeal, spiritual, spatial and temporal. For example, Stines argues that dancehall provides an opportunity for participants to construct a terrain on which they can reconceive the world as secure for them, precisely because their bodies and lives are intimately shaped by everyday life in the garrison areas. This is an embodied security that is not open to others (either middle class or overseas) who would like to appropriate dancehall but who do not share in that secure, embodied identity: Stines interprets living outside the garrison areas as a source of insecurity that must always be negotiated against any alternative claims to embodied or cultural security (racialised, diasporic or knowledge-based). Similarly, dancehall's intimate relationship with the forms of security and insecurity that come from a clear awareness of the spiritual in everyday life features in each of the chapters as a fertile terrain for negotiation. Patten (p. 86), for example, demonstrates precisely how the movement vocabulary of dancehall's Bogle dance resonates directly with the more explicitly 'African/neo-African spiritual dance vocabulary and codes' of revival. Intriguingly, Patten also notes that, when Bogle travels to Jamaican diasporic communities in the UK, its arm movements shifted to 'gun-fingers (two fingers pointing from a fist)' which might be interpreted as a move away from African-centric spirituality. Indeed Hall (p. 33), who also notes the emergence of what he calls 'gun Bogle', insists that this was a profound misunderstanding of Bogle's essential spirit: "the soul, where he's coming from". In fact, it is that link between spirit and movement that Prestø seeks to maintain in his coining of the phrase 'cosmo-technical' in relation to African and Caribbean dance techniques.

Dancehall In/Securities, then, moves the study of in/security onto new terrains, pressing down harder on the everyday workings of negotiation. The negotiation of in/security is able to take place not only through music and language but also in a range of *material* forms, each of which offers a range of affordances for how the negotiation of in/security can be staged and what it can achieve. Stanley Niaah, for example, recognises the material implications of the legislation on the lives and livelihoods of dancehall performers, not only critiquing the violence of policing, but also recognising that the need to engage in dancehall is not just about livelihoods but is also an important form of release for the many who have to deal with 'sufferation' in their everyday lives.

Notes

1 See www.birmingham.ac.uk/research/activity/cariscc/index.aspx and www.ukri.org/news/ahrc-announces-edi-engagement-fellowships/.
2 The 'Sleng Teng' (1985) riddim by Wayne Smith is often cited as the first major computerised dancehall hit. Norman Stolzoff notes, "What was new about Smiths song is that it used the drum machine and synchronized instruments as a backing track rather than a live drummer and bass player" (2000, p. 106). This highlights in/security within dancehall's creative process as technology opened new avenues for exploration, whilst replacing and decreasing the level of live artist needed.
3 The modellers, divas and flossers are the individuals who help set dancehall's stylistic trends and fashions. Hope (2006) and Stanley Niaah (2010) both provide detailed accounts of the roles dancehall practitioners play.
4 'Winding the waist' is shorted as wining. It is a colloquialism which has been normalized in dance jargon.

References

Abrahams, R. D. and Szwed, J. F. (1983) *After Africa: Extracts from British Travel Accounts and Journals of the Seventeenth, Eighteenth and Nineteenth Centuries Concerning the Slaves, Their Manners and Customs in the British West Indies*. New Haven: Yale University Press.

Anim-Addo, A. (2018) Reading Postemancipation In/Security: Negotiations of Everyday Freedom. *Small Axe* 22(3), pp. 105–114.

Aradau, C. (2008) *Rethinking Trafficking in Women: Politics Out of Security*. Basingstoke: Palgrave Macmillan.

Bakare-Yusuf, B. (2006) Fabricating Identities: Survival and the Imagination in Jamaican Dancehall Culture. *Fashion Theory* 10(3), pp. 1–24.

Bigo, D. (2014) The (In)securitization Practices of the Three Universes of EU Border Control: Military/Navy – Border Guards/Police – Database Analysts. *Security Dialogue* 45(3), pp. 209–225. Special issue *Border Security as Practice: An agenda for Research*. Ed. K. Côté-Boucher, F. Infantino and M. B. Salter.

Bob Marley and the Wailers. (1983) Buffalo Soldier. In *Confrontation!* [Vinyl]. Kingston: Island Records.

Bogues, A. (2007) The Politics of Power and Violence: Rethinking the Political in the Caribbean. In B. Meeks (Ed.), *Culture, Politics, Race and Diaspora: The Thought of Stuart Hall*. Kingston: Ian Randle.

Bradley, L. (2000) *Bass Culture: When Reggae Was King*. London and New York: Viking, Penguin Books Ltd.

Campbell, H. (1987) *Rasta and Resistance: From Marcus Garvey to Walter Rodney*. Trenton, NJ: Africa World Press.

Charles, C. A. D. (2002) Garrison Communities as Counter Societies and the 1998 Zeeks Riot in Jamaica. *Ideaz* 1(1), pp. 29–43.

Charles, C. A. D. (2009) Violence, Musical Identity, and the Celebrity of the Spanglers Crew in Jamaica. *Wadabagei: A Journal of the Caribbean and Its Diasporas* 12(2), pp. 52–79.

Cooper, C. (1993) *Noises in the Blood: Gender and the "Vulgar" Body of Jamaican Popular Culture*. Caribbean: Palgrave Macmillan.

Cooper, C. (2004) *Sound Clash: Jamaican Dancehall Culture at Large*. Basingstoke: Palgrave Macmillan.

Cummings, R. (2018) Maroon In/Securities. *Small Axe* 22(3), pp. 47–55.

Fluri, J. (2011) Bodies, Bombs and Barricades: Geographies of Conflict and Civilian (In) Security. *Transactions of the Institute of British Geographers* 36, pp. 280–296.

Fullerton, L. A. (2017) *Women in Jamaican Dancehall: Rethinking Jamaican Dancehall Through a Women-Centered Informal Economy Approach*. MA Thesis. Department of Social Justice Education, University of Toronto, Toronto.

Harriott, A. and Jaffe, R. (2018) Security Encounters: Negotiating Authority and Citizenship During the Tivoli 'Incursion'. *Small Axe* 22(3), pp. 81–89.

Henriques, J. (2011) *Sonic Bodies: Reggae Sound Systems, Performance Techniques, and Ways of Knowing*. New York: Continuum.

Henriques, J. (2014) Rhythmic Bodies: Amplification, Inflection and Transduction in the Dance Performance Techniques of the 'Bashment Gal'. *Body and Society* 20(3–4), pp. 79–112.

Hope, D. P. (2006) *Inna Di Dancehall: Popular Culture and the Politics of Identity in Jamaica*. Jamaica: University of the West Indies Press.

Hope, D. P. (2010) *Man Vibes: Masculinities in the Jamaican Dancehall*. Jamaica: Ian Randle Publishers.

Howard, D. (2016) *The Creative Echo Chamber: Contemporary Music Production in Kingston Jamaica*. Jamaica: Ian Randle Publishers.

Hutton, C. (2007) Forging Identity and Community Through Aestheticism and Entertainment: The Sound System and the Rise of the DJ. *Caribbean Quarterly* 53(4), pp. 16–31.

Huysmans, J. (2009) Conclusion: Insecurity and the Everyday. In P. Noxolo and J. Huysmans (Eds.), *Community, Citizenship, and the 'War on Terror': Security and Insecurity*. Basingstoke: Palgrave Macmillan, pp. 196–207.

Johnson, H. N. and Soeters, J. L. (2008) Jamaican Dons, Italian Godfathers and the Chances of a 'Reversible Destiny'. *Political Studies* 56(1), pp. 166–191.

Mains, S. P. (2018) In/Secure Conversations: Retheorizing Life and Debt, Tourism and Caribbean Geopolitics. *Small Axe* 22(3), pp. 90–104.Nettleford, R. (2003) *Caribbean Cultural Identity: The Case of Jamaica – An Essay in Cultural Dynamics*. Jamaica: Ian Randle Publishers, Markus Wiener Publishers.

Noxolo, P. (2017) In/Security: Global Geographies of a Troubled Everyday. *Geography Journal* 102(1), pp. 5–9.

Noxolo, P. (2018) Caribbean in/Securities: An Introduction. *Small Axe* 22(3), pp. 37–46.

Noxolo, P. and Featherstone, D. (2014) Commentary: Co-Producing Caribbean Geographies of In/Security. *Transactions of the Institute of British Geographers* 39, pp. 603–607.

Noxolo, P. and Huysmans, J. (Eds.). (2009) *Community, Citizenship, and the 'War on Terror': Security and Insecurity*. Basingstoke: Palgrave Macmillan.

Patten, H. (2016) Feel De Riddim, Feel De Vibes: Dance as a Transcendent Act of Survival and Upliftment. In C. Adair and R. Burt (Eds.), *British Dance: Black Routes*. Oxon and New York: Routledge.

Patten, H. (2022) *Reading Religion and Spirituality in Jamaican Reggae Dancehall Dance*. London: Routledge.

Philo, C. (2012) Security of Geography/Geography of Security. *Transactions of the Institute of British Geographers* 37, pp. 1–7.

Rediker, M. (2008) *The Slave Ship: A Human History*. New York: Viking.

Rhiney, K. (2018) Global Change, Vulnerability and the Co-Production of Resilience Among Caribbean Farmers. *Small Axe* 22(3 (57)), pp. 68–80.

Roberts, D. (2010) *Global Governance and Biopolitics: Regulating Human Security*. London: Zed Books.

Smith, W. (1985) *Under mi Sleng Teng [vinyl]*. Kingston: Jammy's/Greensleeves.

Stanley Niaah, S. (2009) Negotiating a Common Transnational Space: Mapping Performance in Jamaican Dancehall and South African Kwaito. *Cultural Studies* 23(5), pp. 756–774.

Stanley Niaah, S. (2010) *Dancehall: From Slave Ship to Ghetto*. Ottawa: University of Ottawa Press.

Stanley Niaah, S. (Ed.). (2020) Dancehall: A Reader on Jamaican Music and Culture. *The Press, UWI*, p. 506, July.

Stolzoff, N. C. (2000, 2003) *Wake the Town and Tell the People: Dancehall Culture in Jamaica*. Durham: Duke University Press.

Thomas, D. (2011) *Exceptional Violence: Embodied Citizenship in Transnational Jamaica*. Durham: Duke University Press.

White, G. (1984) The Development of Jamaican Popular Music Part 2: The Urbanization of the Folk. *ACIJ Review* 1, pp. 47–80. The African-Caribbean Institute of Jamaica, A Division of the Institute of Jamaica.

1 Corporeal in/securities in the dancehall space

Patricia Noxolo

This chapter offers a critical investigation of how bodies in Jamaican dancehall can be theorised as a locus of corporeal in/security. The concept of in/security draws on redefinitions of the lived experience of security and insecurity as an everyday negotiation between the two, played out in a range of aspects of everyday life. Pushing beyond a top-down state-led declaration of levels of security threat, in/security is an understanding of the line between security and insecurity as much more porous, and as constantly defined and redefined in everyday life (Noxolo and Huysmans, 2009). Such a negotiation can be overtly political: for example, it can operate through a range of more or less formal political moves by non-governmental organisations, media and parastate actors (lobbying government, contributing to public debate, declaring and counter-declaring that particular social groups or government actions are a threat) (Huysmans, 2014). However, in/security can also be social and cultural, operating through the everyday conversations and actions of individuals, artists and communities, who begin to conceive of in/security in multiple ways – for example, around criminality and violence, environmental change, livelihoods and basic needs – based on a range of different perceptions and assessments of the sources, meanings and extent of their own safety and unsafety, certainty and uncertainty, or stability and precarity (Noxolo and Featherstone, 2014).

The CARISCC and CARICUK projects[1] focus on in/security in the Caribbean region and on how in/security is negotiated in creative arenas. The seven network members are working towards an understanding of creativity and in/security as pervasive aspects of contemporary life in the region, with a range of actors, but particularly the region's poorest, having to be creative in managing the resources available to them (for example in finding forms of income generation and making money stretch), and negotiating between the competing demands of different kinds of in/security (existential, financial, criminal, violent, environmental) (Rhiney and Cruse, 2012; Jaffe et al., 2012). Moreover historically, a range of differently mobile actors – seamen, tourists, migrants, as well as enslaved peoples – have catalysed new dialogues around in/security through a range of dialogic encounters and through the circulation of radical ideas (Anim-Addo, 2016, 2011; Featherstone, 2016, 2012). But the project also engages with the Caribbean's formidable range of creative cultural practices – literature, visual

DOI: 10.4324/9781003205500-2

arts, dance and music – and understands creativity as a forum within which security and insecurity are constantly re-negotiated (Mains, 2015; Noxolo, 2016). When seen as part of creative practice in the Caribbean, in/security becomes more than a discussion about the precarious tightrope between desired security and undesired insecurity, neither of which is ever total. Where there are conflicting perspectives, for example historically between Maroon and planter communities, creative artists, such as novelists, can redefine in/security through new perspectives on the different technologies of surveillance that the landscape of the islands has afforded to different groups (Cummings, 2016, 2010). Beyond this, in/security is also intrinsic to creativity: creativity can be redefined as a delicious precariousness between success and failure, between the stunning and the nondescript, but beyond this, as the proliferation of generative slippages and ambivalences that in themselves spark new meanings. In literature, for example, in/security can be in the slippage of meaning between words on the page or between the immateriality of narrative and ideas and the monumental materiality of screen, ink and paper (Noxolo and Preziuso, 2012): it can be at the heart of the craft of creative writing.

This generative quality of in/security is the starting point for this chapter. Coming from a nonpractitioner of dancehall, this chapter does *theoretical* workaround corporeal in/security – or how security and insecurity are negotiated in and through the body – and locates this in the context of Jamaican dancehall spaces. The chapter asks this core question: how does the body negotiate between different kinds of in/security in dancehall spaces? After some preliminary work around the concept of corporeal negotiation, and brief contextual analysis about the wider social and political in/securities, both local and global, in which dancehall in Kingston takes place, the chapter theorises the corporeal negotiations of these in/securities in dancehall spaces, through the material forces of sonic vibration on the flesh, the communal affects of lyrics and movement, and the visual effects of dance performance.

Corporeal negotiation

There has been a corporeal turn in the western academy in recent years, and an increasing recognition that something is lost when the body is seen as only a container for the mind: as Julian Henriques (2011, p. 243) succinctly puts it, in the context of dancehall culture: "Very often the privilege of the intelligible over the sensible requires the sacrifice of the qualities and values of our embodiment." True as this is for western philosophy, Charles Mills (2010, pp. 179–180), however, has asserted that this 'sacrifice' has never actually been a choice open to Black people – due to the heavy racialisation of post-enslavement, and through globalised processes of continued exclusion, Black people have been defined by Black bodies. Black bodies demand recognition (Noxolo, 2009), so Mills (2010, p. 180) incites us to "contend with" the body: "recovering it, revalorizing it, relating to it differently". Rex Nettleford taught us that we can contend most closely with the body through dance, becoming attentive to its power as a force that belongs to the Black body and is not determined from elsewhere:

> Sound and movement are the life-making abstractions beyond the reach of external domination. . . . Coupled with music and performed in a context of religious ritual, the dance assume[s] elemental proportions . . . a means of revitalisation, of integrating inner and outer space in the sense that it is seen to serve as a route to self-confidence that underpins the creation of one's own destiny in modern life.
> (quoted in Mills, 2010, p. 180)

Dance is a primary location for thinking about the body.

The body is many things (material, representational, discursive), and can therefore be understood in multiple ways (as fleshy, muscular, boney substance; as a means of communication; and as a 'text' to be interpreted). As Stuart Hall recognised so clearly, this flexibility relates to the Black body as a locus both of its multiple inheritances and of its spatio-temporal contingencies, so that corporeal practices within Black cultures are 'over-determined' by "Selective appropriation, incorporation and rearticulation of European ideologies, cultures and institutions, alongside an African heritage" (Hall, 1996, p. 471), leading to an emphasis in Black popular culture on embodied 'style', and the body as 'cultural capital' (Hall, 1996, p. 472). L'Antoinette Stines' (2014, p. 23) dance-focused neologism 'synerbridging' both interrogates the corporeal content of that over-determination and broadens out the range of traditional influences to Africa, Asia and Europe, in recognition of the diversity of the Caribbean body. Her example of the corporeal content of selection, appropriation, re-articulation and literal incorporation (as mentioned previously) speaks to the choreographic choices made by dancers as they knowingly negotiate these different traditions: "A dancer can execute a grand plie while simultaneously disrupting the rigid line of the back with the circular rotations of the hips as done in a daaance'all bubble" (Stines, 2014/15, p. 13). Stines' dance philosophy recognises the "deliberate and planned" but also unforced and fluid capacity of the Caribbean body to move across and draw from these diverse traditions: "Synerbridge . . . encourages the dancing body to traverse cultures fluidly" (Stines, 2014, p. 23).

As matter, the dancing body's bone, muscle and flesh can be disciplined and controlled by the individual dancer, working within a range of traditional techniques and within the contingencies of its spatio-historical contexts. However, at the sub-atomic level, as Wilson Harris, the Guyanese novelist and philosopher, highlights, the corporeal matter is constantly changing, remaking itself molten and chaotic (Noxolo and Preziuso, 2012). Wilson Harris' 'quantum' vision, inspired by his understanding of the diversity of Caribbean culture – which notably incorporates Amerindian, as well as European, Asian and African traditions – links bodies together through quantum 'gateways' (Henry, 2000, p. 106). Sub-atomic particles of one body (human, animal, flora or fauna) pass through to another, each bringing a tiny aspect of shared consciousness, a 'fossil' in Harris' terms, to which the human person might or might not be consciously alive. Where Stines (2014/2015), as a dancer/choreographer, works with and on the biomechanics of the body (see Henrique, 2014), deploying the 'synerbridge' as a recognition of the body's capacity for disciplined fluidity in crossing cultures, Harris (1999, p. 242) works through his understanding of deep matter to "help us to arrive upon unsuspected bridges, bridges of innermost content that have a deeper, stranger luminosity and incandescence than the purely formal appropriation by one culture of another's artifacts". Although Harris is concerned with the language of fiction here, his recognition of material bridging allows us to imagine the body as deeply communal.

The concept of corporeal negotiation that I want to develop in the dancehall context draws from these combined senses of a dancing body that (as a material, representational and discursive entity that is over-determined by a range of traditions and contemporary contingencies) has the capacity both to negotiate in/security through a conscious, disciplined agency, and also to slip the bonds of conscious control, operating at sub-atomic, uncannily communal scales that we can only intuit. This duality is crucial; it is part of the racialisation of the Black body for it to be understood as purely uncontrolled, animal, irrational. Dance introduces technique and recognises embodied agency in corporeal negotiation, but this is by no means incommensurate with an appreciative contention with the body's deeper capacities, its material relationships. The next section places dancehall in the context of in/security before the following sections focus on corporeal negotiations of in/security in dancehall spaces.

Dancehall contexts

The other chapters in this volume (see also Patten, 2016) give a more comprehensive analysis of in/security in Jamaican dancehall, in relation to the corporeal dancing body. It will suffice here to draw on the commentaries of key academics (Sonjah N. Stanley Niaah, Carolyn Cooper, Donna Hope) to sketch out a number of contexts for theorising the corporeal negotiation of in/security in dancehall.

Stanley Niaah's (2010) focus on the spatio-temporalities of dancehall highlights the in/security that comes from the construction of dancehall spaces in the middle of the urban outdoor spaces of downtown Kingston. Rather than walls or boundaries, it is the styles and activities of dancehall that transmogrify the ordinary into the event: "Ordinary spaces are transformed into dancehall performance spaces once the selector's turntable and speakers, the drinks bar and the patrons are put in place" (Stanley Niaah, 2010, p. 53). Situated in heavily policed areas of Kingston, dancehall performers and crowds have often been subject to "raids, beatings, lockdowns and arrests" (Stanley Niaah, 2010, p. 64), exacerbated by strongly enforced legislation necessitating permits and prohibiting noise (Stanley Niaah, 2010, p. 55). Nonetheless, the 'celebratory culture' (Stanley Niaah, 2010) of dancehall is burgeoning, with, by some accounts, "more than 1400 live events in Jamaica every day" (Stanley Niaah, 2010, p. 66). At the same time, dancehall's downtown spatial location has often linked it with the kind of urban violence[2] that leads "young males [to] expect death as an affirmation that they have lived" (Bogues, 2007, p. 211): dancehall's accommodation of violence leads the 'shotta', 'don' and other violent characters to be "superimposed on the lyrics and parodied in the performances" within the dancehall space (Hope, 2006, p. 98). This existential in/security (which bears the marks of the divides that Carolyn Cooper's, 2004, early analysis of dancehall identifies as "a fundamental antagonism in Jamaican society, between uptown and downtown, high culture and low culture", p. 171) is negotiated in many ways: through the 'contest' between dancehall organisers and police; through spatial agility that means that dancehall venues are 'nomadic' (Stanley Niaah, 2010, p. 55) within Kingston; but also through the capacity of the dancehall form to connect with audiences worldwide (Stanley Niaah, 2010; see also Patten, 2016). Dancehall travels: not only through the global tours of its most well-known artists, but also through the growing importance of music videos (Stanley Niaah, 2010, p. 173), and through instant digital communications.

Donna Hope's analysis of the 'video light syndrome' draws attention to the cultural, and in particular sartorial, shifts that relate to these technological shifts (2006, p. 127).[3] However Hope (2010, p. xv) also questions the layers of in/security of meaning set up by dancehall's translocality, particularly in relation to lyrics:

> Many of dancehall's very location-specific themes traverse international boundaries to be consumed and interpreted in places that are so far removed geographically, socially and culturally from their site of creation that meanings are transposed, transformed and oftentimes lost in translation.[4]

In Carolyn Cooper's (2004) 'Sound Clash' a range of such misinterpretations and reinterpretations are critically discussed, in encounters and dialogues both within Jamaica and in other countries, such as Barbados and the UK. Perhaps most potently, the recurrent issue of dancehall's misogyny is given a nuanced, iterative discussion throughout the book, that includes both the insight that "Jamaican dancehall DJ philosophers themselves offer alternate readings of the sexualised female body that reclaim the potency of embodied spirituality" (Cooper, 2004, p. 106) and the later concession that "the line between celebration and exploitation of the Black female body is rather thin, as thin as some of the fashionable garments sported by women in the dancehall" (Cooper, 1993, p. 245). This negotiation of meaning by one of the foremost Jamaican cultural analysts, in relation to the lively and dynamic dancehall culture, is interesting here in demonstrating that in/security of meaning is not just a feature of translocality, but is inherent to the dancehall space.

Donna Hope also questions how dancehall meanings circulate in and with global culture, bouncing back to increase the in/security of meaning in Jamaican dancehall space. In her discussion of masculinities, Hope (2010, p. 119) argues that the celebration of 'bling bling' in, for example, the lyrics of the British Link-Up Crew, offers "a tripartite ideological orientation", paying homage to middle-class Jamaican cultural values, to colonial allegiances to Britain, and to global capitalist consumerism. The emphasis on imported wealth (Rolex watches, suits from Paris, etc.) appropriates hegemonic value systems, claiming them for the sense of secure global belonging of the young Black men who are in the crew; but at the same time, the celebration of 'bling bling' highlights and underscores the distance between the wealthy artists and the working-class young people who listen to the music in Kingston, who may even access some of the luxury labels but have little access to the secure wealth from which they emanate: "The postmodern dancehall male eagerly slakes his thirst in riotous and celebratory moments of 'bling bling' and consumption that becomes an end in itself, in the absence of visible and accessible means of true social mobility" (Hope, 2010, p. 122). A consumption-driven negotiation of in/security in dancehall spaces becomes limited to people appropriating signs of financial security whilst remaining financially insecure.

So, from this brief sketch of the dancehall context, key contexts for theorising corporeal negotiations in dancehall space include existential in/securities, including both the presence of diverse forms of violence and the shifting spatialities of dancehall; technological shifts and the multiple in/securities of meaning occasioned by the complexity and translocalities of dancehall; and the in/securities of livelihoods that is only emphasised by the hyper-valuing of hegemonic cultures of consumption.

Corporeal negotiations in dancehall spaces

In this final section, the chapter seeks to theorise the corporeal negotiations that are available in dancehall spaces. The focus will be on dance, rather than on the 'soundings' (Henriques, 2011) of music providers, though of course, the music is dance's condition of existence: sound is dominant in the dancehall space (Henriques, 2011). Understanding dance both as a disciplined technique and as an uncanny quantum community (as mentioned previously), the attempt here is to theorise the dancing body as negotiating its in/secure contexts (existence, meaning and value) across both of these modes.

Sonic forces and existential in/securities

Julian Henriques (2011, p. 277) influential contribution to a 'kinetic turn' in the study of dancehall, locates the sonic dominance of the dancehall space within the material movements of the body. Where 'Sonic bodies' (Henriques, 2011) is more concerned with the 'sounding' bodies of the engineer, selector and MC, Henriques' (2014) more recent article on 'Rhythmic bodies' engages more with the dancing bodies of the 'bashment gal'. Henriques' suggestive comment that dancers' 'bumper-grinding' is "the bass note . . . struck by the body itself – celebrating its own fecundity" (2011, p. 18), aligns with a wider consensus on the importance of the pelvic base as a means of rising above death and celebrating sexuality as the medium of life and as part of "frenetic, spiritual rituals of self-affirmation and renewal" (Hope, 2006, p. 128). As such 'bumper-grinding' is a form of corporeal negotiation with the existential in/securities that surround dancehall and the spaces in which it takes place. Beyond this though, the idea of the 'bass note' specifically locates the dancing body within the material presence of the sound culture of the dancehall space, and it is with this that I want primarily to engage in this section.

Henriques (2011, 2014) makes a number of interesting moves around the body. In a move highly reminiscent of Harris' fossil bridges between very different forms of matter at the sub-atomic level (as mentioned previously), Henriques (2011, p. 27) splits the body into three different corporeal forms: the corporeal "flesh-and-blood agents" (including a range of embodied performances, for example dancing); the sociocultural/communal "corps of men or women or social institutions, with beliefs, feelings and ways of understanding in common" (including dance crews and sound system crews); and "corpuscles or particles, such as air molecules in the gaseous medium of auditory transmission". In carefully crafting these heuristic distinctions between "practices, beliefs and particles" as embodiments, Henriques (2011, p. 27) reveals corporeal negotiation in the dancehall space as a range of dialogues between different *kinds* of bodies. The negotiation element of this is brought out more sharply when Henriques (2011, p. 61) deliberately goes beyond the "transport model" (in which music travels from an active source to a passive hearer) to invoke a system of "reciprocation and affordance": sonic forces do not simply act *on* the body, but are negotiated *by* the body.

This point is illustrated more keenly in 'Rhythmic bodies', where Henriques (2014) moves to incorporate both the disciplined dancing body and the uncanny material body (as mentioned previously) into corporeal negotiation within the sound-dominated space. Henriques (2014, p. 86) quotes the 'bashment gal' Yvonne as immersing herself in the sound from the speakers: "It's not just enough to hear it, you got to feel it." He notes (2014, p. 87) that this locates the dancer within the sound, senses fully open to reciprocation with the sound particles in which she is immersed: "The bashment gal is consumed within sound, 'bathed' and 'immersed' in it, making her part and parcel of multisensory flux, rather than at the receiving end of a discrete sensory channel." She develops a "listening skin" (Henriques, 2014, p. 101), where the entire surface of the body becomes "transductive" (Henriques, 2014, p. 101), transforming sound into movement. At the same time, Henriques (2014, p. 99) notes that the disciplined and practised 'bashment gal' (the dancehall space is one of the skilled practitioners who choreograph and rehearse their moves, often producing coordinated routines) also creates and amplifies the rhythm, working skilfully along the grain of the soundscape: the dancer's skilled movement "inflects the rhythm with and through her body. She is a rhythmatician." The flow between performative *intention* – "There are times where you know exactly what you are doing" (Shelly-Ann, quoted in Henriques, 2014, p. 105) – and materialised *attention* to the music – "You are consumed by the music . . . lost to the point where you have no idea what's happening to you" (Shelly-Ann, quoted in Henriques, 2014, p. 105) – is a to-and-fro corporeal negotiation that for me expresses the existential in/security of dancehall spaces: the dancer disciplines her body and hones its capacities, demonstrating her belief, capacity and right to move in a dancehall space whose existence has been heavily contested; and at the same time, in the sonic space, the life of the body itself – its skin, muscle, vitalities – asserts itself independently even of the dancer herself, speaking (albeit ephemerally) in many ways just as eloquently as the violence and death that more stubbornly haunt urban spaces.

Affect and livelihood in/securities

Much has been written about dancehall lyrics, and with my focus on embodiment, I do not seek to intervene in these discussions. Carolyn Cooper's (2004, p. 24) groundbreaking work of 'mediation' has been hugely influential in the "translation of the street into the argot of the academy", and has long since opened up dancehall lyrics to serious consideration as lyrical poetry/social commentary. My concern here is more with the affective entanglements that lyrics, sound and movement bring together in the dancehall space, and how these relate to the negotiation of livelihood in/securities. My thoughts in this section are summoned by the closing paragraphs of Sonjah N. Stanley Niaah's (2004, p. 114) paper on dancehall, where, after quoting from Buju Banton's 1990 lyrics for 'How the World a Run', in which he "names the distributive injustice of postcolonial society", Stanley Niaah (2004, p. 115; my emphases) says this: "The consumption of these lyrics in dance halls *through bodily movement and around specific themes* reveals potent modes of community throughout history, signalling developed forms of commentary, problem solving, and memorializing." I want to revisit (see also Noxolo, 2009) this emphasis on consumption through movement, leading to the community, in relation to the British geographer Ben Anderson's (2016) article on neoliberal affects, in order to more closely consider the generative political capacity of embodied affect in dancehall spaces.

Ben Anderson's (2016) article does the useful work of re-ordering the relationship between neoliberalism and the kinds of affect that set the atmosphere of particular spaces. Affect can be understood in multiple ways and often reduces down to emotion or feeling. My own, as yet rather informal, work on affect specifically in relation to dance (Noxolo, 2014), understands affect as a form of embodied 'thought', literally incorporating emotional as well as sensory data, and embedded within the biomechanical and quantum structures of the body. I would largely agree with Anderson that affect in its more inter-corporeal, communal forms, as a more or less communally organised structure of feeling within a space or community, can be described as 'atmosphere'.[5] It should be clear from the previous section that such an atmosphere is never completely open to being organised or orchestrated: it is negotiated between bodies.

Anderson points out that affect is often understood as subject to powerful neoliberal ideologies, particularly in work around neoliberal governmentality: "By focusing on governmentalities, affect becomes a material to be manipulated or moulded to form subjects in conformity with neoliberal polices or programmes" (Anderson, 2016, p. 738). However, Anderson usefully points out that the kinds of large-scale affective or atmospheric shifts (most notably dominated by fear) that can be argued to have led recently to Brexit and the rise of Trump, are just as much drivers of neoliberal ideologies as orchestrated by them. I would see this as quite close to Stuart Hall's use of articulation and contingency: there is a complex configuration of events, conditions and affects that enable and sustain large-scale economic and political processes at particular times and in particular places.

Reader, you may be starting to wonder what this has to do with Jamaican dancehall. Stanley Niaah's (2004) observation around the consumption of lyrics through bodily movement (as mentioned previously) gives a leading role to embodied affect. As was established through Henriques' (2011, 2014) insights in the previous section, this does not, of course, mean that people are not thinking with their minds in the dancehall – they hear the lyrics and think about them. What I take 'consumption of lyrics through bodily movement' to mean in the context of this chapter is that people do not stop thinking when their bodies take over, and within the dancehall space that to-and-fro negotiation between intention (to listen to lyrics, to dance in a skilled and disciplined way, and, crucially, to take pleasure in doing so) and attention (of the body to what might be called the sonic regime of dancehall) is at the heart of corporeal negotiation.

Livelihood in/securities arrive within this negotiation as part of a politics around the "distributive injustice of postcolonial society" (Stanley Niaah, 2004, p. 115), or within the capacity to at least partially resist the hyper-valuing of hegemonic cultures of consumption. Anderson (2016, p. 738) reveals the possibilities here: affect is not only a bodily reaction but it is an arena for thinking, such that "collective affects form part of the conditions through which economic-political formations come to form and are lived." Now, I do not wish to suggest here that dancehall is a necessarily redemptive space politically, much less that we should look to dancehall adherents to organise themselves into the vanguard of a counter-hegemonic anti-neoliberal revolution anytime soon. Certainly, there is nothing in the literature to suggest this, and some literature to suggest the opposite, not least Donna Hope's critical concept of dis/place (2006, p. 26). Rather, I am suggesting that the corporeal negotiation between livelihood security and insecurity (in/security) in dancehall spaces is indeed, but can also be more than, a stark recognition of the distances between wealth and poverty (as mentioned previously): beyond this, it can *also* be a dagger-by-dagger, bubble-by-bubble affective reflection on ways in which that distance is made and maintained. And, if Anderson (2016) is correct, both sides of that affective negotiation are potent ingredients in the formation of the surrounding economic-political regimes in Jamaica.

Effects of visual performance and in/securities of meaning

Finally, I want to consider corporeal negotiations around the visual effects of dance performance. In this section, I want to contrast the visual culture of dancehall space with that of rave spaces, as set out by Rietvald (2013), and to think beyond the video-light alone, drawing on Michelle Stephens' (2013) analysis of Ebony Patterson's dancehall aesthetics.

Rietvald (2013), writing about the role of the DJ in international rave culture, draws on Julian Henriques' (2011) work on sonic dominance (as mentioned previously) to note that in dance cultures where the DJ controls and manipulates complex light displays, a "hierarchical ocular regime" (Rietvald, 2013, p. 95) is created. Rietvald (2013, p. 97) contrasts this with darker spaces, such as dancehall in the UK, where people dance together in dark, enclosed spaces, feeling the movement of other bodies around them, but without the divisive impact of "differentiating daylight", emphasising gendered and racialised differences. This embodied sensory communality is even more dissipated in large venues where the DJ is on a centre stage and commands a huge light display, and in which people become isolated spectators: "where the visual performance takes centre stage, we find fans massing together as atomized individuals, distracted from their sense of isolation by engaging in the spectacle" (Rietvald, 2013, p. 95).

In Jamaica, where dancehall takes place outside, the intensity of darkness is not the same as in the UK – there is always some light, even if only streetlights and video-light amplifies (to repurpose Henriques, 2014, sonic term) the prevailing luminescence. Of course, video-light is not just light, and Donna Hope's (2006, p. 127) powerful description of 'video-light syndrome' (in which people compete to dress and dance in more and more eye-catching ways) is not just about being seen but is about being "documented, photographed and, in particular, videotaped", so that the image can circulate globally, through digital technologies. However the eye-catching dancehall aesthetic – "elaborate and expensive jewellery and regalia; conspicuous purchase and consumption of expensive, brand-name beverages . . . ; along with wearing revealing clothes and the performance of erotic, X-rated dances" (Hope, 2006, pp. 127–128) – is also seen by all in the dancehall. The visual effect of the dancehall aesthetic is a pervasive element of dancehall space, and though it may be encouraged by the selector (see Orville 'Xpressionz' Hall's description of the power of the selector, in Henriques, 2014, p. 104), it is a communal experience that is not controlled by an all-powerful DJ.

Ebony Patterson, as a visual artist, engages with light effects within the dancehall aesthetic. In particular, her large-scale wall-hanging 'Entourage', is said by Michelle Stephens (2013, p. 24) to display "the black body . . . lit up, irradiated . . .", in a posed family scene that to me is reminiscent of the 'smadditising' (Mills, 2010, p. 164) self-making induced by the video-light. However, what both light and shade in 'Entourage' pick out is "an explosion of blackness, color, pattern, figure, flesh, form, and décor" (Stephens, 2013, p. 24), pattern on pattern, texture on texture that catches and dazzles the eye, in a similar way to the pervasive dazzling variety of textures and colours worn in the dancehall space. By recognising the complexity and eye-catching beauty of the dancehall aesthetic, Stephens (2013) sees Patterson as contesting and problematising voyeuristic stereotypes both of the Black body and of dancehall spaces, negotiating between their simple inscription as violent, misogynistic spaces, and the undeniable presence of some of these features in the space.

Nadia Ellis (2014) picks up on this sense of dazzlement in the dancehall aesthetic, focusing on the sparkling rhinestones and sequins that Patterson sews into her work, particularly her commemoration of the 72 people killed in the disturbances of May 2010, 'Of 72'. In this 72-panel piece, which more obviously engages with violence and insecurity, Ellis links the sparkle of the rhinestones to the 'shine' of the oiled skins of enslaved people, who were displayed as so much 'bling' by plantation owners. The meaning here is taken to link present violence with past violence, and both to the subjugation of human lives to consumption.

The work of Ebony Patterson, and other visual artists, draws attention to the visual aesthetic of the dancehall space, and to the dancing body not only as sonic and sensual but also as visual. Above all the visual commentary on dancehall – silently presenting itself for analysis – highlights the in/security of meaning in dancehall space, its openness to reinterpretation.

Conclusion

This chapter has sought to define and explore the corporeal negotiations around three different forms of security and insecurity – existential, meaning and livelihood – linking these with a range of existing analyses. In doing so, it aims to craft and incite a field of enquiry around corporeal in/securities in relation to the creativity of dancehall, with a view to linking this with the larger cross-genre field of Caribbean in/security and creativity explored by the CARISCC network. I hope it might also make a small contribution to the more specialist field of dancehall studies.

Notes

1 See www.birmingham.ac.uk/research/activity/cariscc/index.aspx and https://caricuk.co.uk/
2 However, Yonique Campbell's (2015) work has shown that the garrison community phenomenon, with its attendant violent in/securities, is often identified as urban but is also a feature of some rural communities.
3 Dennis Howard (2016) gives a helpful decade-by-decade breakdown in relation to the digitisation of production, which provides the ongoing throb of activity that underlies consumption: dancehall emerges during the 1980s out of a "neoinnovation revival" (Howard, 2016, p. 62) of rhythms from the 1960s and 1970s, influenced by the birth of the sound system. The year 1985 saw the birth of digitisation in studio production (Howard, 2016, p. 64), and the 1990s was a peak in terms of "marketing, distribution, product development and international outreach" (Howard, 2016, p. 65), and the early 2000s have seen the "democratisation of music distribution and promotion" (Howard, 2016, p. 67) through the addition of MP3 technology.
4 Carolyn Cooper (2013) gives an amusing anecdote around this kind of misunderstanding, albeit not about dancehall as such. She relates how the omission of a comma after the first 'no' in the record sleeve song lyrics for a German distribution of Bob Marley's 'No Woman, No Cry', combined with a lack of familiarity around Jamaican grammar and syntax, leads German enthusiasts to believe that the song is "a seemingly misogynist, homosocial chanting down of demonised woman".

5 This concept gives a pleasing sense of the multiple embodiments suggested by Henriques, 2011 (as mentioned previously): there is an ongoing discussion within geography about the relationships between the affective atmospheres experienced by people, and other more strictly 'airy' atmospheric conditions.

References

Anderson, B. (2016) Neoliberal Affects. *Progress in Human Geography* 40(6), pp. 734–753.

Anim-Addo, A. (2011) 'A Wretched and Slave-Like Mode of Labor': Slavery, Emancipation and the Royal Mail Steam Packet Company's Coaling Stations. *Historical Geography* 39, pp. 65–84.

Anim-Addo, A. (2016) *Post-Emancipation In/Security: A Working Paper.* http://epapers.bham.ac.uk/2227/1/CARISCC-Working-Papers-Anim-Addo-final-v2.pdf. Last accessed: 13 January 2017.

Bogues, A. (2007) The Politics of Power and Violence: Rethinking the Political in the Caribbean. In B. Meeks (Ed.), *Culture, Politics, Race and Diaspora: The Thought of Stuart Hall.* Kingston: Ian Randle.

Campbell, Y. (2015) Doing 'What Wisdom Dictates': Localized Forms of Citizenship, 'Livity', and the Use of Violence in the 'Commons'. *Caribbean Journal of Criminology* 1(2), pp. 53–75.

Cooper, C. (1993) *Noises in the Blood: Orality, Gender and the 'Vulgar' Body of Jamaican Popular Culture.* London: Palgrave Macmillan.

Cooper, C. (2004) *Sound Clash: Jamaican Dancehall Culture at Large.* Basingstoke: Palgrave Macmillan.

Cooper, C. (Ed.). (2013) *Global Reggae.* Kingston: University of the West Indies Press.

Cummings, R. (2010) (Trans)Nationalisms, Marronage and Queer Caribbean Subjectivities. *Transforming Anthropology* 18(2), pp. 169–180.

Cummings, R. (2016) *Maroon In/Securities: Kamau Brathwaite on Colonial Wars of Xtermination.* http://epapers.bham.ac.uk/2210/5/CARISCC-Working-Papers-Cummings-revised.pdf. Last accessed: 13 January 2017.

Ellis, N. (2014) Elegies of Diaspora. *Small Axe* 43, pp. 164–172, March.

Featherstone, D. J. (2012) *Solidarity: Hidden Histories and Geographies of Internationalism.* London: Zed Books.

Featherstone, D. (2016) *Caribbean Maritime Labour and the Politicisation of In/Security.* http://epapers.bham.ac.uk/2224/1/CARISCC-Working-Papers-Featherstone-Final_(2).pdf. Last accessed: 13 January 2017.

Hall S (1996) What Is This 'Black' in Black Popular Culture? In D. Morley and K. H. Chen (Eds.), *Stuart Hall: Critical Dialogues.* London: Routledge, pp. 465–476.

Harris, W. (1999) Creoleness: The Crossroads of a Civilization? In A. Bundy (Ed.), *Selected Essays of Wilson Harris: The Unfinished Genesis of the Imagination.* London: Routledge, pp. 237–248.

Henriques, J. (2011) *Sonic Bodies: Reggae Sound Systems, Performance Techniques and Ways of Knowing.* New York: Continuum.

Henriques, J. (2014) Rhythmic Bodies: Amplification, Inflection and Transduction in the Dance Performance Techniques of the 'Bashment Gal'. *Body and Society* 20(3–4), pp. 79–112.

Henry, P. (2000) *Caliban's Reason: Introducing Afro-Caribbean Philosophy.* New York: Routledge.

Hope, D. (2006) *Inna di Dancehall: Popular Culture and the Politics of Identity.* Kingston: University of the West Indies Press.

Hope, D. (2010) *Man Vibes: Masculinities in the Jamaican Dancehall*. Kingston: Ian Randle.

Howard, D. (2016) *The Creative Echo Chamber: Contemporary Music Production in Kingston Jamaica*. Kingston: Ian Randle.

Huysmans, J. (2014) *Security Unbound: Enacting Democratic Limits*. Abingdon: Routledge.

Jaffe, R., Rhiney, K. and Francis, C. (2012) Throw Word: Graffiti, Space and Power in Kingston Jamaica. *Caribbean Quarterly* 58(1), pp. 1–20.

Mains, S. P. (2015) From Bolt to Brand: Olympic Celebrations, Tourist Destinations and Media Landscapes. In S. P. Mains, J. Cupples and C. Lukinbeal (Eds.), *Mediated Geographies and Geographies of Media*. Rotterdam, Netherlands: Springer.

Mills, C. (2010) *Radical Theory, Caribbean Reality: Race, Class and Social Domination*. Kingston: The University of the West Indies Press.

Noxolo, P. (2009) 'My Paper, My Paper': Reflections on the Embodied Production of Postcolonial Geographical Responsibility in Academic Writing. *Geoforum* 40(1), p. 5565.

Noxolo, P. (2014) *Dancing Maps Blog*. www.dancingmap.wordpress.com. Last accessed: 13 January 2017.

Noxolo, P. (2016) *Caribbean In/Security and Creativity: A Working Paper*. http://epapers.bham.ac.uk/2208/1/CARISCC-Working-Paper-Noxolo.pdf. Last accessed: 13 January 2017.

Noxolo, P. and Featherstone, D. (2014) Co-Producing Caribbean Geographies of In/Security. *Transactions of the Institute of British Geographers* 39, pp. 603–607.

Noxolo, P. and Huysmans, J. (2009). *Community, Citizenship and the 'War on Terror': Security and Insecurity*. Basingstoke and New York: Palgrave Macmillan.

Noxolo, P. and Preziuso, M. (2012) Moving Matter. *Interventions: International Journal of Postcolonial Studies* 14(1), pp. 120–135.

Patten, H. (2016) Feel de Riddim, Feel de Vibes: Dance as a Transcendent Act of Survival and Upliftment. In C. Adair and R. Burt (Eds.), *British Dance: Black Routes*. London: Routledge.

Rhiney, K. and Cruse, R. (2012) Trench Town Rock: Reggae Music, Landscape Inscription and the Making of Place in Kingston, Jamaica. *Urban Studies Research Journal*. www.hindawi.com/journals/usr/2012/585160/. Last accessed: 13 January 2017.

Rietvald, H. (2013) Journey to the Light? Immersion, Spectacle and Mediation. In B. Attias, A. Gavanas and H. Rietvald (Eds.), *DJ Culture in the Mix: Power, Technology and Social Change in Electronic Dance Music*. London: Bloomsbury.

Stanley Niaah, S. (2004) Kingston's Dancehall: A Story of Space and Celebration. *Space and Culture* 7(1), pp. 102–118.

Stanley Niaah, S. (2010) *Dancehall: From Slave Ship to Ghetto*. Ottawa: University of Ottawa Press.

Stephens, M. (2013) What Is an Island? Caribbean Studies and the Contemporary Visual Artist. *Small Axe* 41, pp. 8–26, July.

Stines, L. A. (2014) *Soul Casings: A Journey from Classical Ballet to the CARIMOD Daaance Technique L'Antech*. Kingston: Zight.

Stines, L. A. (2014/15) From Dance to Daaance: Embracing the Ancestral Ridims. In M. L. Soukaina Edom, G. M. Francis, R. Kempadoo, P. Parson and L. A. Stines (Eds.), *Creolizing Dance in a Global Age*. London: Serendipity.

2 Practice, vision, security

Orville 'Xpressionz' Hall

Dancehall in an insecure city: 1980s and 1990s Kingston

In my experience, when I was growing up there were two types of dance space: the dancehall space in the inner cities where we as inner-city youths would dance, we couldn't truly dance in communities, there were the uptown parties and the downtown parties, the trouble was the downtown parties was really troubled with violence because of the politics.[1] So in the '80s, inner-city parties, because of the different rivalling factions, the men could not dance in the middle of the dance floor; that is the easiest place for them to get hurt. There was always the Jamaica Labour Party (JLP) and People's National Party (PNP) factor. Men danced against the walls; women danced in the middle. If we wanted to enjoy ourselves, we had to go to the uptown parties. The uptown parties didn't play dancehall; they saw dancehall as the thing that brought violence into the party. People would fire shots in the air because they were enjoying the music. If this was a dominant JLP area, the JLP guys would just fire shots in the air to show that this is their turf and they have the dominance; if it was a PNP area the same thing would happen. So, for us, who were not deemed as gangsters and loved dance, we would go to the uptown parties.

In the '80s we had two different types of dance styles in the uptown parties: we had the Michael Jackson for the individual dancers, and then break dancers; movies like *Beat Street* were popular in those days. These are the parties we would go to have fun in those days because, in the inner-city parties, the men couldn't commit. You'd just have to stand there and watch women dance. We were fresh out of the rub-a-dub era: they would play a version of the song itself. There was a lot of beats. Most of it was couple up. Men would dance against the fence and women would dance with them: men danced with their backs against the wall, and the women would dance up against them so that the men could see around them. So, the space was uncomfortable for us to dance. Havendale and Fairfax Drive are some of the places we went to for those uptown parties. They wouldn't let you in if they knew you were from an inner-city area or if you just dressed differently; they could identify that 'he's not from this community' because they did not know who was going to follow you. Guys used to follow guys to parties for a confrontation. That is the easiest

DOI: 10.4324/9781003205500-3

place to catch them, outside of a party or in the centre of a party; that is why guys did not party in the middle if you were downtown. Being uptown, there was the freedom to just dance.

In the '60s it was the same thing. They used to call them soul boys, dancing to hits out of the US. They wouldn't dance in the hardcore sections of the inner city. It was the same thing in my generation: we were fresh out of the 1980 election, one of the bloodiest elections in the history of Jamaica. That trend follows through up to 1985; by that time Michael Jackson was part of our culture. Breakdance was also a part of our culture from the '80s.

Dancehall goes global

In the '90s the video light became a more integral part of the dancehall parties. People started to video parties to send the videos overseas to sell. The dancehall space, even though some people might not admit it, is a spiritual space, but it's almost spiritual without dancers understanding what is happening; the spirit is there that sends them into a trance when they dance. The dancehall space for us is a space where we go to release bad energies, forget about not having any money, not being able to deal with some of the bills. The beats pull out a different spirit in us because some of these beats were created from our traditional music such as Kumina and Revival. The '80s is what I call the golden decade of dancehall because it is the decade that established the name and the space locally. The '90s is the decade that put dancehall on the international market because this is when dancehall was seen as more than just music and dance, but as a lifestyle. Gerald 'Bogle' Levy, who is seen as our dancehall king, was responsible for the development of the dancehall language, whilst Carolyn Smith, a.k.a dancehall queen Carlene, was responsible for the development of the dancehall queen dress code. The beats of the '90s were born out of the Jamaican inner-city experience, which made the sound unique alongside the dance moves as well.

Bogle and Carlene were largely responsible for the movements that defined the male and female dancehall styles. Whilst the females did a full 360-degree rotation of the waistline, men would move their waistline to represent the infinity sign. Carlene would write the story of the dancehall queen, dress code and how women should dance in dancehall, the sexuality and sensuality. Bogle showed that men do not have to dance against a fence. He danced in the middle of the dancehall space. We as inner-city dancers could not do that. Bogle always had his crew present, so he was always protected. Bogle invited other male dancers in the space when he realised their talent or ability to dance, and they danced because they felt safe dancing around Bogle.

The video light started to pick up some of these dancers and with the trend of sending DVDs and cassettes overseas, and many of them started getting work as dancers in Jamaican parties and clubs in the US to give a Jamaican flavour. Those already living overseas thought that the culture was being washed out, so this is why promoters started sending for authentic Jamaican dancers to heighten the energy in the space. Dancers realised that, just by dancing in the space and really showing what they could do, they would have a chance to really travel. Many dancers travelled to Brooklyn, the Bronx and Queens because these were the places with the highest population of Jamaicans. They were there as party dancers; they were there to nice up the party. Some of them earned good money. Dancers love foreign name-brand clothes; some of them would get money and some would get money plus clothes as payment and they would come back and tell stories about their travels, as it is every dancehall dancer's dream to travel. Some would say that they toured; some of them would dance at a barbecue in a backyard or in a few clubs within the New York area and come back and tell people they've toured and become popular based on that.

Some people used to say it was because of the drug dons wanting to wash money, why they became party promoters. They would keep parties to show their legitimacy, but it was never about making a profit. As law enforcement started to clamp down and a lot of drug busts started happening some of these people, drugs dons/party promoters, were sent to prison; the ones that were not had to come up with strategies to bring people to their parties, as they had to transition into real party promoters. Now they had to depend on the party itself. There was no marketing strategy because previously it was just about putting a lot of money into a party and making it work, but now it was actually about making a profit, as the parties became their main source of income.

Between the 1990s and mid-2000s, after Bogle died in 2005, overseas travelling for dancers took a nosedive. Dancers were just in the street dancing, hoping the dance profession would rise again. It wasn't until 2010 that new opportunities opened, as a different set of people started travelling to Jamaica, interested in learning about dancehall dance. The profession began leaning more towards teaching rather than just performing. The focus shifted from the US to Europe, as Europeans wanted to learn the culture of the dancehall moves, whilst in America they just wanted dancers to be at the party to entertain.

Crazy Hype, leader of the group M.O.B (Men of Business), and Raddy Rich, a solo dancer, took the first trip that I know of to Europe; it was Russia that they went to first. It was a studio setup. It wasn't about entertainment, for Europeans: Europeans saw where they could make money from dancehall using a classroom setting. They would take a dancehall dancer on tour as a teacher. At first, they were watching the moves on YouTube and taking the moves and teaching them without a real understanding of the technique or cultural significance. That was one of the problems I identified when the trend first started. An Internet war of words started on Facebook around 2009/2010 when I saw overseas dancers taking the moves from local Jamaican dancers, renaming them and teaching them to students. Some of them had never travelled to Jamaica or even taken a class with a Jamaican dancehall teacher. What needs to be understood is that dancehall moves, especially '80s and '90s dancehall dances, have significant meanings. We dance what we live, so 'gulley creeper', 'S 90s skank', 'water pumping', 'cool and deadly', 'horseman scabby' – these moves all came out of a lifestyle. My argument is that you have to understand the cultural significance, rather than just the aesthetic value of a dancehall move, looking at it on YouTube, taking and teaching it back. It was when I started pointing out the cultural significance within dancehall that promoters started making more efforts to get Jamaican dancers to tour and teach. In 2012, I was invited to Russia for the first time, to teach dancehall exclusively. If you saw dancehall at any event, it was a big hip-hop event, or some other dance genre like jazz. Dancehall was usually a small part of a bigger festival and sometimes there were no more than 20 students attending. By 2012 we were seeing 300 students from around Russia and Europe attending exclusive dancehall camps; it was phenomenal! Now we are seeing up to 500 students, coming out for exclusive dancehall workshops. You have a big campsite, a big open space, you have parties every night. You have classes in the morning, parties at night, '90s parties; all these things are happening in Europe and in Russia. Major things are happening on the international scene that our government does not have a clue about.

Teaching and appropriation: dancehall as an insecure cultural resource

I have been chastised as a sell-out because of teaching dancehall to foreigners. I understand clearly why some dancers see it that way, especially those dancers who have failed to make the transition from dancers to teachers. Many feel that we should not teach our culture to others. However, the truth is that whether or not it is taught to them in a formal way, they still have the advantage of visiting Jamaica and learning it in an informal way. I prefer the formal; that way real local dancehall practitioners will be engaged to teach proper techniques and give real and correct information about the culture. Outside of the formal approach, foreigners are left to draw their own conclusions about things in the culture that they do not fully understand, which obviously leads to misrepresentation. As a culture keeper, I believe practitioners are instrumental for the preservation of Jamaican culture generally and dancehall culture specifically.

I remember opening my studio to dancers to say, 'listen, I have an advantage, I was lucky enough to get into an institution, to learn the art of teaching; we now have an opening for teaching'. Once I was just a dancer; I had to learn the art of teaching. Dancer and teacher are two different things. I had to learn the art of teaching, different genres of dance. There were two places – Excelsior Community College and Stella Maris Dance Ensemble – where I got my formal training. I tell dancers that it doesn't deter you or change you as a dancer; what it does is enhance and develop your dance skills. When I go to Russia and Europe, they're translating how you dance, how you're standing, using dance words and jargons to explain what the body is doing. For example, 'first position', 'second position', 'plié', 'relevé' and 'contraction'. Many dance students overseas interested in learning dancehall are ballet-trained: they understand, 'parallel', 'contraction', 'isolation', so you can use the language. That is what I do.

I have realised in recent times that dancehall is at a place where the guys are taking off their shirts and dancing for white girls to swoon over them. It is less about actual teaching. When your feet cease to work, you have to have information to empower yourself with knowledge. Most of them are afraid to link dances that they create now, to dances that existed before. They're having problems because of a lack of education, dance education. I am not saying that dancers are dunce, but if they research, they will be able to make the link between the traditional and popular and have a clearer understanding of how the movements have evolved. You always have to be a student of your craft; you always have to be seeking higher knowledge, understand different traditional forms. I had to understand people to say what looked like what. I learnt it from somebody. This was taught to me by my mentor, Patsy Ricketts.

Dancers promote themselves and love to say, 'I created these 10 dances', but never research or try to link them to anything traditional. To anybody who comes to them, they are willing to tell them 'I'll teach you' without understanding how to teach; there is a big difference between being a dancer and being a teacher. Some dancers don't understand that when foreigners come here and say 'I created a dancehall dance move' – which is impossible – it is to get them to promote it, not knowing it is the worst thing you can do. If local dancehall dancers tell foreign dancers that they are able to create dancehall moves without even understanding the culture, why would they need you from Jamaica to teach in their country? The math is this: it costs 1,500 to 1,800 euros to fly a Jamaican dancer from Jamaica to Europe, put them up, feed them and they will be there for a month; it's an expensive venture, and many times they don't make this money back because the dancer they booked is either not as popular as they thought or not able to teach. However, if the foreigner can get the Jamaican dancers to verify their moves as dancehall moves and also help them promote it then eventually Jamaican dancers would no longer be needed overseas to teach, especially now that foreigners can create their own dancehall dance moves. There are unwritten rules as to how a dance move is created and gets popular in the streets of Jamaica: (1) The dancer creates something based on a beat that he/she hears that evokes emotion from a real-life experience; (2) the move is done repeatedly in parties; (3) others (not necessarily dancers, but ordinary patrons) start doing the move; (4) the move catches the attention of the selector and he asks the name; sometimes there is no name at the moment and it is created at the moment or the selector gives it a name based on the energy of the move and the issue the move seems to be addressing; (5) most times the moves come from local slangs; these are the ones that stand the test of time in my estimation. This is why I see it as impossible for overseas dancers who understand little or nothing about the culture to create dancehall moves.

I remember the first time I stood on stage and saw 200 people standing in front of me, for a dancehall class, teaching my dance move. It's a different feeling. If your head is not screwed on properly you give away everything for the promise of touring. We have to be careful of what we say, because foreigners will feel empowered and say, 'you have just legitimised me, so I am now going to teach'.

So many foreigners live completely from dancehall, hosting big dancehall camps, and have never set foot in Jamaica. One of the popular talks in recent time is that 'we have to change the game in dancehall, as we are the new generation.' I say, 'you are playing games; this is my culture. You can't classify the culture I live by as a game, especially the fact that you're not even Jamaican.' Some realise you can buy some Jamaican dancers, because everyone wants to travel, so they take sides with these culture vultures because they say 'I want you at my camp this year but I want you to help me promote my new dancehall step.' Their reply is 'anything you want me to do; which dance do you want me to promote?', so it is big business.

If you want people to take dancehall seriously you have to find a way to formalise it. All of the dances that have come off the street, such as, ballet, contemporary, jazz, have been formalised. Jamaican people are afraid to do that with dancehall, so now other people take it and run with it. They're trying to rename it, change the music, the dancehall beats and call it 'tropical house' or 'trap'. Richie Stevens, one of our most prolific reggae and dancehall singers, had to stand his ground and prove that Rihanna's 'Work Work' song was a sample of his beat created more than a decade ago, and after proving it he was able to benefit and most importantly be recognised. We should not be afraid to formalise our dance moves. That's how the rest of the world owns their genre and styles: there is a technique that is used in hip-hop, jazz and so on. The same should be for dancehall.

Re-creating cultural security in the dancehall space

So, I am telling them there is an unwritten rule as to how a dance becomes popular in Jamaica. People walk to a party because they don't have any money. They make up a move. A selector sees the move – four persons pick it up, then ten persons pick it up. They make up a name on the spot, then the party starts a dance. That is the first part of it. The next part is to go to every dancehall party for the week and try to get that same energy. Remember – you are hungry and thirsty, but this is your sacrifice. Your dance is nothing until the public start doing your dance. The public start doing a dance, somebody sends you a video, telling you, 'you know that people are in the party doing your dance and you didn't know?' People like Ding Dong, so everybody is flinging their shoulder. That's what every dancer tries to reach, that's the level you try to reach. You have to campaign your dance because dancehall is a social dance. The aim is for the oldest person to attempt your dance and the youngest child to do your dance. That is how you know it will be a hit: when old people and young people are trying to do your dance. Dancehall is not a spectator sport.

There were beats first, not lyrics. This is the difference between dancehall and hip-hop, even though they grew up together; one of the founding fathers of hip-hop is Jamaican, DJ Cool Herc. They dance the lyrics. Dancehall is drum and bass; if you listen to old rhythms like Toxic, it is the drum and bass we dance to, so the body flows with that, and we listen to the lyrics after. Bogle came in 1992. He helped to open the door for dancehall when he came back with these dances in the '90s; that is what brought dancehall onto the international scene. After Bogle died in 2005, we started to look back at everything that was happening in the US: *You Got Served, Step Up, One Two Three Four*, all of these dances; then when there was more cable in homes it was, *So You Think You Can Dance?, America's Top Dance Crew*. They started adding choreography to dancehall, but dancehall is not about choreography. Bogle used to do the whole night and people would not stop watching, because it is not just the move, it is the soul, it is where he is coming from. I started cussing at people overseas, people who teach about guns. Bogle never used a gun, but he was shot for that dance. They labelled Bogle as a socialist dancer because he came from Trenchtown, a jungle: Bogle was not using a gun finger. We call them funk arms. Dancehall is a packed space, you put your hands up in the air. If you look at Bogle's body language; he made dancehall popular. I love him; he was the dancehall king. His body was doing a traditional dance, limbo, by pushing the pelvis forward; and the deeper he goes back with it, it is like when you are going under the stick; and he uses the waist because it is the pelvis you use to go under the stick. A lot of people do not look at it from that angle.

What is happening in dancehall now is that there are a lot of relationships. Sixty or seventy per cent of the women who come from Europe and South America have relationships with dancers: he is touring because his manager is his girlfriend. They do not have to be known in Jamaica. They are social media dancers, pushing themselves on social media saying they're the baddest thing in dancehall. They get a rude awakening when they come to Jamaica and look in the streets at dancehall. These are internet dancers; they tell people a lot of lies about dancehall. That's when you get conflicts and confrontations with everyone clashing. If you want to see true dancehall again, play some '80s or '90s dancehall. You cannot be in the dancehall doing a different move. This is what it tells you. But now every dancer is creating moves for themselves, cussing one another, 'this was my move first, this was my move first'. I say, 'it's not your move, it's a "kumina" move, it's a "bruckins" move, all of them are linked'. They do 'higher level' and do not talk about 'bruckins'; they do 'summer bounce', and do not talk about 'bruckins', which are pieces of traditional dance. If two dancers are arguing over 'higher level' and 'summer bounce', they should pay homage to kumina and bruckins.

Now everyone wants to create dancehall moves, that is why we are having so many problems. We used to wait on Bogle and Ovamarz, wait for them. When they came on the street with a move, we asked what's next, we used to wait, we never used to tear it down. I saw my part already: I'm a teacher. I don't create dancehall moves, but when it comes to teaching, I can put my hand up. I'm not running behind you creating moves; everybody is competing with each other. Don't be afraid. Have you ever seen leaves hanging without branches? Everything is connected. Link them to something. People will have more respect. This dance was inspired by this or that. It has a story to tell. You mash them up.

For the last two or three years, I've intentionally put off tours to Europe. I want to focus on camps here in Jamaica. Shelley had a bad knee, and she won't go on her head like the new-school females. Last year when Shelley toured, this year's tour was booked from the end of that tour. Then she went and did two months again this year, and next year's tour is already booked. Because of her knowledge, she showed women what they are supposed to be in dancehall. In dancehall in the '80s, when Carlene and the Ouch girls had their big hairstyle and big earrings, who would dance on their heads? Who would split in the dirt? It's about the waistline, sensuality; the true essence of dancehall queens is self in dancehall. Men are looking at them because of how they dance and the sexiness, it's not about jumping off things. More power to you because it's youthful exuberance, but you have to be able to show them the transitions.

Dancehall secures livelihoods in Kingston

For some of the dancers, there is security the minute they start to travel. Now you can buy things for yourself and for your children. Insecurity comes where more dancers start coming into the market and seem to threaten their area. Because of lack of education, your five moves are now deemed as old moves compared to the younger youths coming up. Everyone is trying to dethrone people: that is the constant insecurity. Young dancers are not just secure with being better than you – they want to kill the king because the king will use his experience to dethrone you. They know this. They are worried about the king's legacy: time and time again they realise that expertise, knowledge and experience can get rid of them after a while.

In 2013, when I went on my second European tour, I said to myself, 'why not try to bring dancers here to Jamaica? They will never get authentic dancehall in Europe.' Shelley and I decided to start a dancehall dreamcamp. A guy lived right in front of my house where Buju Banton's studio was. There was a break-up between him and Buju; the studio was non-existent, but the house was still there, a nice two-storey place. I woke up one morning and said, 'I wonder if he would consider turning this place into a hostel?' These people like hostel-style if they're going anywhere; they just want a room and shower because they're not staying there. They are going out to party. I said, 'let's turn this place into a hostel'. He was interested but did not have money to fix up the place. So, I got some bunk beds on hire and fixed up the place. Twelve Russians came to Jamaica. That's where it started.

Now the dancehall hostel holds 34 persons from 16 different countries. This is now his livelihood. When Buju's concert was here, he was fully booked; there are certain times of the year when he's fully booked. The house beside us and our parents are the first settlers in that community. The people who live beside him now sublet their place to him to be a part of the hostel. In 2017, the hostel got an award for the No. 1 hostel in Kingston. We're in the inner city, you know. At the end of last year, bookings.com gave us the best guest review. The guest said 'that's where you can stay, go to the dancehall hostel because of the hospitality and all of that'. Plus, between January and December 2018, we took 425 people into the community.

It impacts the community, makes the community eat. There's a girl down the road selling chicken and fries, a girl down the road selling ice cream and a youth up the road selling ground provision. We literally walk with them through the community and make them get things; they walk up and down and they eat their box food on the sidewalk. They want to do it like that. The whole community thrives. When they come to Jamaica, because of loving dancehall, I'm not knocking the five-star hotels, but you cannot get that image when you go to a five-star hotel. They want to live with the people. Syl, who grew up with me, who runs the hostel, is one of the best hosts. Technically it's a historic site. The community has so much history. His studio is partners with Buju Banton; he was also the engineer on Shabba Ranks's *As Raw as Ever* album, on the two albums that got a Grammy. There's a history in the community. Some of the guests do not want to call a taxi and prefer to walk to the bus stop, and there are some youths in the community who will walk with them to the bus stop and get a little money just from doing that. The only other community I know doing that, and just a little bit more, is Trenchtown. They have a programme because it is Bob Marley's birthplace. Trenchtown wants to partner with my community, Jacksontown.

Community tourism, I said this on the radio for the last ten years, is part of the healing. I am my community. I bawled out on the radio, so many times, and it wasn't happening, so I did it myself. Just the thought of knowing that 425 people came into our community in just one year, a little over one a day! It can work. It can work to reduce crime. The community feel too far away from what is happening where tourism is concerned. I just want to put up tents down the road. Everyone will do something in the community; just put up a tent and people will come and take ackee saltfish, and bammi and fish. These are the things we want to do. People will ensure that there's no crime. It used to happen in Passa Passa. In spite of what they say about Tivoli, it was the safest place when Passa Passa was going on. It brought money into the community. Everybody earned. I saw a youth parking a car with an M16 rifle over his back, thrown over his shoulder. When you come out of the car, he tells you 'good night, have fun'. The community protects. If you know there is crime and violence in the community, try different things to bring the community into what is happening.

The movers and shakers need to have the understanding that Jamaica was made popular based on sports and entertainment, and look at some of the areas, listen to us. I have been trying to get ministers to come and look; I want the road to be fixed in my community. At election time, we begged them, so our member of parliament came through the area; I cannot remember seeing him after he won his seat. We bring a lot of traffic, a big tourist bus, just like at the five-star hotel. We want the road fixed; just pave the road. We're not asking for handouts.

Note

1 This chapter was transcribed and edited by Patricia Noxolo, from an interview with Orville 'Xpressionz' Hall, which was carried out by MoniKa Lawrence, in collaboration with H Patten

3 Me badi a fe me BMW (my body is my BMW)

Engaging the badi (body) to interrogate the shifting in/securities within the co-culture daaance'all

L'Antoinette Stines

I stand under the stars in an area surrounded by monstrous speaker boxes pounding every genre of music. The people anxiously file in. There is a little window through which we pay. Bend down. Look under the little slit. Yes someone is hidden behind the slit collecting the money. Fear of the gate being robbed, demands strict security at the gate. The vendors line the adjoining street, the pungent smell of jerk chicken, mannish water,[1] curry goat, fry fish and bammy[2] permeate the air. Children rush to pick up the used liquor bottles as they need to sell them; it is tomorrow's lunch money. The outfits glitter as the style and fashion of the avid dancehall participants change weekly re-shaping fashion design from Jamaica to Paris. I hear oldies reggae of the 60s; present day reggae; American hip-hop; religious music; and the gyrating African call and response contrapuntal rhythms of dancehall music. Rhythms, vibes, fashion, a voice for the voiceless. *Daaance'all* is definitively Jamaican.[3]

The Jamaican society is framed inside a journey beginning with the Tainos, whose presence has for many centuries been ignored. The history of enslavement and sovereignty dominates the historical maps in Jamaica. However, these evo-revo[4] paradigms have morphed into a new world society with multiple levels of social and cultural engagements. These have impacted the lives of each and every individual in multiplicities of ways. As such, securities and insecurities naturally occur developed from a variety of influences. We are presently experiencing a society partially led by Generations X and Y. However, they are about to experience yet another journey between themselves and Generation Z. Herein lies the issue of cultural data being created or destroyed within a framework of in/securities. With inventions such as cell phones, the internet, wi-fi, and the many forms of social media, cultural data in some instances becomes misrepresented. Outsiders give their onlooker interpretations that are tainted by individual in/securities. I humbly present from a generation called baby boomers who with very limited technological instruments proudly found methods to honestly document cultural data.

DOI: 10.4324/9781003205500-4

My focus on in/securities in this chapter will be informed by the journey from the time of plantocracy till the now. This journey impacts significantly on the present and shapes the future. I admit that the term in/securities as it relates to culture can be both confusing and vague, as such I isolate my theories using the lens of Jamaica's most dynamic popular culture creation called daaance'all. I challenge in/securities through my lens as mine is the lens of a lived experience. I hope to offer a more concrete overstanding[5] of how I personally view in/securities in daaance'all.

Daaance'all is a phenomenon I love for its dynamic energy, contrapuntal musical rhythms, cultural representation and social commentary. My phenomenological experiences allowed me to be closely entwined with the source as a practitioner. One such source is "Tippa"[6] an inner-city ground breaker, dancer and choreographer whom I regard as a colleague and friend in the struggle. Tippa was one of my assistants alongside Amanyea (my daughter) for the World Reggae Dancehall Competition, which is held annually in Jamaica led by The Jamaica Cultural Development Commission. His definition of daaance'all begins with how it is really pronounced by the practitioners.

> First ting – me call it *daaance'all* – not dancehall! Daaance'all is everything, the food, the music, the location, the clothes, the vibes, the everything is daaance'all. Daaance'all is a Jamaican culture divided into two parts, one is music and one is daaance. Daaance'all reflects ghetto. How we talk, how we live, how we communicate. It is just a way of life for youth from the inner city areas.
>
> (personal interview June 2006)

Daaance'all, daaance, and yaad are the phonetic spellings of the common Jamaican pronunciation of those words in Jamaican patois. As a born and grown Jamaican daaance'all practitioner who also has the lived experiences in the Seal yaads of Kumina, I choose to use those pronunciations. I aim to share my phenomenological experiences by offering an overstanding of the Jamaican co-culture and focus on the in/securities I view in the daaance'all yaads. There is evidence of in/securities not only by the participants but, in my opinion, primarily by the observers. Hegemonic as well as short-term partially involved interpretations often present miss/conceptions of this revolutionary explosive co-culture.[7]

My ability to be accepted as a daaance'all dancer allowed me the opportunities to experience the daaance in daaance'all not merely as a movement but as a cultural tool with a purpose within a historical framework. I came to overstand that the screams in daaance'all represented many people globally. Tippa's discussion on daaance'all informed my hypothesis that Jamaicans daaance in Patois and validated the oral distinction I make between my explanations of what I refer to as daaance[8] and daunce.[9]

My auto-ethnographic overstanding of the phenomenon from a socio-cultural perspective was arrived at from participation in sessions in which

38 L'Antoinette Stines

I daaanced. Early in the 1980s, I ventured into daaance'all with the creators and choreographers of many of the movements such as Bogle,[10] Crab[11], and others fully aware that, at the time, the phenomenon was regarded as socially unacceptable by both the working and upper classes. In strict opposition to that were the views of Jamaican inner-city, ghetto or garrison population who considered daaance'all to be a major voice of protest and resistance as they struggled for acceptance and acknowledgement of their presence and needs in a country that in many instances ignored them.

I am the choreographer who first presented my lived daaance'all experience on a proscenium stage and ventured to contemporize it as a nation dance language. I also spent many years training the competitors of the World Reggae Dancehall Competition. Recently for L'Acadco, a United Caribbean Dance Force 2018 Season of Dance named Daaancing Crystals, I choreographed alongside Amanyea Stines a piece we named Lovey Dovey featuring one of Jamaica's daaance'all queens Kimiko Miller to the music of upcoming Artistes Royal Blue featuring Runkus.

In contrast to Tippa's explanation of daaance'all, the lexical explanation of the word is: "a large room set aside or suitable for dances and a public hall offering facilities for dancing".[12] This definition places importance on an enclosed and covered space for the purpose of social interaction through dancing. In Jamaica, such dancehalls may be found throughout the island in nightclubs such as Cactus in Portmore, Asylum in New Kingston, Roof Top Inn in Negril, and Margaritaville in Montego Bay in the 1980s. However, presently there is a return to the original outdoor sky roof to find dances such as Uptown and

Figure 3.1 KIMIKO VERSATILE IN HOT GYAL MUSIC VIDEO (Photographer: Britney Holung)

Me badi a fe me BMW (my body is my BMW) 39

Figure 3.2 L'ANTECH MEETS REGGAE choreographed by L'Antoinette Stines, PhD (Photographer: IAN GAGE)

Figure 3.3 L'ANTECH MEETS REGGAE choreographed by L'Antoinette Stines, PhD (Photographer: IAN GAGE)

Figure 3.4 L'ANTECH MEETS REGGAE (Photographer: IAN GAGE)

Figure 3.5 BRUCK IT UP choreographer Dr. L'Antoinette Stines (Photographer: IAN GAGE)

Mojito Mondays, Nipples and Boasy Tuesdays, Weddy Weddy Wednesdays and Magnum Wednesdays, Day Rave on Thursdays, and Yeng Yeng on Fridays to name a few. All these dances are located in Kingston; however, similar dances are held in different parishes with different names all over the island of Jamaica. Daaance'all is alive and reigns strong with dynamic and talented daaance'all queens and kings in every parish.

Daaance'all – the underground faaambily

The work of Norman Stolzoff (2000), a senior research fellow at the Centre for Research on Information Technology and Organizations at the University of California, Irvine, USA, offered the first in-depth examination of dancehall.[13] He posits that:

> Perhaps the human body is where the most significant symbols and practices of dancehall circulate. However, through fashion, speech, and techniques of the body, ghetto youth mark their participation in dancehall . . . haircuts, and jewelry worn to dancehall sessions have now become daily garb . . . Because dancehall is driven by fashion cycles, it is tempting to think of it as a merely superficial cultural style. Yet dancehall plays a deeper role in shaping notions about personhood – that is, the motivations, values, and worldviews of young children (2).

Stolzoff reminded me of the importance of the practitioners' lived experience as his 'outsider' explanation would have differed if he had engaged the phenomenon through the eyes of the life lived participants. Stolzoff's documentation has undergone *evo-revo*[14] changes since the time of his writing. Perhaps the most marked is the impression he gives that "Dancehall is driven by fashion" (Stolzoff, 2000). Today, most of those acquainted with daaance'all will argue that daaance'all is driven primarily by the constant creation of daaance movements, which is married to music and to fashion. Prominence has been given to the word *daaance* in daaance'all, and the argument will be put forward that perhaps it was always so, even if disguised by the layers of fashion that embellished it in its early stages.

Daaance is one of the tools which enamour the participants with liberation and security in the space. Lady Saw's[15] lyrics validates the "sexual liberation of many African-Jamaican working-class women from airy fairy Judeo-Christianity definitions of appropriate female behaviour" (Cooper, 2004, p. 99). This liberation of spirit, mind and body of the males and females in the daaance'all is not one of insecurity but one of pride and sanctuary, exhibiting that they are all comfortable in their own skin.

I must emphasize that Caribbean dance is never without a purpose, and over the years some of the purposes of the daaance in daaance'all are to present males and females as sexy, fashionable, talented and warriors. This has led to a global acceptance of the movement structure, fashion and attitude. As such, large groups of international dancers are consistently arriving in Jamaica to live the experience and learn how to become daaance'all dancers with the assertiveness and the body language of Jamaican practitioners. They also aim to learn the rich cultural explosion of movements in order to become internationally famous as a choreographer.

To interrogate this concept of in/securities within the framework of the daaance'all yaads, I considered the interrelated strands of history, geography, ethnography, anthropology, sociology, economics, fine arts, music, gender studies and philosophy which are interwoven to create this postmodern Jamaican art form including dance. Fortunately, daaance'all is attracting much interest in academic circles, and resource material includes the ground-breaking work of scholars such as Donna Hope, Carolyn Cooper, Norman Stolzoff and Sonjah N. Stanley Niaah, to name a few. In examining the concept of securities/insecurities in daaance'all I also looked at the definitions presented in the works of the scholars highlighted as well as those shared by the organic scholars I was privileged to interview. My approach to the frame called 'the dance' is not focused on language or spatial arrangements in the daaance'all but on how the social and psychological dynamics, which lead the aesthetics of the spirit, mind and body within the daaance yaads, are all factors that inform the in/securities of the space.

Stolzoff (2000) states that "Dancehall is a multidimensional force, at once symbolic and material, that permeates and structures everyday life in Jamaica (1)." This "multidimensional force of Daaance'all" has its beginnings within the underground faaambily on the enslaved plantations, which were originally located in open-air 'social and spiritual' yaads. Today the memories of the underground faaambily have evolved into sessions held on streets and unorthodox locations (e.g. out-of-use car parks), and at stage shows in which the daaance'all movement and the accompanying "chanting" (deejaying) occur. The primary purpose of the attendees is the same as the enslaved on the plantation many centuries past, that is, to celebrate life, which for many inner-city youths is often numbered. The daaance is celebrated *via* body energy, moving unrestrainedly to the vibrations of characteristic rhythms, quaint (unfamiliar to the outsider) word usage, carnivalesque adornment (masquerading), and the uninhibited use of space which are the expressions of the ancestral shouts retained within them, making life endurable in the ghettoes of Jamaica (Pinnock, 2010, p. 100). In the inner cities/garrisons/ghettoes, the residents define who they are by appropriating the freedom to reshape and redefine their standards however and whenever they choose. These uninhibited uses of body, word sound and space are all expressions of ancestral shouts retained within the daaance'all yaads, all of these making life endurable in the inner cities/ghettos/garrisons of Jamaica. Daaance'all kings and queens of music and daaance lead the revolution to redefine themselves within their chosen paradigms while seizing the freedom to reconstruct their standards however, and whenever they chose and within their own socially morphed in/securities.

I was having a casual conversation with a daaance'all dancer and admiring her outfit on that specific night, after which I asked her how she afforded such fashionable clothes and expensive boots. She responded proudly and said "My Badi a fe me BMW (my body is my BMW)". This badi (body) interrogates the shifting in/securities within the co-culture daaance'all.

Yes massa – switching codes

In a personal interview with the late Rex Nettleford, he spoke to the ability of Caribbean people to "code switch".[16] In daaance'all communities code-switching is a feature of daily 'livity', as a survival tool. It is evident that the ancestors were highly successful due to constantly and fluidly switching codes. An aspect of code-switching is the practitioners' attitudes that mirror that of the enslaved Africans, smiling for massa while conniving to overthrow him. The 'massas' in this case are those members of society who autocratically make uninformed decisions about the less privileged, fringe-dwellers of society – but it is they, the downtrodden, who are the organic daaance'all practitioners, the creators of its music and movement and the progenitors of its spirit.

At any session, the careful observer may recognize audible, physical and conscious code-switching in the music played and the dances performed. The DJ (or deejay) takes the participants through a melange of reggae music (inclusive and dominantly daaance'all), traditional rhythms, African American R&B and hip-hop, with gospel thrown in if, or when, he/she elects to code-switch to a fleeting mood of reverence, possibly when the session has run through the night into early Sunday morning. The musical safari typifies the dynamics and fluidity of the organic practitioners to code-switch spontaneously in their music and the related dance movements.

The rhythms, lyrics and daaances emerging from the belly of the inner cities are conscious efforts of inner-city dwellers to document themselves and their creations under Brand Jamaica. Daaance'all is the twentieth-century revolutionary process through which marginalized people have claimed their own space and created their own identities. Daaance'all represents a bloodless revolution against a class hegemony that erected invisible walls to maintain the *status quo* of disenfranchised people (Cooper, 2004).

A multiplicity of sub-liminal hegemonic issues causes those who are not of similar circumstances to misunderstand and therefore misinterpret the actions of the daaance'all practitioner who has kept code-switching alive as a performance tool of resistance and revolution.

Warrior wo/men[17]

I have worked in many capacities over the years on daaance'all movies, videos as well as a lecturer and a teacher of the dance, resulting in me developing many students, friends and children. These relationships inspired me to name the practitioners in daaance'all warrior wo/men. As a practitioner of the Yoruba religion, I *zight*[18] in them the Yoruba Orishas[19] Oshun,[20] Jemunja,[21] Oya,[22] Shango[23] and Ogun,[24] to name a few.

44   L'Antoinette Stines

The world is enamoured by the Jamaican daaance'all dancers, and as such, they are very often called upon to daaance in videos and movies. These locations often bring to light the placement of securities and insecurities, which exist in the space. I share two such occasions. On one movie set, which I prefer to remain nameless, a Black American choreographer was hired to lead-choreograph the dancers for the movie specifically focused on what I refer to as the 'contrived winning group' in the movie. They gave the group, which was to be the 'forced losing group' the job to choreograph themselves, but the African American choreographer had the power to dictate to them as well. When the "forced losing group" with the warrior women returned to the set with their choreography, they outshined the "contrived winning group" whose dance was choreographed by the foreign choreographer. The insecurities of the outsider[25] choreographer who had already received international acclaim for, what is referred to by most Jamaican choreographers as, watered movement structure with Jamaican similarities was publicly evident. The securities of the forced losing group comprised daaance'all diva warrior women born and bred in the daaance'all yaads, and in some cases the creators of some of the famous daaance'all steps were also apparent.

It must be noted that the warrior wo/men movements are an exploration of all their daily cultural lives. The sound, shape and energy of the movements remember the sound and constant vibrations of gunshots, the conversations while sitting on the roadside doing manicures, pedicures and braiding hair, the fights that occur with Mattie,[26] the struggle to survive by bridging light,[27] and running boat[28] so that the community can have a meal while publicly and proudly breastfeeding, posturing their stretch marks called beauty spots, as this is her proof of fertility. The group choreographed by a team of daaance'all warrior women was immediately asked to tone down their choreography so that the "contrived winning group" could visibly win. The questions therefore arise: Why would the foreign organizers come to the home of daance'all and bring a foreign choreographer who has not spent time living and researching like the famed Tanisha Scott,[29] who although grew up abroad is of Jamaican heritage and has made focused efforts to overstand the innuendos of the movement? Why is it not clear that being Jamaican and living inside the experience enables an overstanding of the movements, which reflects life in the inner-city yaads?

The insecurity in the contrived winning group led by the foreign choreographer who rarely visited Jamaica was noticeable. On the other hand, the secure Asante warrior women decided that they were being disrespected and made their choreographer even more challenging. They decided that the opposing foreign choreographer must enhance her choreography. The concept of the movie became real on the set.

On another set, a Black American stylist was brought to Jamaica to dress the cast. He decided that he would allow the Jamaican dressers to dress the extras and he would focus on the main artist. On arrival to the set, the artist asked for one of the dresses to be removed from the cast and given to her, as the warrior woman's outfit was definitely outshining the one chosen for her by the foreign stylist. The girl who was undressed remarked "IF DEM EVEN LEF

ME NAKED WHEN ME DANCE DEM AFE SEE ME" translated "If they remove my clothes and leave me naked, when I dance everybody have to see me." The girl was one of Jamaica's daaance'all queens. The stories are many.

Daaance'all fashion is created in the inner cities by the warrior men and women, therefore, 'why wouldn't one consult them?' The answer might be that even before landing in Jamaica, the egos are flying and they are possibly unaware of their insecurities or lack of education that Jamaica is the daaance'all capital of the world.

The security began on the bodies of the enslaved on the plantation in Jamaica, where Asante warrior principles reside and remain until today. Another question arises: Why are outsiders deciding that they are now the source and not conceding to the origins of the phenomenon called daaance'all? Why is it not accepted that Jamaican inner-city youth dug daaance'all from the bowels of ancestral memories, which reside here in Jamaica?

It has been my good fortune to choreograph for several international artistes, such as Patra,[30] Sean Paul,[31] Shabba Ranks (Rexton Gordon),[32] Etana, Diana King and Foxy Brown. It was while choreographing for Shabba Ranks that I was made aware of the level of disregard experienced for the organic Caribbean choreographers. I had heard stories of how they were often slighted by foreign record labels, but I had to experience it for myself.

My Shabba Ranks experience began after being asked to go to New York to choreograph dancers for Shabba's tour of the United States. When I arrived at my first rehearsal, Shabba was waiting for his musicians. I was reminded of Bob Marley[33] who was reputed to have been always punctual for rehearsals and performances. The musicians arrived and so did three other choreographers. One musician pulled me aside to tell me that he did not like the choreography and hoped I would improve it.

I waited patiently until three dancers arrived. I could not help noticing their 'diva' attitude, nor could I fail to sense the insecurity of the three choreographers when they strutted in. I was introduced as the 'Jamaican choreographer'. What puzzled me was why Shabba needed four choreographers, so I openly questioned that point by asking: "Why are so many choreographers needed?" I was answered with a tint of condescension, "I am the hip hop choreographer, she is the African choreographer, and he is the *daincehawll* (ebonics) choreographer. We work for the record label." I did not find the response elucidating.

The rehearsal began and what I saw shocked me. There was not a hint of Jamaica reflected in the choreography! The daaance'all choreographer was Guyanese and had never been to Jamaica. His entire repertoire of daaance'all steps was isolated to roughly three or four basic ones. But as Shabba's choreography had to be completed in a few days, there was no time to dwell on problems. My job was obviously to find solutions. I visited a nearby Jamaican club and contacted three women who could do authentic daaance'all. They were invited to join the rehearsals the following day in order to demonstrate to Shabba's dancers the correct way to daaance. The daaancers brought with them authentic daaance'all razzmatazz. There was the fashion, the attitude, the body language of Jamaica as yaad and of course most important the purpose.

When Shabba entered the room and saw who had joined us, he looked at me and sneaked a wry smile. The rehearsal began. The Jamaican dancers proceeded to "bubble".[34] One girl placed the top of her head and both arms on the floor. She raised both legs above her head as in a handstand. Then, with her elbows on the ground and with her arms and fingers pointing forward for better balance, she demonstrated a "head-top bubble".[35] The Jamaican musicians instantly related to the authenticity of the movement and applauded wildly. The African American dancers and the other three choreographers were silent. For all of us present, it had been a moment of truth. The African Americans were accustomed to jazz and hip-hop as reflections of their 'self-identity.' The lived experiences of the marginalized and denigrated socio-cultural "garrison" dwellers had, through their struggles to survive, developed movements that reflected their struggles. They defied gravity and contorted with the ease of acrobats because their lives in Jamaica's ghettoes were full of sequences of defiance of logic, social norms and the law. They were masters at overcoming the topsy-turvy and of falling but landing on their feet.

The African American dancers made every effort to master the bubble and other daaance'all steps in an atmosphere of friendly give-and-take and sharing. In some instances we purged, and in others we compromised and synerbridged.[36] The choreographers, whose error had been that they assumed that daaance'all is movement devoid of any cultural history, changed their attitude and followed my instructions. Perhaps, because our bodies all claimed Africa as our source and sustenance, we got the show ready on time with no further hitches or confrontation.

In Jamaica, it is common to experience financially destitute young men cleaning car windows. This man with nothing to offer financially sees himself as a king because of his physical prowess. A friend of mine shared her story, which took place while she stopped at a corner in her BMW, where he told her about her beauty and his love for her and informed her of his ability to give her the best loving. The woman with all her education and wealth became insecure at that moment due to his confidence in his male powers. If she opened that car door he might step in and step up to the plate. It is that security that results in Jamaica's many megastars such as Jimmy Cliff, Marcia Griffith, Dawn Penn, Judy Mowatt, Burning Spear, Shaggy, Sean Paul and, of course, the honourable Robert Nesta Marley – Bob Marley.

Jamaica has successfully given birth to Sizzla, Buju Banton, Tanya Stephens, Lady Saw,[37] Spice, Chronixx and the legacy of Bob Marley lives on through his lineage of Damian Marley, Stephen Marley, Ziggy Marley and so on. In the world of sports, it is that Ashanti warrior security that has given birth to the worlds' fastest woman and man Shelley Ann Frazier and Usain Bolt.

We recognize the famous creations of daance'all dances by Bogle, Mr Wacky aka Gerald Levy with dance steps such as bogle, zip it up, wacky dip, world dance and more recently Ding Dong and the Ravers Clavers crew with such movements as flairy, and fling. I remind everyone that in daaance'all there was a time of female dominance in fashion and dance, then the males dominated with the daaance movements. However, women like Kimiko Miller, Dancing Rebel – Christine Nelson, Happy Feet – Tony Gay O'Meally, Latonya Style, who has written a book on the dances she created, Stacia Fyah and Shelley Callum are a few of the many who have securely forged through the dominantly male barriers and are admired for their creations alongside the men.

Many posit that the daaance'all practitioners are seeking attention because of their insecurities of being born inside poverty and always being downtrodden. These sexy erotic bodies are comfortable in their own skin, becoming international fashionistas garnering the runways of France, New York and London to name a few locations. The ghetto daaance'all dancers are gatekeepers of popular dance and envied by the other socio-economic classes who endeavour to look and dance like them. The Eurocentric canons of a dancing body state that one should have a flat stomach, no derriere/bottom, no big breasts, no knife marks especially on the face, no stretch marks (which the inner city regards as marks proving strength, and fertility).

These are warrior women who fight to feed their children, fight for their lives, fight to be equally accepted, fight for dance in daaance'all to be viable, and fight to be recognized and respected. Where have we seen these women in the history of Jamaica? These women who carry arms, present their bodies, and are fierce and fearless. Nanny of the Marroons, Portia Simpson (Jamaica's first and only female Black Prime Minister), Marion Hall a.k.a Lady Saw, Ventrice Morgan a.k.a. Queen Ifrica, Grace Latoya Hamilton, a.k.a, Spice and Carlene Smith a.k.a Carlene first to be called daaance'all queeen, whose carnivalesque fashionable display of the body led to her crowning as daaance'all queen Carlene Smith. I was the first to choreograph Carlene for the Uptown versus Downtown fashion show. Carlene, a soft-spoken intelligent woman, told me that she was going to make a difference in daaance'all with her fashion ideas. Carlene is an iconic figure in daaance'all and a difficult act to follow. When I assisted her to dress, I realized her in/securities about her weight and even the presentation of flesh; Carlene was never really naked. She wore skin-coloured tights and made certain her flesh was covered but she successfully achieved the impression of nakedness. However, she securely accepted herself, which includes flaws alongside her beauty. Her acceptance of her weaknesses and strengths became her superpowers. Carlene brought 'high fashion nakedness' to daaance'all which was deemed socially unacceptable. She was controversial and loved especially by the men.

Zight: don't judge me unfairly

In daaance'all the primary text is the dancing body married to the music. The lifestyle of a people in most instances has been transferred on the street by observation. Today it is becoming more institutionalized and offered in dance classes and the observation of individuals from YouTube. However, that could pose a problem if either of those conduits is infested with any form of hegemony, inaccurate research information or incorrect validating canons. Through *zight – the eyes of dance*, one is brought to the realization that Caribbean dance has been misunderstood for a variety of reasons, which include the following:

1) A canon system that has no relationship to Caribbean cultural and historical information is used to judge and classify Caribbean dance.

2) Eurocentric validating values were not eliminated or purged from the consciousness of those liminally or subliminally drafting the existing canon system.
3) Drafters of the existing canon system fell victim to 'reverse hegemony', which classified all Caribbean retentions as African, thereby disregarding or devaluing other influences or presences.
4) Conversely, the drafters fell victim to the hegemony that decided that European constructs were those through which the artistic and cultural components should be hierarchically positioned.

Those factors have resulted in the following:

a) Incorrect naming systems or creation of names for existing retentions with no regard for the names already designated by the source practitioners (the organic scholars).
b) Practitioners or artistic directors of African dance sequences/schools have made uninformed decisions on Caribbean dance continuities, assigning them to arbitrarily selected categories.
c) The use of classical ballet's philosophical constructs became the given standard used to validate the Caribbean dancing body as well as Caribbean movement structures.

The normal paradigms of Eurocentric canons cannot clarify or validate the African and other presences in Jamaica; and similarly, American or African American canons cannot validate the Caribbean. The canons of the "other" can only guide Caribbean dance researchers to achieve the following:

i) Establish comparative cultural values, that is, use the values of the "other" to make comparisons
ii) Accept and utilize different values when applicable
iii) Identify instances where values have been borrowed or copied
iv) Experience the 'tidalectic'[38] trading over time

Within the perspectives of Caribbean dance, I propose the following as the nucleus of a rational canon system that could move positively towards an epistemology of ontological dance. My phenomenology lens suggests that the missoverstanding[39] and onlookers' inexperience be reviewed through a new lens assisted by a Caribbean dance canon system as follows:

1) Although Christianity, as the dominant theology throughout the Caribbean, must be included in the canon system, marginalized religions of ancestral worship found throughout the Caribbean, for example Jamaica's Kumina and Revival, Trinidad's Caballa and Chango, Cuba's Santeria, Lucumi and Palo, Haiti's Voudun, and Guyana's Confi, should be included in the dance training to enhance a better understanding of the cosmology in which they are embedded.

2) Source persons interviewed or in any other way consulted by dance researchers must have their contributions acknowledged. Failure to do so would amount to plagiarism pertaining to the written word. The shared knowledge can be regarded as textual. Erna Brodber (1983, 1997) makes a claim for acknowledging the authority of oral traditions and body language:

> One of the consequences of scholarship's function as the matrix, which joins the sectors of Caribbean societies together, is the disvaluing of any other source of knowledge but book learning. Thus, contrary to what happened in other non-literate societies, a vigorous oral tradition in which a group's history was handed down, did not develop here. There were personalities, however, who were very particular that certain events and their involvement with them passed on to posterity. We are suggesting that the Caribbean historian makes himself into a *griot* and set about to collect these accounts. (45)

3) Research teams should always include the representation of the "organic intelligentsia", that is, the grass-roots griots who are knowledgeable practitioners in their specific area of expertise. The field workers/researchers/theorists are the persons who come from outside the source space to 'dig up' information, manipulate the information and hypothesize. They must interact and hypothesize with an understanding of the Caribbean canon system, accepting that Eurocentric canons are not the ultimate validation systems.
4) A valid naming system should be compiled. Naming here applies to all or any variations of cultural or geographical modalities. It is not necessary for the theorist to create names for the organic practitioner but should instead document the name given them by those grass-roots griots.
5) Categorizing Caribbean popular and contemporary dance within a Caribbean framework as it relates to body types and uses of the body in the indigenous and traditional dance are the guidelines to be included in the contemporary dance.

One must daaance the dance, feel the warm blood of the goat on one's forehead, "trump"[40] with the revivalists, experience the presence of the ancestors, and at a Missa[41] listen to messages from the Orisha, sit on the Kumina drums and beat the Nyahbingi[42] bass drum. The participant/observer eats with the Maroons,[43] holds the waists of the Bruckins[44] dancers and feels the point of initiation of the "break"[45] in the back, learns *Kwale Kwale*,[46] rivets one's bare foot into the earth, and knows the difference between a "duty", a "session", and a "groundation" in order to be able to identify the retentions that have become continuities. One should Bruk up u back, Flairy and Fling with the daaance'all dancers, acquaint themselves with the warrior women and men without fear, and get to know about their lives before one can truly validate it in writing or employ it in further creative forms.

Daaance'all is a co-culture within a culture whose retentions are many with many faces and diversity of hidden shades of code-switching. According to Chevannes (2001, p. 129): "Being and defining Jamaican, being and defining Canadian, being and defining anything is a necessary and urgent task".

Plantation spirit daaances on daaance'all

In Jamaica, plantation ritualistic spirit daaances are also found in Gherreh, Dinki Mini Tambu, and Etu. In other Caribbean islands, we find Yanvalou (Haitian), Palo (Cuban), Winti (Surinamese) and Cumfa (Guyanese). Such indigenous and traditional dances have informed daaance'all in terms of the use of space, language form, freedom to formulate fashion, food and culinary features, music, and movement.

Daaance'all remains close to the traditional Kumina, to the indigenous Bruckins and to the indige-traditional Nyabinghi. Retentions from these are preserved in many of the movements. The grounding of the knees, almost always bent, is served in both Kumina and Bruckins. The Kumina pivot step is adapted into a daaance'all style. Bruckins is represented in the 'breaking' of the shoulder blades and back. Limbo, another African preservation, may appear in daaance'all, as well as, the intricate footwork (seen in Ghana and Guinea).[47] The open hips (turn-out) of classical ballet is the normal stance of the male daaance'all practitioner, but the female, by isolating the gluteal muscles vibrates and pulsates them. The hips move either in smooth circular action or in staccato jerks referred to as *tick tack*. In short, many traditional and indigenous movements such as the convoluting back of Gherreh, the breaks in Tambu and Etu, the inching of Kumina, the knock-kneed progression step of Dinki Mini, the elevations of Binghi, the gliding leg work of Bruckins, and the silent trumping of Revival are reissued in daaance'all. They may be given different names or the names may remain the same, but there can be no doubt that traditional movements inform daaance'all choreography. The body memories of the plantation's religious spirit daaances, the Jamaican cultural infant, recently weaned from the breast of plantation support, had become a lively adolescent and has risen tall and on its own daaancing feet.

The social and popular daaances in the plantation period included the maypole, quadrille, Jonkonnu (a West-African retention) and Bruckins. Those daaances with their own musical rhythms, costumes, elements of masquerade and predictable code-switching also inform the apparel, body movement and sense of theatre displayed in modern daaance'all.[48] Bruckins, although morphed to meet modern and economic demands, remains culturally ingrained in the daaance'all genre. For example, the carnivalesque quality of the apparel worn in daaance'all today is reminiscent of the set girls of the 1700s. In 1790, William Beckford documented the first reference to 'set girls'.

> At Christmas, the Negroes upon the neighbouring estates are divided in different parties, some call themselves the blue girls and some the red; and their clothes are generally characteristic of their attachment. . . . Each set had a sponsor usually the mistress of the plantation. The sets were intensely competitive. They sought to outdance, outdress and outsing their competitors. They practiced their routines with discipline and vigour, and they placed great stock in the outcome of the competition.
>
> (79)

Set girls were present in 1834 at the Bruckins parties held to celebrate the Emancipation. Beckford recalls the groups under the name courtiers and set girls, and his account is comparable to a description of today's daaance'all posses.[49] Posses first emerged in the 1970s. Groups of men and boys (mirroring courtiers) and women and girls (mirroring set girls) wore similar outfits and colours and adornments and danced in groups. The fashion re-emerged in the late 1980s in a modernized version, where the women's dresses became sparser and the men donned jewellery that they called *bling*. As in the nineteenth century, however, when Bruckins was based on keen competition between rival plantations, with kudos to the winners, strong socio-political statements were made by winning daaance'all groups and clashes, usually representing rival areas of depressed communities in the nation's capital city. Their kudos was the admiration of their peers and adulation of their community. When we look at the historical perspective of traditional daaance in Jamaica, we come to realize that they all impact upon the daaance'all yard.

It should not be forgotten that daaance'all preserves the memories of Africa in the movements of the bodies, in the arrangements of the music, in the utilization and choice of space, and in the purposes that steer the gatherings. Daaance'all will not allow the nation to ignore its links to Africa as its homeland. Neither should it be forgotten that, like the steel pan of Trinidad and Tobago, the only new musical instrument created in the twentieth century,[50] so too, I propose that reggae and daaance'all are among the new creations of the twentieth century. Yet we find that daaance'all is still regarded by some as a cover-up or front for many illegal business transactions, and its practitioners assessed as a cultural sub-stratum created by and for the uneducated and unsophisticated of the country.[51]

Conclusion

Jamaica is a predominantly Christian society in which many find everything daaance'all disturbing. However, against all odds, this dynamic phenomenon revolutionized from the bottom as a sub-culture, has evolved into a co-culture, and in some instances a dominant cultural representation due to its international exposure. Insecurity occurs in daaance'all more commonly from the non-practitioners. Hegemony is construed inside invalid canon systems with which Caribbean dance is judged. Misunderstandings of the dance and the bodies who execute them are evident among those who both live inside and outside the space. The common saying that a little bit of knowledge is worse than no knowledge at all in many cases arise when Caribbean dance is being critiqued, both by the onlookers and even among insiders within the Caribbean yaad.[52] The lack of phenomenological experience has in many instances resulted in biased opinions.

Many years have passed, and I note that there are improvements to outsiders' execution of daance'all movements; however, the downtrodden attitude of disrespect to the organic practitioners still remains. This is evident in outsider–insider and insider–outsider academic documentations of the space as well as by artists, especially choreographers who create videos without the acknowledgement of their sources.

In contrast, those who are 'dissed' for their daaance'all connection regard it as an underground route that moves them from entrapment and deprivation to social mobility and recognition of their abilities, creativity, skills through the music, the daaance, the fashion, and now the business ventures they undertake. Daance'all, against bitter criticism, is lauded by a majority of all Jamaicans for the international impact, empowering, economic viability resulting in the upgrade of the practice from the position of being a *sub*-culture to what I classify as a *co*-culture. Based on daaance'all's global visibility, political negotiations and artistic ingenuity, it can no longer be accurately labelled 'sub'. It is now a recognizable partner in the socio-cultural affairs of Jamaica. To use its own parlance, it is "married to livity". Daance'all no longer struggles to hold a place on the periphery but has claimed a central spot on society's consciousness. The massive achievements are signs of securities among the practitioners. Daaance'all has been analysed and documented by scholars who conclude that daaance'all will securely continue to "wake the town and tell the people".[53]

Notes

1 Highly seasoned soup made from parts of slaughtered goats including the heads and intestines.
2 Bread-like loaf made from pounded cassava tubers.
3 Presented at the University of the West Indies as a series of Lectures for Dr Carolyn Cooper in 2001. My experience of the daaance'all scene of the 1990s.
4 Evo-revo: the phenomenon of evolution and revolution occurring concurrently.
5 Overstanding: Practitioners of Rastafari Levity use *over* instead of *under*. For Rastafari, the use of under in this specific word means lexically below, beneath, insufficiently, incompletely which is the same as to not comprehend while to 'ovas' is to fully comprehend.
6 Fredrick Moncrieffe (2007) – founder, artistic director, and choreographer of the Squad One group from Rollington Town, an economically deprived section of Kingston.
7 Co-culture: A designation I offered in my PhD thesis to define daaance'all. Co-culture is my placement daaance'all as it resides equally alongside all the cultural artefacts in Jamaica and is now one of the tools representing Jamaica internationally.
8 Daaance: I also call Spirit Daaance which is the natural movement that represents precise identity for people of different cultures and is found specific to each nation state; Spirit Daaance are dances of purpose that communicate the spirit of a people.
9 Daunce: Refers to the movement structures dominated by the vocabulary of foreign European Classical ballet, which remains the dominant procedure for the training of modern contemporary dancers. Daunce represents the culture of Europe and is focused on the elevation and execution of geometric shapes.
10 Gerald Levy Bogle – creator of several well-known popular dance steps, for example, 'The Bogle', 'Sesame Street', 'Sweeper', 'Zip it Up', 'Row You Boat'.
11 Crab: also a creator of popular dance moves.
12 See also Hope (2006, p. 26).
13 Faaambily: this is the pronunciation of the word family given to genetic family and those loved and regarded as family.
14 Evo-revo: the phenomenon of evolution and revolution occurring concurrently.
15 Arguably for many years the leading female Jamaican singer of 'pop' music, known for her often raunchy lyrics and suggestive movement, although she also offers daring lyrics

Me badi a fe me BMW (my body is my BMW) 53

about socio-sexual problems that have tended to be swept under the carpet. Lady Saw is now a Christian and has given up her daaance'all career; however, her queenship still remains valid and gives a voice to many problems.
16 Nettleford (1993, p. 84.)
17 Wo/men to designate both women and men.
18 Zight: My newly coined word heavily influenced by Zee, Zeen from the Rastafari lexicon meaning spiritual sight.
19 Orishas: spirits.
20 Oshun: The name of the Goddess of the river whose attributes are love, and fertility in the Yoruba pantheon.
21 Jemunja: The names of the Goddess of the ocean who lives alongside Jemunja Olocun the God/dess of the deep ocean.
22 Oya: The Goddess of the graveyard.
23 Shango: The God of thunder
24 Ogun: The God of war.
25 Outsider: A person who has lived outside of the consciousness of the space.
26 Mattie: A person who is in an affair, who is in a relationship with another person's man.
27 Bridging light: Illegally reconnecting the light for their houses after the Jamaica Public Service (JPS) has disconnected it for lack of payment or in the case of inner cities to connect and never inform JPS.
28 Running boat: each person gives some funds in-kind or money so that one big meal can be made to be shared in order for each person to have a meal on that day.
29 Tanisha Scott: Internationally acclaimed choreographer of Jamaican descent.
30 A DJ who worked with Shabba Ranks and was the featured singer with him on his hit record 'Family Affair'.
31 An internationally recognized reggae and dancehall vocalist, recording artist, and DJ.
32 A dancehall exponent and reggae recording artiste. A protégé of Jose Wales, he was the First Jamaican DJ to gain international recognition, in spite of some people's reservations about the "slackness" of some of his lyrics.
33 Honorable Robert 'Nesta' Marley OM is Jamaica's most famous reggae singer, composer, performer and folk philosopher. He is accredited with originating reggae, along with Bunny Rugs and Peter Tosh (other members of Bob Marley and the Wailers). Reggae blends R&B, Jazz, Mento and Binghi, a highly classical sound that has captured the world's attention.
34 Bubble: A dance step usually executed by the women. The movement of the hips is circular or in a figure-of-eight pattern, forwards and backwards. The movement is smooth and sensual. (See Appendix 19.)
35 This dance, first demonstrated in the 1980s, is said to have been created by 'Crab'. To perform it, the dancer puts her head on the ground using her elbows and arms to balance, moving her feet in various positions, usually kept wide apart, while the dancer moves her hips in a bubble as described earlier. The movement is similar to American street dancers' acrobatic dance motifs.
36 Synerbridged: fluid traversing between cultures.
37 Lady Saw: Stage Name for Marian Hall.
38 Tidalectic: Brathwaite, 1994, pp. 240–241 "the movement of water backwards and forward as a kind of cyclic motion rather than linear". www.hawai.edu/cpis/psu/literature/lit_arch.htm.
39 Miss-overstanding:
40 A characteristic movement of Revival worship, where heavy breathing accompanies movement that usually induces spirit possession (from an unpublished paper given to the author by Mr. Seaga, titled Kumina, A Pure Gem of African Retention).
41 A ritual held to call Orishas and ancestors to communicate by using a worshipper's body as *a horse* for the deities, Orishas or ancestors to verbally *carry* their messages to their adherents. Normally practised in Yoruba, Santeria, Candomble, Shango, Vodun and Palo.
42 Suggested by Chevannes (1995) to mean "death to all black and white oppressors". Also the name of an order of Rastafari.

43 Runaway slaves whose descendants may be found throughout the Caribbean, especially in Jamaica and Suriname.
44 Festivity originally created by newly freed slaves to celebrate the abolition of slavery, with costumes and dance patterns mimicking the slave owners and overseers. Bruckins was accompanied by drumming and songs. It is still practised in parts of the Caribbean, mainly in Jamaica. Hill 247–249, Lewin 113–118.
45 Movement in Kumina, Bruckins, Tambu, Etu, Santeria, etc., where the dancers and drummers come to a halt in unison. In Bruckins, there is another type of 'break' which is marked by a mimed snap of the wrists to symbolize the breaking of chains at Emancipation.
46 See 'The Spirit of African Survival' *Jamaica Journal* #43, documented first by Edward Seaga and by the Oriental Institute of Languages, London, as the *Lord's Prayer* in Kikongo.
47 Stanley Niaah, 2004, p. 102.
48 See Hope (2006, pp. 71–79; Stolzoff, pp. 56–57, 110–111; Stanley Niaah, 2004, n.p.).
49 Posses: Group of men or women who dress alike usually to attend street dances and other fetes.
50 Manuel, Bilby, Largey 205.
51 Hope 86–121.
52 Yaad: Barry Chevannes' phonetical spelling of yard representing spiritual and cultural yards such as Seal Yaads and Kumina Yaads.
53 Original title of URoy regarded as Jamaica's first DJ in the 1960s.

References

Brathwaite, K. (1994) *Trench Town Rock*. Providence: Lost Roads Publishers.

Brodber, E. (1983) Oral Sources and the Creation of a Social History of the Caribbean. *Jamaica Journal* 16.

Brodber, E. (1997) Reengineering Black Space. *Caribbean Quarterly. The Plenaries: Conference on Caribbean Culture in Honour of Professor Rex Nettleford* 43(1–2).

Chevannes, B. (1995) *Rastafari Roots and Ideology*. Syracuse University Press Series. Jamaica, Trinidad and Tobago: The University of the West Indies, Barbados.

Chevannes, B. (2001) Jamaican Diasporic Identity: The Metaphor of Yaad. In P. Taylor (Ed.), *Nation Dance*. Bloomington, IN: Indiana University Press, pp. 129–137.

Cooper, C. (2004) *Sound Clash: Jamaican Dancehall Culture at Large*. Basingstoke: Palgrave Macmillan.

Hope, D. (2006) *Inna di Dancehall: Popular Culture and the Politics of Identity in Jamaica*. Kingston: University of the West Indies Press.

Moncrieffe, Frederick (a.k.a Tippa). (2007) Personal Interview, June.

Nettleford, R. (1993) *Inward Stretch Outward Reach: A Voice from the Caribbean*. London: Palgrave Macmillan.

Pinnock, T. (2010) Rasta and Reggae. In S. Sloat (Ed.), *Caribbean Dance from Abakua to Zouk*. Gainesville, FL: University of Florida, pp. 95–106.

Stanley Niaah, S. (2004) Kingston's Dancehall a Story of Space and Celebration. In *Space and Culture*. Vol. 7.1. Thousand Oaks, CA: Sage Publications, pp. 102–118, February.

Stolzoff, N. C. (2000) *Wake the Town & Tell the People: Dancehall Culture in Jamaica*. Durham and London: Duke University Press.

4 Interrogating in/securities in the recording studios of Kingston

Dennis Howard

"Cut! You can play bass? leave the studio I don't want you inside here!"

This chapter will interrogate the concept of in/security as it relates to the popular music scene in Kingston. The recording studio can be a secure space for those who are accepted by the creative collectives that govern and police that space. Hence the issue of in/securities in this chapter centres around the negotiations needed to gain acceptance to this creative space in order to express their creativity with the ultimate aim of making an impact in the entertainment business. There is also the in/security that surrounds making it to the studio but still having to prove oneself by making hits, which itself creates its own fragility when one has to repeat success for a sustained period. The production processes in the studios of Kingston present an intriguing manifestation of creative democratization on one hand, where the music-making process sets up scenarios that facilitate easy entry for some, while, on the other hand, the gate-keeping process still exists in a very forceful and unforgiving way which affects modes of production, star creation, hit music creation, and leads to endless frustration and disappointment for the majority of entrants to the music scene. This in/security is prevalent, even necessary, despite the glamorous stories of major successes that are associated with the industry. Using case study and ethnographic enquiry, this chapter attempts to shed light on the complicated process of selection, production and acceptance which plays out in the studios of Kingston and how it affects the output of music production, which is so influential globally.

Kingston's creative in/security

The concept of global in/security has been delineated through three distinctive elements. However, for the purposes of this chapter, I will interrogate in/security from perspectives that are "characterized by forms of negotiative agency that are amenable to exploration via creative practice". According to Patricia Noxolo (2018), creative practice is seen as "a resource for examining

DOI: 10.4324/9781003205500-5

specific modes of negotiative agency"; she gives examples such as "discursive, corporeal, and visual modes". She continues,

> Creative negotiation is at the heart of creative agency: the risk that the artwork will not go well or will not arrive at all is played out through negotiation with the possibilities and limits of a wide range of accessible media, whether words on a screen or page, ink on paper, the dancing body, or the sound of music or spoken words.
>
> (p. 40)

In analysing the creative process involved in the making of sound recordings in Kingston's music scene, the systems model of creativity (Csikszentmihalyi, 1988) is a useful tool for theorising on the outcomes of the making of popular music.

Drawing on the work of Csikszentmihalyi (1988), McIntyre (2008, p. 41) states, "The systems model proposes that the confluence of a number of factors must be in place for creativity to occur, and sees creativity resulting from a complex process that is less individual-focused than systemic in operation." A critical aspect of the systems model of creativity as outlined by Mckintyre is that "this system comprises of a domain of knowledge, a field or social organization that understands that knowledge, and an individual whose task it is to make changes in the domain. The system, in this case, has circular causality, as it may not necessarily start with an individual but may be instigated by any component within the system."

So far, this chapter has focused on laying out the theoretical terrain, which will guide the chapter going forward. The following section will discuss the concept of in/securities in Jamaican popular music, reggae and dancehall, in particular, through the lenses of livelihood in/securities, environmental in/securities and creative risk.

Creative risk in genre labelling in/securities

For this chapter, I have deliberately omitted the use of the term dancehall to describe both the genre and its cultural manifestations. In my view, dancehall in terms of a musical expression with a particular signature and musical identity has hardly been practised for the last ten years. The lack of acknowledgement that the music style has shifted and needs to be labelled as a new genre is one of the main obstacles in the progress of Jamaican popular music. This lack of clarity in terms of identification of genre trends is a result of the power of the cultural and sociological gatekeepers, who wish to romanticize particular eras, making the music static. This is not the nature of culture. Culture evolves and music is one form that records the evolution.

There have been attempts to rebrand our music: producers Sly and Robbie introduced reggae bangara and la trengue during the 1990s, in recognition of the work they did by fusing bhangra, mento and salsa into the music.[2] Richie

Stevens introduced ska tech, and Supreme Promotions, owners of the infamous dancehall concert series, attempted to rebrand dancehall as EDH (electronic dancehall). There have been recent attempts of cultural appropriation of Jamaican popular music by rebranding it as tropical house.[3] I have written on these genre changes and the need to label the forms of musical styles (Howard, 2012). This highlights issues of cultural erasure and appropriation which have been a major issue for Caribbean music from as early as the 1950s. Mento at that time was labelled as kalypso in order to cash in on the calypso craze of the 1950s in the United States. The British group the Police refashioned reggae in the 1980s and became international superstars. Recently Justin Bieber and Rihanna reworked Jamaican dancehall and fusion sounds to create major international hit songs "Sorry" and "Work". In Kingston, the music has been experiencing transitional and in-between periods of genre modification which have moved the music away from the dancehall label, a label that is proving an inadequate signifier for the music being produced. I have labelled the new syncretic styles that have emerged *one beat* (Howard, 2012).

Genre blending is not a new phenomenon and has been practised in many music scenes including Kingston, Port of Spain, New York Liverpool, London, Miami and Atlanta. What is of major concern is the appropriation without acknowledgement which is practised by the major music conglomerates of the Anglo-American music industry. As Harley Brown (2016) accurately noted,

> The real issue here isn't technical or branding differences between genre signifiers, it's that arbiters of musical knowledge are contributing to the continual whitewashing of dance music's roots in black, Latino, queer communities – in other words, artists who already could and should be represented in the mainstream.

These attempts at rebranding and labelling have so far made no impact, despite the realization by the industry that the current musical output has evolved into a new form of music and creativity alongside established genres such as reggae and dancehall.

Syncretism is not a new phenomenon for Jamaican popular music: in fact, it has been one of the essential features of music-making in Kingston. The original dancehall sound was a revival of the rocksteady and reggae roots with a different vocal and mixing style – a more singjay and deejay style. In terms of recording, it employed the sound system and dub aesthetic, such as the "mixing" of the fader. It was an extreme challenge to label music dancehall, and it began with journalists and disc-jockeys. It was Sugar Minott who came up with the name for the genre, and when journalists and radio deejays started to call the music dancehall there was major backlash saying that no genre can be called dancehall, because dancehall is a space where popular music of all types are played for entertainment purposes. The original dancehall music was not readily distinguishable from reggae and rocksteady due to the reusing of old rocksteady and reggae "riddims". In a dancehall live show, the backing would recycle a set of riddims, including "answer mi question", "full up", "throw mi corn", "heavenless" and "rockfort rock", for the entire night; top backing band Sagittarius would play the same riddims and all the deejays would perform on these backing tracks. The riddims were easy to sing on as it used only two chords and, usually, the keys were in the lower register which allowed almost anyone to perform on them.

This is where democratization comes in – persons, who in the earlier days could not go into a studio because they could not sing, hold high notes or had not mastered singing styles such as legato and melisma, now had a chance to become recording artists. In this case, one of the major insecurities of cultural labour was averted by the production techniques and the acceptance of unique singing styles such as singjaying. The uncertainties of genre formations, the lack of a central collective to identify and claim the latest developments in music trends, have created creative in/securities that have created a serious conundrum for the Jamaican music industry, which is now in a crisis of identity. There's a clear need to acknowledge the existence of a new genre, and that the phenomenon of popular music culture has gone past labels such as dancehall.

Creative in/security is at a peak and must be resolved if the music is to move and thrive internationally. The ambiguities and identity crisis we are now experiencing have to be resolved in the shortest time possible to alleviate the creative flux and brand confusion the Jamaican music industry is experiencing. This while other new genres such as trap, grime, afrobeats, amapiano and dubstep are establishing a footprint globally. The important thing about culture is that it is never static. It is always changing based on environmental influences such as geo-political conditions, technology and socioeconomics. It is unfortunate that oftentimes cultural practitioners, theorists, and intellectuals constrain the phenomenon under study by holding on to outdated analyses of culture and as a result resist growth. We often hold on too tightly, even in the popular cultural space.

For example, veteran and established producers, artists and even radio presenters have complained about the fact that younger artists/producers are creating recordings that do not fit any discrete Jamaican genre classification. In the absence of any classification of these new musical styles, these new recordings are erroneously labelled as hip-hop or fusion. These "purists" consider them a waste of time, unworthy of any merit, and admonish the new sound with declarations of returning to roots. Ironically, this was the same conversation when dancehall was being birthed. It was said that it was "foolishness," that we must go back to reggae, that we must go back to rocksteady. So it is with every innovation, that it suffers the rebuke from the last great formation.

In the 1970s, Bob Marley and Chris Blackwell experimented with albums like *Kaya* and *Exodus*, to appeal to the rock market, they were criticized in Jamaica and other places, who claimed that Marley had sold out or that he had watered down his content. When the One Love Concert was done, Bob had just released *Kaya* which was doing well worldwide. When Jamaica was introduced to it, the mature fans hated it, but younger music fans were more open to the inclusion of other sounds and textures in the music; they loved it. The criticism by the reggae purists affected Marley's choice of songs so much that during the "One Love Concert" he never performed a song from *Kaya* and opted for songs from *Rastaman Vibration* and *Natty Dread*, which by that time were dated recordings. There was great pressure meted out on him by many, who said he had sold out with songs such as *Is this love*, not remembering that Bob Marley always used to sing "It Hurts to Be Alone" and other love songs. His own success as a militant rastaman who "bun dung Babylon" always fuelled the belief that there was no other side to him, and so he was never expected to have any softer feelings and should not experiment with music.

Bob's *Catch a Fire* album was a disaster in Jamaica. Allan "Skill" Cole, recounted in a personal communication, stated that they could not give the albums away, because no one wanted to hear it – it was considered watered down and devoid of the bass sonic texture that was critical to reggae. Chris Blackwell had introduced the blues guitar with *Catch a Fire* which changed the sonic architecture of Jamaican popular music. Every band now include a guitarist who plays blues and rock type riffs and solos. The notion of merging blues/rock aesthetics in reggae before *Catch a Fire* would not have been an accepted practice. However, culture evolves, and what better to record this evolution than music? The change is rejected initially until it becomes normative. Then, when something new comes along it is again rejected, and the cycle continues.

In/security in the streets

Environmental in/securities[4] are a major feature of popular music production from a safety standpoint, especially in the first 20 years of recorded music history. Studios were located in inner-city areas of Kingston. In the dancehall period, more so, the top studios were located in communities such as Waterhouse, Maxfield Avenue, Rollington Town and Olympic Gardens. These communities had a very high incidence of violence, and a lot of the recording talent stems from these same communities. Violence was a constant feature of everyday life for most inner-city inhabitants so many escaped it through the sanctuary of the studio. In these areas, which are called garrisons, musicians are protected from violence due to the exalted position they enjoy in these areas and are given political immunity (see Howard, 2010). This also enables them to move freely in areas that are divided and are restricted to opposing community members. However, free movement is sometimes restricted for Kingston's creative labour force due to ongoing gun violence and the artists are warned by the community against visiting the studio until the gunfights are over or interrupted by police intervention.

This level of insecurity in the recording music industry is a critical factor that is usually ignored by academic or journalistic accounts of Jamaican popular music. Environment plays an important part in any creative process: in fact, Richard Florida (2000, p. 95) states that "places that offer stimulating, creative environment" is a critical component for the viability of a creative class. Charles Landry (2008) also states that a stable, violence-free environment is essential to the survival of creative city initiatives aimed at the revitalization of urban decay. However, for the first three decades of music creation in Kingston, studios were located in violence-prone areas and recording artists lived in these areas, which could hardly be described as creative zones. In the Kingston music scene, it is hazardous being a music industry member, a fact that has not had sufficient interrogation. Creative personnel have regularly been the victims of crimes ranging from robbery, assault, fraud, kidnapping and murder. There are several famous cases of murder, including DJ Pan Head, Major Worries, Dirts Man, Nitty Gritty, Tenor Saw, Oniel Voicemail, dancer Bogle, producer Roache, promoter Fada Fowl and producer Winston Riley.

Creative labour in/securities

Patricia Noxolo (2018, p. 40) observed that "creative negotiation is at the heart of creative agency". While there is a democratic process of music-making in the studios of Kingston, it is still one that is hierarchical in its organization. In the studio environment all around Kingston, there are aspiring singers, singjays, deejays, musicians and engineers who have no access to the studio facilities; generally, they are not even allowed in the studio yard. They are relegated to the periphery (at the gate) and often spend years at that position. A change of status from outside to the studio yard requires negotiation with the gatekeepers depending on circumstances such as who they know, their ability to convince an insider to get them into the yard[5] or, most importantly, recognition of the level of their talent. These will determine how quickly they are granted access to recording for the producer or studio owner.[6] The recognition of potential talent is another significant process that needs some elaboration. As a record producer and radio personality[7] I have been a part of the process of recognizing talent and affording them the opportunity to gain access to the recording studios of Kingston. Garnett Silk, acknowledged as one of the most talented singers of his time, is an example of this process of development. Garnet started to hone his talent in a bus park in Mandeville in the parish of Manchester. This was the only space available where he was able to deejay at the time. At that time, he could not even entertain the thought of venturing to Kingston because no one invited him. When he eventually made it to Kingston, he stayed in the studio yard for a very long time and transformed from a deejay into a singer. He was then granted access to the studio where he spent another long period before being allowed into the voice room. During the process he shifted his focus from being a deejay[8] to being a singer, which was where he eventually enjoyed his short-lived success.[9]

This social organizational structure is influenced by a myriad of other sociocultural and economic factors such as, who mentors you, who you "flex"[10] with, who you want to support, and who you are willing to give your talent free of cost. Sometimes, to get in the favour of the producer, engineer or studio owner, potential artists work without any compensation or promise of royalties.[11] For example, a lyricist will write songs for an established recording star for no compensation or credit for the song. They endure this exploitation as they know that any mention of demanding their intellectual property rights or record royalties will have them returned to the gate of the recording studio. It was more important to have bragging rights of being the ghostwriter than to secure pecuniary benefits from their composition. This is the daily dynamic process within the music industry – for some it is an easy passage because of who they know, for some it is very hard, and for others it never happens because circumstances have never led them to the point where someone grants them recognition.

Without the recognition of the opinion-shapers and individuals who count, such as the producer or an external person such as a radio announcer or sound system operator/ selector, there is no stamp of approval, and they are doomed to remain on the periphery of the recording studio system and the music industry. While other music scenes have similar processes of selection, Kingston was unique in the sense that there were no record companies to sign artists and work with them over an extended period to record, develop an image and promote the artist and his recordings (Power and Hallencreutz, 2002; Howard, 2016). Hence the domain of knowledge had unique features that were difficult to replicate elsewhere. The Jamaican system was a series of fragmented production labels and recording studios. Most recording artists were itinerant creative labourers not aligned to any specific label and recorded for any producers that would invite them to record. Again, the field was particularly different from the Anglo-American music industry, with which the Kingston music scene has had to interact in order to gain international access and exposure.

There are innumerable persons in the music industry who remain as journeymen and "wanna-bes" for many years. Unfortunately, sometimes it is not a reflection of talent (or lack thereof). There have been many individuals with limited talent who have gotten through the gate and become stars. There is the inevitable decline of these artists because they do not have the capability to endure. They are able to deliver a few hit songs but eventually fail in the wider music industry. Factors such as the hit-making strategies of the particular studio of limited talent are major factors to consider when analysing their success. This process also highlights the fact that "creative practice offers accessible insights into how negotiative agency around a specific form and location of in/security actually takes place" (Noxolo, 2018, p. 40).

Making the sound recording

Turning now to the making of sound recordings, it is generally acknowledged that hit songs do not just come by accident. It is a combination of the hard work of the producer, and attendant personnel such as the songwriters, musicians or engineers (Johansson, 2010). These creative personnel work at developing a "hit" sound and repeat this formula until the trend has outlived its popularity in the market. Once a recording artist gets into a hit-making production unit or system, talented or otherwise, they tend to eventually score a hit, based on that formula of the production team. However, people with limited talent experience transient success in the music industry. The nature of Jamaican music is a dynamic and moving process. An individual who is successful in a system but then thinks he is greater than that system and leaves, usually "crashes" because their talent cannot be sustained outside of the system which created the hit songs. The reason is that talent is not the greatest and only factor for success. Sometimes the talent moves into a studio system that is more successful but there is no chemistry between the artist and the production team, no dynamics or support to make another hit song. For example, an artist working with producer Dave Kelly might see Sly Dunbar and Taxi Gang as international hit-makers and decide to align with them. However, their talent might only suit Dave Kelly's creative process. Consequently, in order to succeed with the Sly & Robbie team, the artist needs to have the competence to excel in the international marketplace – be it voicing a song numerous times, singing on key or other activities necessary which might not be normally required in a Dave Kelly structure. Kelly may assemble a riddim which anyone can sing on whilst Sly, who is considering an international situation, will create for an international audience.

Therefore, this individual who is acclimated to Kelly and tries to move into the Sly machinery may not transition successfully and is likely to fail to impress. A case in point is Shaggy. Reggae pop artist Shaggy, in his nascent work with Sly Dunbar, had creative challenges because he was accustomed to a particular way of making music. Shaggy's regular producers like Sting and Robert Livingston knew how to make songs that suited his styles. Dunbar required a different type of presentation, production and performance from Shaggy and, hence, it proved problematic in terms of the process of making the songs. In addition, prior to working with Sly Dunbar, Shaggy had enjoyed a track record of selling ten million copies of an album which brought the ego into play and that would lead to Sly having to express his proven abilities and accolades received as a hit-maker and musician.[12]

Leave the studio

Much of the dynamics in the studios and the production process is in determining the winners and losers. My position as an industry insider has allowed me to experience the music-making process at diverse levels, including creative, legal and administrative. An example of this immersion was the experience of being in the studio for the birth of the sound recording of "Twist & Shout", which was a British hit song performed by Chaka Demus and Pliers and Jack Radics. Originally, the song was intended to be performed only by Jack Radics. It was to be included on an album that Sly & Robbie subsequently got a Grammy for – *Sly Dunbar & Friends*. The dynamic process in the studio saw Jack Radics recording, then, just by vibing. We all said that this needed a deejay, and incidentally a deejay was around. He expressed his interest in voicing on the track, to me and singer/producer Anthony Red Rose, which we shared with Sly Dunbar. Sly would be influenced by us because, as previously said, music-making in Jamaica is about contacts and influencing the players to make decisions. Subsequently, the deejay got an opportunity and failed miserably. Sly said, "let's try again tomorrow". He started to panic; he called us again and said, "this could be my big break for me – I want to be on this song." We assured him he would get the opportunity to try the next day which he did. He, again, failed to impress. At this point, Sly called Chaka Demus with whom he had a working relationship and who he was confident understood the dynamics of "riding riddims" and how to take instructions. Chaka voiced the song successfully, and immediately this deejay was out. Now that Chaka was on the song, the decision was taken to add Pliers who had scored the big hit "Murder She Wrote" with Chaka Demus.[13]

No one can predict which song was going to be a hit. Nonetheless, they did a compilation of all the songs to be included on the album, and when executives at Island (Records) listened to "Twist & Shout" they decided to release it immediately as a single. They felt it would be a hit song. Originally, "Twist & Shout" was an Isley Brothers song that was redone by the Beatles and went to No. 6 on the charts; the Jamaican version rose to No. 1 and spent approximately 10 weeks on the chart.

Technology and the way in which it has impacted the making of music especially beats has democratized the creation process, allowing more people with limited vocals or deejay skills to record a song. A beat in the Jamaican context, whether reggae or dancehall, is a basic chord structure – usually two, accompanied by minor keys. When the beat is played anyone can sing on it successfully – this, in itself, democratizes the process. However, the gatekeeping hierarchy, which is very rigid, limits accessibility.

Conclusion

Creative practice as outlined by Csikszentmihalyi (1988) suggests that creativity is a complex process that is systemic and not reliant on notions of individual creative genius as espoused by western philosophical thought. In/securities are manifested within this milieu, including livelihood in/securities, environmental in/securities and creative risk. The politics of labelling in the music industry has created major challenges in terms of identity and authenticity for the makers of music in the music scene of Kingston. This has led to numerous claims and counterclaims as to what is and what is not a particular genre. Expedient labelling as was the case for mento, which was rebranded as kalypso in the 1950s, has resulted in a significant devaluing of mento and its critical role in the development of Jamaican popular music. The dancehall labelling conundrum continues to be a source of creative insecurities and genre confusion. Creative risk is rampant in the Kingston music scene through the problematic situation of labelling politics. Moreover, music insiders are still reluctant to abandon genre signifiers.

Environmental insecurities in the Kingston music scene had debunked two guiding characteristics espoused by the theoretical concepts of the creative class and creative city. These concepts suggest, that a peaceful and conflict-free environment are prerequisites for their sustainability: so far Kingston has proven to be a hotbed of hyper-creativity while also experiencing violent and environmental insecurities. As in the case of most music scenes, barriers to entry are low on the one hand but complex gatekeeping processes can inhibit access to the music-making process in Kingston. This chapter has attempted to elucidate the dynamics of Caribbean in/securities from the perspectives of creativity, artistic expression and cultural production. Noxolo sees "Caribbean in/security as located but unfixed, as relational, and as characterized by forms of negotiative agency that are amenable to exploration via creative practice" (2018, p. 46). Creative practices in Kingston's music scene present us with the opportunity to interrogate this formulation.

Notes

1 This line comes from the recording "Skanking in Bed" by Lorna Bennett, featuring Scotty. The song is interrupted by Scotty who stops the session and asks an intruder why he is in the studio. He is asked if he can play bass or drums. He's then asked to leave the studio and the song continues.
2 Recordings such as "Murder She Wrote" by Chaka Demus and Pliers, La Bamba Amblique and "Poor People Fed Bounty Killa" are examples of this fusion of genres
3 www.okayplayer.com/news/rihanna-drake-work-is-dancehall-not-tropical-house.html
4 Where Noxolo (2018) uses environmental in/security in relation to pollution, mining and other forms of change in the natural environment, I use environmental in/security to refer to conditions in the built environment.
5 Most studios in Kingston are set in a fortress-like manner. Usually there is a main gate which is over 10 feet high with a courtyard leading to the studio building which usually has an admin office before access to the studio facilities.
6 Most recording studios are located in areas where there is a courtyard with a main gate and another entrance to the studio. So you have to gain entrance to the property and then get access to the studio, a process that might take years.
7 Here I'm operating as a cultural intermediary, see Bourdieu (1984). See also Howard (2016).
8 He was known as Bimbo.
9 He died at an early age in unfortunate circumstances.
10 Flexing in this case is the entourage of popular artists who are present everywhere with the artist as support and protection.
11 Music royalties are the monies generated from the licensing of copyrighted songs and recordings and is the primary payment for musicians and recording artists.
12 Personal interview with producer Sly Dunbar.
13 On listening to the song, one will realize that Pliers did not perform many parts, as he was added at the tail-end.

References

Bourdieu, P. (1984) *Distinction: A Social Critique of the Judgement of Taste*. Cambridge: Harvard University Press.
Brown, H. (2016) *Rihanna Was Making 'Tropical House' Before Justin Bieber – It's Called Dancehall*, 1 February. www.spin.com/2016/01/rihanna-tropical-house-dancehall-kygo-charlie-puth-justin-bieber-selena-gomez/.

Csikszentmihalyi, M. (1988) Society, Culture and Person: A Systems View of Creativity. In R. Sternberg (Ed.), *The Nature of Creativity: Contemporary Psychological Perspectives*. New York: Cambridge University Press, pp. 325–339.

Florida, R. (2000) *The Rise of the Creative Class and How It's Transforming Work, Leisure, Community and Everyday Life*. New York: Basic Books.

Howard, D. (2010) Dancehall Political Patronage and Gun Violence Political Affiliations and Glorification of Gun Culture. *Jamaica Journal* 32(3), pp. 8–15.

Howard, D. (2012) *Rantin from Inside the Dancehall*. Kingston: Jahmento Publishing.

Howard, D. (2016) *The Creative Echo Chamber: Contemporary Music Production in Kingston, Jamaica*. Kingston: Ian Randle.

Johansson, O. (2010) Beyond ABBA: The Globalization of Swedish Popular Music. *Focus on Geography* 53(4), pp. 134–141.

Landry, C. (2008) *The Creative City: A Toolkit for Urban Innovators*. New York: Routledge.

McIntyre, P. (2008) Creativity and Cultural Production: A Study of Contemporary Western Popular Music Songwriting. *Creativity Research Journal* 20(1), pp. 40–52.

Noxolo, P. (2018) Caribbean In/Securities: An Introduction. *Small Axe: A Caribbean Journal of Criticism* 22(3), pp. 37–46.

Power, D. and Hallencreutz, D. (2002) Profiting from Creativity: The Music Industry in Stockholm, Sweden and Kingston, Jamaica. *Environment and Planning A* 34, pp. 1833–1854.

5 The mask for survival
A discourse in dancehall regalia

MoniKa Lawrence

Introduction

Dancehall fashion is multi-layered and influential. As descendants from Africa, the love of pageantry and adornments is embedded, as portrayed in the early masquerade of the enslaved on the plantations in Jamaica. During enslavement, masquerade was used to sustain cultural identity and to mock what suppressed it so mercilessly. The sustaining lifeblood of these festivals was the creation by the participants "of mask to disguise, of music to affirm, of dances to celebrate, as well as the germination of ideas beyond the reach of those who brutishly supervised them" (Nettleford, 2006). This chapter is based on Rex Nettleford's (1995, p. 16D) insight that "Old characters like Pitchy Patchy have their counterparts in contemporary Dancehall." Pitchy Patchy is a distinct character, known for its multi-layering of fabrics, vibrancy of colours, ripped pieces of cloth hanging and framing the body which allows for exaggeration of movements and vibrancy almost bordering on overkill. The masking in the masquerade is now transformed into dark glasses, neck scarves, hoodies, designer labels, and elaborate coloured wigs flowing mid-back. Designer labels are an insecure mask, a display of affluence for those who may not actually have any money. Conversely, the skimpiness of attire reveals the voluptuous body. This masking through nakedness is in direct contestation with powerful elements of middle-class Jamaican society, who view such displays of sexiness as lude and vulgar, and whose secure respectability is threatened by 'the body no ready' syndrome.

Historically, the masquerade was celebrated on the plantation as a means of mockery of the ruling class. It can also be viewed as a temporary respite from a world of drudgery, hardship and toil, whether under the enslavement era, during colonialism or post-independence in Jamaica. The year 1962 marked the culmination of the change in political representation in Jamaica that had started in 1944, with Universal Adult Suffrage. The fundamentals of power and control over the economic and social system were now fully in the newly independent Jamaica's control. However, recognition and status of a nation do not automatically produce social, economic or psychological freedom for its individual citizens, and this was evident.

In keeping with the Jamaican creole vernacular as an expression of dancehall, Mills (1997, p. 55) states that "a single word that encapsulates the many

DOI: 10.4324/9781003205500-6

dimensions of struggle of those historically subordinated in the Caribbean is the Jamaican creole term 'smadditizin'." In Jamaican creole, words take on different meanings depending on the context in which they are used. For this chapter, 'smadditization' is "the struggle to have one's personhood recognized in a world where, primarily because of race, it is denied". It is a representation of oneself, which is utmost to defining self on one's own terms and not what society expects of you. It challenges the status quo since it views these players with contempt. This struggle among dancehall participants is a cultural struggle through the rejection of the privileged class norms and values and as such they create their own rituals, which is evident in the regalia and adornment in the dancehall space. The objective is to become 'somebody' even if only for a moment, and to be recognized as such.

Bakare-Yusuf (2006, p. 2) articulates that "fashion allows Dancehall women to challenge the patriarchal, class-based and (Christian and Rastafarian) puritanical logic operating in Jamaica". It is also an expression of self-definition and the way one views society. Self-definition refers to the ability of human beings to make definitions about themselves on their own terms and to follow through creatively with action on the basis of such definitions.

Martin Budder expresses the view that there are two aspects of an individual, namely: 'image man', which is taking on a creative persona, and 'essence man', which is who you really are. It is evident that dancehall practitioners become 'image man' and adorn themselves with the mask of deception since masquerading gives one the sovereignty to transform oneself into any character one wishes, if only for a moment in time. As a means of liberation from the restrictions society places on sexuality and beautification, the dancehall artists have adorned this translucent mask, reflected in their regalia and bodily discourse, as they express bodily confidence.

This escape from the reality of the real oppressive world is liberating and invigorating to the participants, as they now become the law in society and assume control. This mask shields them from reality, oppression and governance. They now become the controllers, casting insecurities on their spectators who view them with intolerance. These artists then mock society through their bodily discourse, costuming and the lyrical content of their songs.

Drawing on interviews that I conducted with various dancehall participants from 1990 to 2018, the chapter looks at two different sources of insecurity in and around the dancehall space: first, the dancehall participants' masquerade through colourful costuming and designer labels; and second, the insecure respectability of Jamaica's middle-class population, who watch as the imaginary line of demarcation between themselves and dancehall's traditional participants extends well beyond dancehall spaces.

Image is everything: masquerade in the dancehall

In an interview in 2017 with moderator Winfred Williams on the programme *On Stage,* aired on Jamaican television, Carlene (2018), Jamaica's original dancehall queen, stated whilst elaborating on her profession as the most popular dancehall artist, "I am selling sex but you can't buy it." In this statement, there is the expectation that she is available. However, it is ironic that what is seemingly packaged beautifully, tempting, appealing and seemingly available, is out of your reach. Jamaica's original dancehall queen displays comfort in her own skin; she does not mean there is a deliberate attempt to tempt or physically seduce. Carlene revolutionized the dancehall space in the '90s when she brought originality in style, fashion and dance, to a male-dominated and bullish space. She further stated, 'sex always sells'. This places pressure on females to tauntingly reveal their bodies to generate arousal by sight, augmented by the gyrations and undulations of the various parts of the body, while moving provocatively to the rhythms of the music.

The regalia worn for this seductive appealing showmanship is deserving of recognition and must be given due diligence. In an interview in 2018 with this researcher, Carlene commented on the process of deciding on what to wear at various events and the painstaking task of conceptualizing original ideas and working with designers and seamstresses in the '90s. This period of dressing demanded one-of-a-kind fashion and in achieving this they were regarded as the trendsetters for others to emulate.

Interestingly, Bettelheim (1998, p. 70) confirmed that in masquerade and performance "Female performers do not conceal their identity. There is no secrecy". In this 21st century, this is evident even today, as females within the dancehall space do not don any form of disguise but instead pride themselves on decorating and bearing it all because they are liberated sex symbols, goddesses of perfection, and their bodies are revered and celebrated through not only movement but also their regalia.

In my 2018 interview with Danielle 'DI', a popular dancehall artist, she expressed the view that the image in this space is everything, and depending on the event and audience one would dress X-rated or accordingly. She reiterated that in the '90s the ladies' emphasis on dressing was showcasing one-of-a-kind, custom-made garments for each event. Carlene confirmed that even if it was initially bought off the rack, it was modified by seamstresses and designers as originality was tantamount to the image one wanted to portray. Originality was then the secret to maintaining and preserving that image. Orville Hall (2018), dancer and director of Dance Expressionz, quantified this originality in the '90s in these terms: "One of the main things the women ensured not happening is that you enter into the party with another person and you in the same suit. The elaborate and original tailor-made outfit was the style that set you above the average person."

However, Danielle dubbed today's dress code as 'cheap and clean' meaning that you buy off the rack, as it is incumbent that it must be the current style of the day. There is little regard for suitability of fit or relevance to body type because what is in fashion is the order of the day. The dancehall space screams freedom and autonomy to be whoever you want to be, and this is reflected in one's style of dressing.

Alphonse Tierou (1992, pp. 36–37) talks about the criteria of beauty, stating that: "the curve and the round are also the basic criteria of African beauty" in that: "Africans are indifferent to a flat stomach." In Jamaica, curved lines and developed buttocks are accepted signs of beauty. In Africa, women who are not "favoured in this area, make padding for themselves which they wear beneath their clothes during big ceremonies". The length of their legs does not matter "the only criterion is their muscularity". Tierou makes an interesting point about the buttocks:

> In order to understand the problems which follow from the standing position when it is subjected to tension, it is necessary to understand the mechanism of the body in which the buttocks play an important role because these two muscular masses joined to the hind lilt of the pelvis furnish the structural support of the standing position. The contracted buttocks and pelvis tilted outwards produce a state of partial slump in the body.

The buttocks and hips are focused on in the dancehall space and as such are adorned for emphasis, whilst expressing sensuality, sexuality and *joie de vivre* (love of life). It is clear that women are highly visible in this space and anything to enhance the 'video-light' is embraced. Carolyn Cooper (1993, p. 155) states "The dancehall is the social space in which the smell of female power is exuded in the extravagant display of flashy jewellery, expensive clothes and elaborate hairstyles and rigidly attendant men that altogether represent substantial wealth."

In *The Sanctified Church*, Zora Neale Hurston (1981) has a chapter called 'Characteristics of Negro Expression' in which she delineates certain characteristics that she feels are keys to Black expression. Although her work is mainly situated in the American south, I find her work useful and applicable to Jamaican culture and aesthetics as well. For example, her description of a young woman passing a 'corner lounger' or in Jamaica known as a 'Rum bar' is apt and I quote:

> A Negro girl strolls past the corner lounger. Her whole body panging and posing. A slight shoulder movement that calls attention to her bust that is all of a dare. A hippy undulation below the waist that is a sheaf of promises tied with conscious power. She is acting out I'm a darned sweet woman and you know it.
>
> (50)

This can be played out in any Jamaican, Caribbean or African street in terms of this cultural attitude that the Black woman has with her knowledge of the power of her feminine wiles. This aspect is what Hurston calls 'drama'. She is not talking about concert drama but everyday drama in life. Our use of words, attitudes, even our walk, all imply a dramatic flair. The second characteristic that Hurston talks about is, the 'will to adorn' and simply said, it is the ability to make anything prettier or more attractive. This can be seen in hairstyles, use of colour, language, dance and so on, all being played out by women in the dancehall.

An attempt to seem affluent is evident in the number of bottles of expensive alcohol that are displayed on their table and the daring and outrageous costumes that are worn without regard for bodily suitability and tailoring. Kudos must be given to these patrons, as it is costly to attend these functions which are held nightly, seven days per week. Not that all will attend daily within any given week, but their appearance on any occasion must be impeccably reflected by the weaves, wigs, make-up, jewellery, nails, garments and shoes. It is a complete ensemble. The spotlight is up for grabs, as all participants in the space are competing for visibility.

Orville Hall (2018) also supports the idea that "one is afforded the right to dress in the most outlandish and crazy way as it comes with the fact that you have money". This is more evident if one can display the most expensive liquors on his/her table, even at times pouring a bottle on the floor just for show. This affluent display would be perfectly timed during the night because it was necessary for all their rivals to witness this pouring of libation and wanton disregard for money.

This space is owned by the patrons who are all dancehall queens vying for visibility and status, if only for one night. They confidently and proudly showcase their womanhood without regard for onlookers who are governed by societal norms, looking and responding in shock. Do they care? No, because it is liberating and empowering to demonstrate the look without the onlooker's ability to touch. This illusion of affluence makes them feel relevant under the 'video-light' through perceived recognition and popularity.

The appearance is expensive, the fashion is current, and everything screams thousands of dollars, yet how do they afford this opulence nightly, given their humble circumstances? It is interesting to examine this ritualization expressed by John S. Mbiti (1969) in his seminal book *African Religions and Philosophy*. Mbiti highlights five categories in terms of man's relationship with God. These categories include God, spirits, man, animals and plants, as well as phenomena and objects without biological life (pp. 15–16). He further relates these to "the African concept of time as the key to our understanding of the basic religious and philosophical concepts" (p. 16). He maintains that an understanding of the African concept of time can help to explain the beliefs, and behaviours of the African people. The African concept of time is also critical to understanding the mindset of the early enslaved Africans and offers entrée into the creation of spirituals. "Actual time is therefore what is present and what is past. It moves 'backward' rather than 'forward'; and people set their minds not on future things, but chiefly on what has taken place" (p. 17). For the Africans, there is a past and a present, but there is essentially no such thing as a future and "what would be 'future' is extremely brief" (p. 21). Hence, events that have not yet occurred and are not imminent are situated in the realm of 'no time'. Could this philosophy be embedded in the minds of these patrons in the dancehall space which gives scant regard for tomorrow's bills? As Vybz Kartel et al. (2012, pp. 30–31), in *Voice of the Jamaican Ghetto*, states "some gyal go a dance and dem pickney ah suffer". He further elaborates:

> I really don't like to offend 'dance-goers' because is them mek Kartel reach where him reach but in one song I mention some unfortunate behaviour by women. Straight to the point, do me a favour, don't come to dance and leave the children at home alone. The children never beg to come into the world, so you have to take responsibility. Going to a dance seven days a week is irresponsible parenting if you don't earn a living from Dancehall. We know the pretty girls like their Street Vybz rum and to be in VIP and they deserve it. Also, big man thing, mi thugs please don't come dance come show-off with champagne when the same day your mother water cut off, fridge empty and light gone.
>
> (30–31)

Earl McKenzie (1973) in his essay, "Time in European and African Philosophy;" argues that "the nature and significance of time are among the most fundamental features of human experience" (77). McKenzie views Mbiti's concept of time as "not considered real until it has been experienced. Time is composed of events, so a day, month, year or whatever, is simply the sum of its events" (82). McKenzie then concludes that "since time has to be experienced before it is considered real, actual time consists only of the past and the present" (82).

Mbiti is speaking of 'time' as conceptualized in traditional Africa. The future is now a reality for most Africans and people in the African Diasporas. The power of the traditional concept of time was that it enabled millions of enslaved Africans to survive in extraordinary times. What continues to be operative is the idea that time is cyclical. In this way, the future is not only ahead of us, but also behind us.

The use of designer labels reveals how insecure the mask of affluence can be. At the turn of the 21st century, the high-end brand names out of the USA and Europe were the craze and the inner-city youths in Jamaica clambered to own and wear these designer brands, showing that they in fact could afford these items. This resulted in the fashion statement of prominently displaying the price tags on pieces of garments worn, such as hats, tops, pants, and particularly shoes. This style was manifested to showcase that the items worn were indeed purchased new and were from prominent designers. The higher the cost, the more eminence was given to the person wearing them. In the '90s, the advent of dancers and other performers securing jobs overseas to display their roots on the concert stage and at promotional shows saw them often offered payment in kind. The offerings included slightly used designer clothing for their work to offset a cash transfer. As stated by Orville 'Xpressionz' Hall, artistic director and dancer for the renowned Dance Expressionz, they took second-hand clothes because they could not travel overseas without bringing back something to prove their trip. Consequently, when the locals discovered this trick, they were not impressed that these garments were in fact not new, hence showing little financial affluence.

This sleight of hand has only deepened the significance of the new in designer labels. These practices ushered in the tag style display which shouted, "I went to foreign. I bought it new. I have money." To the locals who were their fan base, irrespective of how new the items appeared, if the tag was not displayed, it was not the artist's original and not newly purchased. Sufficing, leaving the tag affixed was proof of purchase and a status symbol. He also explained that the pants worn below the waist were to display designer underpants, with sometimes as many as two worn at the same time, one beneath the other.

Confrontational space: the middle-class masquerade

The quest for self-definition as a nation and as an individual requires acceptance and an embrace of one's heritage, even when that heritage has been torn asunder and denigrated. The oppression and struggle of 'becoming' are common not only in the lower class but actively in the middle class. Hence, the desire to "satisfy the soul and project their own aesthetics onto the world is at the core of Dancehall women's sartorial practice" as stated Bakare-Yusuf (2006, p. 4). In the interview with Carlene, which I mentioned earlier, what is noteworthy is that Carlene is considered a middle class 'browning' (light-skinned), who hails from upper St. Andrew in Jamaica. Yet she embraced this practice and felt the urge to express her bodily discourse, unveiling it all provocatively in an attempt at self-definition/'smaddization'. As a Jamaican, there is a shared history of intrusion, enslavement, colonization and independence and all that each evokes. Carlene's dilemma was that of not being readily accepted in the dancehall culture at one level and being looked down on, at the other. In the Caribbean, that is the duality and ambiguity that one lives daily in order to negotiate multiple spaces and to navigate one's self on several planes. Ambiguity refers to the fluid and multi-layered realities of Jamaican identity. According to Barry Chevannes (2001, p. 15), "the Negro is both black and non-black African, but not African. On one and the same page, Negro shifts in meaning." Carlene uses 'ambiguity' as a tool in all of its contradictions and inversions in her quest for self-identity.

In Norman C. Stolzoff's book, *Wake the Town and Tell the People*, (2000, p. 227), he states that dancehall

> is also an important institution that generates, mediates and reproduces the social order – that is, the hierarchical divisions of race, class, gender, and sexuality running through Jamaican society. Dancehall has thus played a primary role in the formation of a distinct lower-class culture for more than two centuries. From slavery until the present . . . dancehall has been an important medium for the black masses to create an alternative social universe of performance, production and politics.

This statement implies that the social order existing in dancehall is something that people have been governed by since 'slavery'. However, Stolzoff needed to make a distinction between dancehall in the '50s through '70s as compared to the 1980s to 2000 and beyond, which initially incorporated the Jamaican working class, not only the 'distinct lower class'. This statement is inaccurate and rather than dancehall, "reproducing the social order", it serves to dictate certain behavioural patterns within particular strands/elements/factions of the lower strata of Jamaican society. Dancehall has in fact transformed the counter-hegemonic potential as it has now penetrated the middle and upper classes through the dress code, behaviour and language of the people.

Cultural performance has been conceptualised for some time as a means of transforming accepted class distinctions. Edward Seaga (1997, p. 82) stratifies Jamaican society into two layers, namely, "traditional society shaped by the experiences of folklife and the contemporary society moulded by metropolitan influences". He further states that "Jamaica is a well-defined model of this

Figure 5.1 The original Dancehall Queen - Carlene

74 *MoniKa Lawrence*

dual society; two Jamaica's blended at points of contact." Seaga (1997, p. 86) also attributes the abundance of creativity among Jamaicans to the "absence of regimentation". Whilst 'regimentation' exists, it can be manipulated to structure 'process' to stimulate creativity. Nettleford notes that "a child learns the meaning of process and is [thus] better able to relate outcome to effort". Nettleford (1993, p. 94) goes on to say, "it is the opportunity to exercise the creative imagination from an early age that is likely to ensure safe passage through that life". Stuart Hall (1997, p. 29) uses the phrase 'narrative of loss', which refers to the absence of 'something' missing in the development of a generation. This 'something' is what Nettleford describes as the 'process'. During this process, these practitioners distil, abstract and then reconstruct. An extension of this comprehension of 'process' is "dispelling the myth of social hierarchy that suggests that what is European is good and at the top and what is less and

Figure 5.2 The original Dancehall Queen - Carlene

The mask for survival 75

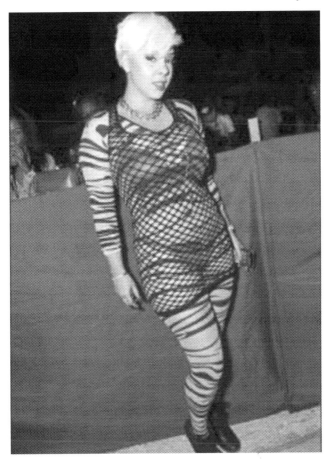

Figure 5.3 Danielle Dl

at the bottom is everything else, particularly African" (Lennox 27) because in the realm of excellence there is no hierarchy.

Finally, we can see the dancehall space even surpassing the boundaries of the nation. Orville 'Xpressionz' Hall dubbed the dancehall space as highly confrontational, as dancers competed at all levels, not only for the 'video-light' or a 'buss', but to create a style of dance with which they can associate their names, as well as making a grand entrance into the venue for recognition. The grand entrance has now become so competitive that they delight in enhancing it by having Europeans and Asians walk with the local group as a gang. This merger of foreigners and locals showed that the local group was in demand by foreigners who have travelled to Jamaica for training by their escorted host, who wishes to grasp the essence of the dancehall aesthetics and movements.

Figure 5.4 Danielle Dl

The space is indeed confrontational and inflammatory at all levels, even among the dancers who see it as an opportunity for upward mobility, international recognition and increased earnings.

In such an internationally competitive space, dancers have had to fall back on their own forms of security: their self-reliance, innate self-confidence, and logically prioritized area of 'inner space'. They have had to create 'space' in Jamaica for personhood/smaddization in areas such as the originality of movements complemented by their regalia. The suggestive sexual tones of hip thrusting, gyrations and seductive posturing in their movements follow through in the minimalistic and provocative style of dressing.

Conclusion

This chapter has briefly expanded on Rex Nettleford's observation that dancehall gives modern counterparts to masquerade's more time-honoured characters. Vibrant costumes and designer labels provide a mask that fulfils the purpose of smadditisation for dancehall participants, creating some security in an insecure world. At the same time, middle-class and foreign participants find their own culture transformed by dancehall's influential style and fashion.

References

Bakare-Yusuf, B. (2006) Fabricating Identities: Survival and the Imagination in Jamaican Dancehall Culture. *Fashion Theory* 10(3), pp. 1–24.

Bettelheim, J. (1998) Women in Masquerade and Performance. *Institute of Jamaica African Arts* 31(2), pp. 68–70, 93–94, Spring.

Carlene. (2018) Personal Interview.

Chevannes, B. (2001) *Ambiguity and the Search for Knowledge: An Open-Ended Adventure of the Imagination*. Kingston: University of the West Indies Press.

Cooper, Carolyn. (1993) *Noises in the Blood: Orality, Gender and the 'Vulgar' Body of Jamaican Popular Culture*. London: Palgrave Macmillan.

Danielle, D. I. (2018) Personal Interview.

Hall, O. (2018) Personal Interview.

Hall, S. (1997) Caribbean Culture: Future Trends. *Caribbean Quarterly* 1–2, pp. 25–33, March–June.

Hurston, Z. N. (1981) *The Sanctified Church*. New York: Marlowe & Company.

Kartel, V., Palmer, A. A. and Dawson, M. (2012) *The Voice of the Jamaican Ghetto*. Ghetto: People Publishing Company Ltd.

Mbiti, J. S. (1969) The Concept of Time as a Key to the Understanding and Interpretation of African Religions and Philosophy: Potential Time and Actual Time & Space and Time. In *African Religions and Philosophy*. 2nd ed. New Hampshire: Heinemann Educational Botswana Ltd.

McKenzie, E. (1973) Time in European and African Philosophy: A Comparison. *Caribbean Quarterly* 19(3).

Mills, C. W. (1997) Smadditisn. *Caribbean Quarterly* 43(2), pp. 54–68.

Nettleford, R. (1993) *Inward Stretch Outward Reach: A Voice from the Caribbean*. Caribbean: Palgrave Macmillan.

Nettleford, R. (1995) Celebrating Tolerance, Peace and Understanding: Jamaica's NDTC as Cultural Ambassador. *Jamaica Journal* 25(3), October.

Nettleford, R. (22 July 2001, 30 April 2003, 21 March 2006) Personal Interview.

Seaga, E. (1997) The Significance of Folk Culture in the Development of National Identity. *Caribbean Quarterly* 43(2), pp. 82–89, March–June.

Stolzoff, N. C. (2000) *Wake the Town and Tell the People: Dance Hall Culture in Jamaica*. London: Duke University Press.

Tierou, A. (1992) *Doople: The Eternal Law of African Dance. Choreography and Dance Studies*. Vol. 2. Chur: Harwood Academic.

6 Dancehall dancing bodies

The performance of embodied in/security

'H' Patten

Introduction

This chapter explores the multiple levels on which in/security is embedded within reggae/dancehall culture, arguably Jamaica's most popular indigenous form. The dancing body clearly manifests cultural expression within the reggae/dancehall genre. Dance practitioners present their dancing bodies within the multiplicity of nightly dancehall sessions that represent the wide range of birth to death life-cycle events that both provide and create in/secure countercultural spaces (Beckford, 2006). I argue that dancehall participants continually negotiate in/security through cultural expression, producing transformative experiences that manifest the genealogical continuum of African/Jamaican religious and spiritual philosophies embodied within dancehall dancing bodies. Thus, modern-day dance rituals are performed and facilitated within reggae/dancehall spaces (Stanley Niaah, 2010; Torres, 2010; Patten, 2016).

These rituals form in/secure connections between past, present and future corporeal practices that question the nature of what really takes place within dancehall dances. Employing ethnography this chapter seeks to illuminate how in/secure bodies, dance, and the dancehall genre facilitate a level of unification between the material and spirit realms as a survival strategy. It will also explore how gender differences and resolutions manifest within the dancehall space as a liberation strategy. This chapter therefore explores in/security in relation to three main themes. Firstly, dance and what I coin the 'corporeal dancing body'; secondly, the functioning of dance and corporeality amongst and between male and female dancehall participants; and finally, dance as spiritual communication, involving transcendence and the attainment of personhood within the dancehall space.

Dancehall and in/security

Dancehall practitioners quickly learn how to secure hyped (aggrandised) personal profiles by making a feature out of insecurity. Hence, what secures one individual often creates insecurity for another. This is evidenced in the frequently transgressive dress, style and fashion statements individuals boast within reggae/dancehall to attract and secure visibility and agency. Many risk reputations, ideological and sometimes physical harm in constructing and developing

DOI: 10.4324/9781003205500-7

alternative and transgressive gender identities that challenge and reinterpret hegemonic ruling class notions of masculinity and femininity (Cooper, 2004; Ellis, 2011). Numerous individuals extend their dancehall personas beyond the confines of the dancehall space into their daily lives, thereby influencing and shaping normative performativity (behavioural actions) within society.

Increasingly, dancehall practitioners attempt to secure themselves and their communities by developing relationships with visitors and/or outsiders, guiding them to and from the dancehall space in cultivating dancehall tourism (Laemmli, 2006). This is both separate and distinct to the engagement of dancehall within Jamaica's general tourist industry (Johnson, 2012). Countless dancehall tourists wish to feel the thrill of entering notorious, historically insecure, violent and volatile locations. Brokered by dancehall dance practitioners they may do so feeling what I term, 'safely vulnerable'. This entails being secure but not overly so, as although visitors remain safe and protected by the dancehall fraternity, importantly, they must simultaneously feel daring and adventurous. Finally, dancehall dance movements are themselves insecure as dancehall is constantly moving and flowing in a creative process of becoming. Yet the impactful creation of a dynamic new dance movement, or the correct, accurate and masterful execution of an established movement can secure 'stardom' (Hickling, 2009), for both dance originators and/or performers respectively. Thereby, to build secure lives dancehall practitioners must negotiate many insecure challenges.

Reggae/dancehall culture

In this chapter, the use of the term 'dancehall', adopted by most Jamaican dancehall participants and practitioners, is used in reference to the discrete music and dance genre emerging from the late 1970s onward. The term 'reggae/dancehall' signals dancehall as a phenomenon and historical space that incorporates its long genealogical history. Thereby, 'reggae/dancehall' subsumes those spaces that form points of convergence where Jamaican resistance against oppression and spiritual African/neo-African (new African) music and dance expressions connect.[1] This incorporates practices such as Jonkonnu Masquerade, Revivalism, Kumina and other African/neo-African worldviews and belief systems.[2] The genealogical continuities of these African/neo-African practices are evidenced in the dance and performative (behavioural) actions of the body within dancehall and its chronological popular cultural forerunners mento, ska, rocksteady and reggae. This study therefore focuses on the in/security dance and the corporeal dancing body presents for dancehall practitioners as a central theme. The term 'practitioners' references dancehall's performers and artists, as described in the introduction to this book. I shall now unpack my conception of the 'corporeal dancing body'.

The corporeal dancing body

It is in relation to corporeality or the body's boundary that communication and knowledge transfer take place. Thus the 'corporeal dancing body' is central to dance and the dancehall space in particular. Through corporeal dance language, combining the senses, symbolic gestures and kinaesthetic action, individuals are able to occupy the roles Stuart Hall articulates as 'encoder-producer and decoder-receiver' (2001, p. 93), to decipher and comprehend the symbolic meanings corporeality conveys. I coin the term 'corporeal dancing body' to emphasise intentionally the fleshly physicality of Black African dancing bodies. This ideologically progresses Black bodies beyond the exotic gaze, through which they embody historical references of 'otherness' signifying notions of enslavement, oppression and inferiority etched on them in relation to the white race, rendering the Black body an animated corpse. The Black 'corporeal dancing body', signals a reflective, spiritual and physical reanimation in the performance of an embodied African/neo-African genealogy.

Until now, the alternative histories hidden within the vocabulary of reggae/dancehall's 'corporeal dancing body' have been largely overlooked within dancehall scholarship. Thomas Fuchs (2003), determines that corporeal movement incorporates the 'lived body', which is the pre-reflective phenomenological integration of the senses and the actions of the physical limbs, alongside the 'corporeal body', the reflective engagement that manifests as emotion. I extend Fuchs' notion in conceptualising the 'corporeal dancing body' by combining the two, thereby not only re-uniting the physical body, reason and emotion but also integrating the spiritual encoding, embodied and mapped within African dancing bodies. This knowledge, or spiritual coding, passed down both generationally and via departed ancestors is acknowledged in what L'Antoinette Stines (2009) refers to as 'ancestral data' and resonates with what Carolyn Cooper (1993) terms 'noises in the blood'.

The 'corporeal dancing body' also includes Diedre Sklar's notion of 'cultural knowledge' (1991), the historically situated constructs that enable cultural continuities both sacred and secular. Stated alternatively, the notion of 'corporeal dancing bodies' facilitates the 'cultural memory' of a people, the 'gender, race, and class identities and identifications' (Hua, 2005, p. 201) handed down over generations as symbolic gestures, connecting communities with locations. Thus, 'corporeal dancing bodies' are argued here as manifesting what I term 'ancestral knowledge', which includes 'ancestral data', 'cultural knowledge', 'noises in the blood' and 'cultural memory' within contemporary cultural expressions performed within in/secure dancehall spaces. Having outlined the 'corporeal dancing body', I shall now address the functioning of dance for dancehall participants.

Perceptions of dancehall culture

Primarily focusing on the slackness (vulgarity) and violence tropes, critical attention within dancehall scholarship has contributed to perceptions of dancehall as functioning as both a secure and insecure space. Notions of in/security are inherent within the many tensions that exist in relation to the performance and performative actions of dancehall bodies. This raises debates concerning popular culture in relation to society's moral fibre (Detweiler and Taylor, 2003). Vis-à-vis dancehall, critics argue that the genre fuels the negative behaviour projected by the youth within Jamaican society, whilst supporters argue that dancehall merely reflects the slackness and violence within the wider society. As Gordon Lynch succinctly advocates, '[s]tudying popular culture can therefore involve both the analysis and critique of contemporary society' (2005, p. 19). Dancehall certainly provides and reflects both a critique and celebration of contemporary Jamaican society and culture. It is hoped that this analysis and exploration of in/security within dancehall cultural expression will foreground and inform attitudes towards it both in Jamaican society and globally.

Although slackness and violence are undeniable and therefore a major focus in dancehall authorship, it has also been explored with respect to: the lyrical content (Cooper, 2004), music industry and rhythmic structure (Stolzoff, 2000; Howard, 2016), issues of gender (Wright, 2004; Hope, 2010), sexuality (Laemmli, 2006; Ellis, 2011), and fashion/aesthetics (Bakare-Yusuf, 2006), amongst other discourses. However, Sonjah N. Stanley Niaah's (2010) geographical study and Julian Henriques' (2011) auditory examination of dancehall both foreground the body's expansion of the dancehall space. The former focuses on its engagement of external space, whilst the latter explores dancehall's sonic impact on internal space and the body's internal organs. Alongside Christopher Walker's (2008) chapter on dancehall's movement characteristics, these works are amongst the few studies that address the 'corporeal dancing body' directly, although none of them position the dancing body as their primary focus. Due to the fact that few dancehall scholars are dance specialists, most neglect the dancing body and the alternative histories corporeality embodies.

The dancehall space

As a dance specialist and dancehall participant, I attended blues parties, stage shows and outdoor spaces such as Skateland in Half Way Tree (Kingston) prior to dancehall's emergence as a distinct genre; I therefore have the necessary insider experience to explore how the alternative histories dancehall embodies function to secure its practitioners through dance and the corporeal dancing body. Dancehall as a popular cultural practice is a repository of the cultural expressions that precede it. The corporeal dancing body has always been an essential, if in/secure part of Jamaican popular culture, acknowledged by many as an important catalyst in the progression from mento to ska, rocksteady to reggae and on to the present dancehall genre (Bradley, 2000; Ryman, 2010; Patten, 2016).

In addressing the functioning of dancehall corporeal dancing bodies, I begin by outlining the general structure of a dancehall session as articulated by practitioners themselves. Orville 'Xpressionz' 'Dancehall Professor' Hall identifies the dancehall session as being 'sectionalised . . . [commencing with] the "early vibe"' (personal interview 2017), which Stanley Niaah (2010) scholastically identifies as the 'early out' section. I maintain the term 'early vibe' section as it represents a 'self-generated concept' (Lewis, in Henry, 2002) from within the profession.[3] The dance builds, according to DJ/dancer and leader of the Ravers Clavers dancers, Kamar 'Ding Dong' Ottey, with the 'mid-juggling' (personal interview, 2010), which consists of the 'man dem section', followed by the 'female section' before culminating with the climax of the dancehall event, the 'coupling up section'. Although I divide dancehall sessions into these broad sections, none are completely distinct as each frequently blurs. Elements from a previous or forthcoming section may also be found within any given section.

Dancehall sessions are community events, which function to build social cohesion. Those held on the streets are generally free, though some are kept within the restricted car park area of a plaza, on private land, or in an enclosed club space, enabling a 'gate' (entry) fee to be charged. This also facilitates the implementation of security measures including bodily searches in an attempt to eradicate gun and knife violence from the dancehall space. Participants attending the dancehall session contribute to its informal economy on multiple levels prior to even entering the dancehall space. They patronise and engage barbers, hairdressers, seamstresses, tailors, jewellery and cosmetic sellers, clothes sellers and stores etc. On dressing up (transforming themselves into dancehall beings), they negotiate taxi fares and employ drivers. Arriving at the 'session' participants pass and spend money with higglers (vendors) such as the jerk chicken, soup, liquor (alcohol) and knick-knack (cigarette, chewing gum, sweets, whistles, lighters, etc.) sellers, whose products over time have become the established aromas, visual and audioscapes, now synonymous with the dancehall phenomenon.[4]

Dancehall has become a multi-layered phenomenon as many authors have outlined (Cooper, 1993; Stolzoff, 2000; Bakare-Yusuf, 2006; Hope, 2010; Stanley Niaah, 2010; Henriques, 2011; Howard, 2016; Patten, 2016; Fullerton, 2017). Although dancehall may be perceived to be an insecure and volatile space by many outsiders, it functions to secure numerous insiders and those affiliated through its informal economy whether physically, psychologically or economically. Dancehall maintains a global, transgressive and subversive cultural status 'outernationally'.[5] Yet immediately on entering the dancehall space the body is corporeally engaged by the musical 'sonic dominance' (Henriques, 2011) that engulfs, subsumes and penetrates it. This signals a unifying corporeal embodiment of the dance session, which every individual within the space experiences, as the auto/ethnographic observations in the following field-note excerpts foreground:

> UPTOWN MONDAYS 2010: One male group, crew, or squad starts dancing before being joined by other male crew dancers, leading to multiple groups, crews and squads joining in, each performing their own choreographed routines. However, it is the presence of the female dancers that excites those within the space, get the man dem aroused and ready to fully participate in the dancing. On this occasion it was when Dancehall Queen (DHQ) Danger and her sister DHQ Tall Up arrived that the dancing really

took off. Danger moved between the dancers and adherents in the space, performing the male dances juxtaposed with the feminine articulation of her female body. She injected a don't-care, free flow of movement that enabled others to join in the child-like freedom and energy she brought to her dance. The male dancers manipulate their limbs and appendages in angular and dynamic ways, flowing, undulating and pulsating, using levels and directional turns, advancing and retreating within the limited dance-floor space.

The female dancers perform more gymnastic movements, either individually or in pairs, with only few crews such as Team Spice (backing dancers for the renowned female dancehall artist and DJ Spice), performing choreographed routines as a threesome.[6] However, it is noticeable that even the Team Spice members revert to dancing as individuals when it came to show time, the female section. Most females challenge each other, aiming to out-dance and defeat all other individuals to assert their position as dancehall queen, premier dancer, or diva. Females frequently employ the more organic wining, the – *circling motion of the pelvic region and or the torso, counterpointed against the kicking and stretching of their legs* – both in the 'headtop' (handstand) mode, or standing with relaxed knees, or acrobatically executing the splits. The additional element of danger introduced by balancing on railings, speaker boxes, in trees etc., all help female dancers to remain current and central within the dancehall space.

Although absent from this particular session, Dance Xpressionz' female dancers can perform all the female movements and in addition, they also perform the male choreographed routines alongside the male dancers, which demonstrates their high level of skill, dynamism and flexibility. The man dem use competitive dance-offs (challenges) against each other to demonstrate their physical strength, skills, prowess and inventiveness. Somewhere within their corporeal performativity of dance some dancers may slip into an 'inbetween space' (Bhabha, 1994). This is what many dancers perhaps reference when stating that they "get lost in the music" whilst others might say they become inspired and yet others claim that something spiritual takes place within them.

HOT MONDAYS 2010: One yute jumps onto a speaker box with a woman wearing an orange dress and starts to rub down against her body and "dagger" her – *articulating the pelvis in a thrusting forward and back action* – on the box, up against the wall, whilst suspending from a ceiling beam. . . . The space became charged with satellite bursts of energy and couples daggering all over the dancehall space. Women bend over and men dagger, some females go on the ground whilst the man dem go on top and dagger. Others jump up on the man dem, lapping [wrapping] their legs around the man dem waist to dagger. The energy and intensity feels the same as when the spirit is moving in the Pentecostal or Revival church. Some women try to out-dance each other, dancing and – *walking on their shoulders, balancing on their head-tops, wining their pelvis and kicking their legs.* The ground now wet with spilt beverages makes no difference as these women slide, turn, wine and dance to command the video-light.[7] The woman in the orange dress presently dances solo on her head-top, but now seemingly conscious of her performance, she holds the front and back hem of her dress together to cover and hide her pink g-string, "preserving" some dignity.

Patten, field-notes 2010

Creating security – male warrior perspectives

As exemplified by the auto/ethnographic excerpts mentioned earlier, it is clear that the corporeal dancing body within the dancehall space has the potential to secure individual practitioners whilst simultaneously exposing them to multiple levels of insecurity. Within Jamaica's lower-socio-economic strata, many dancehall practitioners adhere to the African/neo-African adage 'necessity is the mother of invention!' The creative use of any and all personal skill is therefore foremost within dancehall culture. Historically, African and diaspora masculinity has been in/securely shaped by hegemonic value systems founded on Eurocentric patriarchy determined by the white male gaze. This legacy from enslavement and colonialism has produced a 'double consciousness' (Du Bois, 1994) through which African/Jamaicans have cultivated the ability to read their own corporeality and condition both through the Western and African/neo-African prism at once. Hence dance within any African/neo-African context may be perceived as ambiguous, bestowing 'smadditisation' (Mills, 1997), that

Figure 6.1 The late Fredrick 'Tippa' Moncrieffe dancehall warrior dancer. Video still, 2010
(Video still, 2010 by 'H' Patten)

is personhood and status within a given cultural practice, whilst signalling male insecurity in relation to Jamaican hegemonic and other cultural outsider readings. As African American theologian Michael Eric Dyson appropriately asserts:

> . . . black sexuality was cloaked in white fantasy and fear. Black women were thought to be hot and ready to be bothered. Black men were believed to have big sexual desires and even bigger organs to realize their lust.
> (Dyson, 2004, p. 224)

Hence, white fantasy and fear have historically been inscribed onto African corporeal dancing bodies, producing what Jarret Brown describes as a 'brand of masculinity which is premised on the notion of sexual prowess as masculinity' (1999, p. 3). African/neo-African bodies therefore become the means through which aggressive violent sex symbolises the attainment of manhood, whilst the female form represents the receptacle of sexual agony, which procures her femininity and womanhood.[8] Thereby, through the Western lens African/neo-African corporeal dancing bodies historically signal sexual availability and readiness. Early written accounts reflect this, representing the dance culture of enslaved Africans in the Caribbean generally and Jamaica specifically as morally debauched, fearful (due to its potential to conceal the planning of insurrection/liberation),[9] and far from being spiritual or aesthetically pleasing to European sensibilities (Abrahams and Szwed, 1983; Ramdhanie, 2005).

Conversely, dance for African/neo-African people serves as a unifying means towards spiritual upliftment through social cohesion. Within African/neo-African communities, as Robert Ramdhanie perceptively acknowledges, 'collective [music and dance] participation provide[s] emotional, mental and spiritual upliftment' (2005, p. 87). Pertaining to dancehall, as the man dem dance (as described earlier), with 'multiple groups, crews and squads joining in, each performing their own choreographed routines' (Patten, field-notes 2010), there are moments when one particular dance, such as Gerald 'Bogle' Levy's bogle dance (made popular in song by Buju Banton in the 1990s),[10] takes over and flows through the whole space. Engaged by the majority of corporeal dancing bodies within the space it creates a strong warrior type sense of social cohesion, leading to the spiritual upliftment Victor Turner terms 'communitas' (1969), the conveying of a deep camaraderie, kinship, emotional connection and/or security amongst the majority of individuals present.

However, dance is complicated in Jamaica by Western ideologies in which dance is also perceived as a feminised activity, which from a male perspective carries the stigma of '"effemina[cy]" . . . a code word for homosexual[ity]' (Burt, 1995, p. 12), particularly within theatrical dance. Thereby, coupled with dancehall's barrage of anti-homosexual lyrics, the erotic or sexual styling of the male body was deliberately avoided within the dancehall genre for decades. This was a direct effect of Jamaica's high art, low culture class divide. Rex Nettleford (2003), former director of the Jamaican National Dance Theatre Company (NDTC), outlines this insightfully as representing the insecurity of the male corporeal dancing body within popular and modern dance. Through the Western lens, male spectacular or theatrical dance is commonly stigmatised, whilst dance in the context of practices such as *Kumina, Revivalism, Dinkie Mini* and other African/neo-African cultural expressions remain permissible and stigma-free.

Aligned with African/neo-African cultural practices through its incorporation of their movement vocabulary, dancehall as a present-day popular cultural form, features and foregrounds the styling, grooming and sexualisation of male corporeal dancing bodies. This positions dancehall in opposition to hegemonic masculinity, making it at once both a secure and insecure cultural phenomenon relating to male engagement. However, the *legsman* era of the 1960s, the rise to prominence of the master (lead) dancer Bogle together with that of his associates *The Black Roses Crew*, have all served to change perceptions of masculinity and dance. Male dancehall dancing although still considered a transgressive activity by some, now operates relatively free of any professed stigma, despite constantly pushing the boundaries of both masculinity and hegemonic morality, as scholars have documented (Pinnock, 2007; Hope, 2010; Philogene Heron, 2012; Patten, 2016).

Bogle's distinctive aesthetic dress sense categorised as 'fashion ova style' by Donna P. Hope (2010), demonstrates the flamboyant braggadocio fashion cultivated within dancehall masculinity (Ellis, 2011; Philogene Heron, 2012). In pushing the ideological and physical corporeal boundaries between dancehall culture and Jamaican hegemonic structures, dancehall's stylistic aesthetic challenges and extends constructions of masculinity. Conversely, dancehall's controversial anti-homosexual lyrics serve to reinforce Western hegemonic patriarchy alongside that of the church and Rastafarian religious doctrine based on biblical teachings, which identify homosexuality as being an abomination (Leviticus, 20:13). Yet dancehall's engagement of transgressive masculinity in its 'resistance fashion' (Charles, 2013) against 'hetero-normative ideologies' (Hope, 2010) including male corporeal dance, simultaneously subverts Western patriarchy, church and Rastafarian sensibilities, which are all too conspicuously masked within Jamaican hegemony.

Corporeally, 'gesture' (Idowu, 1973) and 'signification' (De Saussure, 1959) are key elements that assist the 'encoding and decoding' (Hall, 2001) or the making of symbolic meaning within dance. Dancehall is no exception. Dancehall movements may be viewed as 'signifying practices', a notion developed by the Swiss linguist, Ferdinand de Saussure, where a sign or symbol has two component elements, a 'signifier' comprising a sound, object or image and a 'signified' idea or concept. The Jamaican version of the *Bogle* dance, for example, may be read as a signifier of the African/neo-African underpinning of Revivalism and Bruckins. What is therefore signified by dancehall's embodiment of movement vocabulary from these religious and emancipation dances, respectively, are an inherent spiritual and liberation ethos and underscoring.

In Jamaica, the *Bogle* dance is performed with a forward emphasis causing the torso to – *rise in an undulating motion with the pelvis articulating a pulsating impetus at the initiation of each movement*. This action as I state elsewhere, 'resonates with the Revival breathing or "drilling" pattern – *exhaling, whilst stamping the lead leg, dragging the support leg to meet it* – building to the myal state' (Patten, 2016, p. 118).[11] In the *Bogle* dance – *the body is carried with a backward tilt with the lead leg placed in front, the supporting leg behind and the arms held upwards with relaxed (bent) elbows moving in response to the body's impetus*. This demonstrates how dancehall incorporates embedded security, which strengthens masculinity by the signification, manifestation, integration and transference of African/neo-African spiritual dance vocabulary and codes within its contemporary form.

The *Bogle* dance reflects a sense of liberation signified in the physical and psychological continuities it manifests from the Bruckins dance. This connection is articulated or acknowledged by most Jamaican dancehall practitioners, as well as the wider Jamaican dance fraternity. Former NDTC dancer Christopher Walker clearly communicates dancehall's African/neo-African continuities asserting, '[t]his dance [*Bogle*] relates directly to Bruckins' (2008, p. 53). *Bogle's* Bruckins continuities are corporeally apparent in the circular undulation and pulsation motion clearly manifesting in *Bogle* dance vocabulary. Similarly, numerous African/neo-African continuities are expressly evident in dances like *Pressure Dem* by Sheldon 'Shelly Belly' Lewis, which manifest resonances, in both its aesthetic and 'vibe' (feeling or energy), with the Ghanaian *Adzogbo dance*,[12] particularly the warrior focus of the male *Atsia* section. *Atsia* involves the *backward (contraction) movement of the chest to the beat and its return to the centre (neutral) position on the offbeat. The legs (positioned just over shoulder-width apart) maintain relaxed knees, as the ball of each foot swivels alternately, enabling the corresponding heel to touch in (on the beat) and out (on the offbeat)*. Extraordinarily, the only marked difference between *Pressure Dem* and *Atsia* is the use of the arms and the marginally more upright carriage of the torso in the former dance.

Nevertheless, aspects of dancehall's dances have changed in their migration outside of Jamaica. The arm movements of *Bogle* transformed to – *a forward-circling action with the addition of the 'gun-fingers' (two fingers pointing from a fist)* – instead of – *relaxed open hands or single index-finger pointing* – the torso movement also reversed into a – *contracting, backward-circling articulation* – in Britain and other outernational diasporic regions. This possibly signifies a disconnection from the original African/neo-African source, or a reinterpretation reflecting the insecurity of corporeal dancing bodies within alien and frequently hostile environments. Alternatively, small adjustments made in the migration of Jamaican dancehall vocabulary may simply reflect its hybridisation, broadening its appeal, access and marketability, by accommodating seemingly universal (Western-influenced) contemporary trends, requirements, symbolisms and/or interpretations.

In response to dancehall's appeal beyond Jamaican shores, male dancehall dancers in particular are forced to continually create new dance vocabulary and perform increasingly daring and extreme antics (acrobatic tricks) to attract and maintain the video-light and thereby the outside gaze as long as possible. This

Figure 6.2 Sheldon 'Shelly Belly' Lewis (adjusting hat) - performing Pressure Dem. Video still, 2010

(Video still, 2010 by 'H' Patten)

represents an attempt by many to gain 'smadditisation' (Mills, 1997), meaning, the profile, agency, visibility and personhood that facilitates success and enables individuals to feed and support themselves, their families and community.[13] It also provides a window of opportunity for individuals to perhaps secure relative levels of stardom (Hickling, 2009).

In/security in relation to male dancers is ever-present. The pressure to create dance movements that achieve popularity and success is fierce. This may be easily judged by the adoption and performance of a dance by crowds of people even when the originator is not present in the dancehall space. Orville 'Xpressionz' Hall, artistic director of Dance Xpressionz and resident judge on Jamaican television's *Dancin' Dynamites* dance competition, concurs that 'the performance of a dance in the absence of its creator(s), secures its status as a legitimate hit' (personal interview, 2010). Nonetheless, the popularity of a dance is temporary, lasting only the period it takes for the next big dance movement to 'buss' (emerge and gain popularity), shifting the focus and 'hype' (excitement and attention) from one dance originator to the next. The profusion of dances and dancers such as Della Move (Admiral Bailey), World Dance (Bogle), Chaka-Chaka and Sweep (Ding Dong and Ravers Clavers), Gully Creeper (David 'ICE' Alexander Smith), Signal Di Plane and Pon Di River,

Pon Di Bank (Jonathan 'John Hype' Prendergast), Nuh Linga (Marlon 'Ovamars' Hardy), Cow Foot (Shelly Belly), Big and Nasty and Tender Touch (Dance Xpressionz) all serve as examples of some of the dance creations that have occupied the coveted in/secure dancehall centre-spot.

Unfortunately, as new dancehall movements are created weekly, many successful dances do not attain global popularity. Even amongst those that achieve global recognition, very often the originator does not gain the great level of financial reward most anticipate for their creativity. Consequently, many dance originators choreographers and performers become disillusioned and cease to perform within the dancehall space. Others become part of what I term the 'body-drain' in reference to those who are invited abroad by promoters and/or visitors and seizing the opportunity for a more secure lifestyle, understandably, do not return to face their former insecure life of hardship.

Female in/security – female perspectives – wining

The in/security of the corporeal dancing body within the dancehall space is evident from multiple perspectives, which are encapsulated in the slackness and violence trope. Jamaican dancehall scholar Carolyn Cooper (1993) proclaims that 'slackness' (slovenly, vulgar, lewd and immoral behaviour) is projected on the female form, stating, 'in the Jamaican context, slackness becomes essentialized as the generic condition of [an] immoral woman, not man' (Cooper, 2004, p. 3). This highlights the concept critical race theorist Kimberle Crenshaw calls 'intersectionality' (1991), the multiple layers of oppression that intersect to

Figure 6.3 Dancehall dancer Kartoon performing the Tempa Wine dance. Video still, 2010
(Video still, 2010 by 'H' Patten)

disadvantage Black African/neo-African females. Crenshaw originally describes intersectionality as 'denot[ing] the various ways in which race and gender interact to shape the multiple dimensions of Black women's employment experiences' (1991, p. 1244). However, intersectionality has now expanded to convey the oppression levied against Blackness and marginalised African/neo-African communities. Through the prism of intersectionality, dancehall becomes a cultural expression that subverts hegemonic structures and ideals. Thereby, intersectionality unshackles female agency supporting Cooper's contention that:

> [The] feminisation of slackness in the dancehall can also be read in a radically different way as an innocently transgressive celebration of freedom from sin and law. Liberated from the repressive respectability of a conservative gender ideology of female property and propriety, these [dancehall] women lay proper claim to the control of their own bodies.
> (Cooper, 1993, p. 11)

The control of one's own body and destiny extends also to marginalised male dancehall practitioners especially those involved in dance. Most are positioned outside Jamaica's normative patriarchal 'man as hunter and provider' (Hope, 2006, p. 46) hegemonic masculinity models. Thus, metaphorical, ideological, physical and/or sexual violence is promoted and adopted as a means of demonstrating male prowess, as explored earlier. Conversely, dancehall provides both economic opportunities for survival and alternative models against which success and status may be measured. Concerning the female form, although dance has always been an essential part of Jamaican popular culture the corporeal body became a central part of dancehall discourse in the early 1990s with the advent of the *dancehall queen* (DHQ). Female *dancers, modellers* and *divas*, led by the DHQs, all assist in extending and securing the dance floor through their execution of spontaneous and choreographed movements in unorthodox spaces, as the above auto/ethnographies and the observations of other scholars exemplify (Wright, 2004; Stanley Niaah, 2010).

The queen narrative has a long trajectory genealogically established in the Kumina Queen, directly influencing dancehall according to Martha Delgardo De Torres, through 'the matriarchal structure of Kumina' (2010, p. 19). Yet, the queen narrative stands on the shoulders of Queen Nanny of the Maroons during enslavement, the Red and Blue Queens of the emancipatory Bruckins dance, the 'mother' post or functionaries within Revivalism and most African/neo-African spiritual practices, including Christian religions such as the Baptists and Pentecostalism.[14]

Female corporeal dancing bodies employ 'erotic posing and gymnastic and erotic dancing to claim the status of Queens in the dancehall' (Hope, 2010, p. 136). Hence, some opponents to dancehall read the female form as reflecting insecurity and a lack of agency in their erotic corporeal displays and 'bare-as-you-dare' fashion statements that, at times, render females vulnerable to exposure through costume malfunctions. Alternatively, for many female dancehall practitioners their 'strident confidence . . . oppose and disrupt[s] the chaste respectability of the uptown [ruling class] woman' (Bakare-Yusuf, 2006, p. 15). By subverting hegemonic notions of decency and respectability female corporeality resists Jamaican society's Eurocentric moral coding, whilst contesting its patriarchal structures as scholars, spear-headed by Cooper (1993, 2004) have rightly emphasised. Bakare-Yusuf aptly determines, 'Dancehall women live in such extreme circumstances – of crossfire, acid attacks, rape, spousal abuse, sole caregiver and negation – that fearlessness itself becomes the only mode of survival' (2006, p. 17). This fearlessness is manifested corporeally. The signature 'whining' or 'wining' female dancehall movement exemplifies the fearlessness of dancehall practitioners, involving – *circling or rotating the pelvis, whilst rocking it back and forth to produce a 'tumbling quality'* (Patten, 2016), as I term it, which L'Antoinette Stines (2009) also describes as a 'bubbling' action.

Prominent in almost every dancehall event where females are present, wining is performed with varying degrees of dynamic athleticism. However, wining is not solely the preserve of females beyond dancehall. Across the Caribbean, pelvic wining is hotly performed by males and females, both solo or as couples within calypso and soca dances. This is also true within African/neo-African practices and across the African continent. Male wining is performed in dances such as Kwasa Kwasa (Congo), Lizombe (Tanzania), Makishi (Zambia) and numerous other practices. This genealogical link between dancehall and its African/neo-African antecedence, apparent in the corporeal dancing body's circling or wining of the pelvis, signifies humanities' symbolic challenge to death by the affirmation of life (Ryman, 2010). As the pelvis replaces the life that death removes, through dance the pelvis constantly signals its centrality as the life-giving force.

Pelvic wining and contact during dance provide continuity of African resistance in coupling dances such as the 'grine' or 'grinning' (grinding), as popularly termed in UK reggae/dancehall culture and in 'Lovers Rock'[15] dance (Palmer, 2011). Also called rub, dub or scrub, the slow intimate, full contact pelvic rubbing of the male and female against each other explicitly symbolises a fleshly African corporeal resistance. This is acutely apparent within the hip-thrusting action of the daggering dance (described in the field-note excerpt earlier). Thus, the unification of male and female corporeal dancing bodies is a continuity that runs through Jamaican African/neo-African practices. Jamaican musicologist Olive Lewin asserts, 'music rests of course, on the use of sound; in dance, sex finds its normal expression in Art' (in Joseph, 2012, p. 41). Hence, those who dismiss wining or daggering merely as slackness, critically reduce reggae/dancehall to the mere simulation of sex acts. This fails to recognise the metaphoric rejection of Eurocentric value systems that dancehall symbolises, as shall further be discussed in the coupling section.

For its participants, dancehall is increasingly a liberating, subversive and transformative ritual expression. Scholars such as Cooper (2004) and Beth-Sarah Wright (2004) both propose that dancehall be perceived as embodying modern female fertility and healing rituals respectively. This proposition is corporeally supported by any number of my auto/ethnographic observations within the *Uptown Mondays* dancehall sessions held in Savannah Plaza (Kingston). As described earlier, female dancers such as DHQ Danger and DHQ Tall Up regularly risk life and limb challenging other females and each other in performing gymnastic movements and antics (tricks), 'introduc[ing danger] by balancing on railings, speaker boxes, in trees etc.' (Patten, Field-notes 2010). Sher Rumbar and Stacey Xpressionz independently exemplify dancehall's simultaneous security and insecurity each time they invert and precariously balance themselves on the balcony railings of the Savanna Plaza's upper open-staircase landing. Their performance of dancehall's contemporary female *head-top* dance, balancing merely by the shoulders without holding on whilst – *wining, bubbling and tumbling the pelvis and vigorously kicking their legs* – is spectacularly daring. Risking corporeal security by performing in insecure places, dancers like Sher Rumbar and Stacey Xpressionz secure their artistic profiles by publicly demonstrating vulnerability, daring and skill.

Yet, dancehall's in/security remains evident, as wining continues to be perceived as slackness by many outside of the genre, making slackness simultaneously responsible for the rejection and attraction of dancehall. The slackness trope perception is retained by the majority of outsiders to the dancehall genre including the Jamaican ruling class, Rastafarians and Western white dominant societies such as Britain, Europe and the USA, aspiring African and diaspora Black middle classes, and those who regard Black African/neo-African cultural expression generally as exotic, risqué, vulgar and dangerous modes of misconduct. Thus, female security within dancehall is assured through insecure acts, which many dissenters argue only serves to maintain the patriarchal male gaze but in turn diverts attention from the male body, with the exception of those performing coupling up dances, which I shall now focus on.

Coupling up and in/security – gender differences

As a space where notions of identity are developed and negotiated, reggae/dancehall remains an in/secure counter-cultural space. In the Jamaican context and within dancehall's global and glocal diaspora,[16] Black[17] African bodies are produced and operate in relation to place and are defined by a dominant culture that negates their agency. Yet dancehall represents a space in which the physical and emotional agency of Black African corporeal dancing bodies regain agency. By manifesting secure African/neo-African temporal, cultural and artistic expression, Black African corporeal dancing bodies demonstrate the embodied and encoded symbolisms that remain easily recognisable amongst its practitioners and adherents who decode and make meaning of them. Thus, both male and female dancers express their agency and connection to music as a physical, rational, emotional and spiritual engagement, as many African choreographers and scholars assert (Tiérou, 1992; Nii-Yartey, 2013).

Both genders construct and impose in/secure temporal, private and cultural restrictions through cultural expression in relation to gender construction or 'performitivity' (Butler, 1988). However, corporeally male and female cultural expression to music manifests differently. As earlier highlighted, the tendency amongst male dancers is to dance in groups, crews and squads, performing routines through which dance becomes a route to close interaction facilitating feelings of unity and communitas, manifesting a spiritual engagement (Turner, 1969). Conversely, females operate more independently and competitively, manifesting a transformation and transcendence, which Beth-Sarah Wright expresses as 'something old and otherworldly' (2004, p. 55) via a personal, inward embodiment. This represents 'the nuances of a mind-ful-body responding to the many complexities of the world around' (Dewey et al., in Akinleye, 2018). Thus, in 'coupling up' (partner dancing) both male and female dancers enter the in/security of self-exposure and vulnerability, which Ralph Norman (2008) citing Jacques Lacan's conceptualisation of 'jouissance' interprets as the symbolic and spiritually ecstatic unification of male and female corporeality as one entity. Wright (2004) also references jouissance in relation to the female gaze within the dancehall space. I contend that jouissance occurs in both senses in the sensual circling, spiralling and tumbling of the dancers' pelvic region, when locked together.

The term 'coupling up' is used by dancehall dance practitioners to describe partnering dance movements performed by male and female participants, the 'daggering' dance style in particular. Coupling movements such as the 'grine' (grind) as earlier referenced where – *male and female wine together, connecting pelvises, creating a grinding action* – are contemporary versions of what Cheryl Ryman describes in relation to mento dance as 'the "dry grind", "rent a tile" and "dub" or "rub a dub"' (2010, p. 118). Hence it forms part of both reggae/dancehall and its offshoots such as dub and the British Lovers Rock genre. Termed 'rub', 'dub' or 'scrub', the 'grinning' movement incorporates – *a dipping action to compliment the slow, intimate, full contact of the male and female pelvis rubbing against each other in half or full circles, or scribing a figure of eight*. Although frequently characterised as a 'soft' style of reggae (Palmer, 2011; Campbell, 2012), incorporating the Rub, Lovers Rock represents a resistant countercultural activity.

Lisa A. Palmer fittingly articulates the counter-hegemonic and counter-cultural nature of reggae/dancehall dance stating, 'the erotic . . . intimate "slow wine" dance to lovers rock music, can be interpreted as an open expression and validation of Black male and female sexualities and humanity' (2011, p. 190). Dancehall's danced African continuities, through couples daggering and wining, demonstrate an African resistance which clearly challenges Eurocentric perceptions of African/neo-African people as being purely sexual beings.[18] Simultaneously, it also demonstrates a secure engagement through which romantic relations may be forged. I therefore argue that in coupling up individuals do not merely enjoy carnal desire, though some may do so, but many manifest the genealogical continuum of transcendent African/neo-African religious and spiritual cosmological philosophies that both reinforce and contradict patriarchal ideals and taboos.

Jamaican African/neo-African practices, whilst feeding dancehall cultural expression also serve to underscore the individuals' embodiment of spiritual coding through their corporeal dancing body. According to John S. Mbiti 'it is African religion which gives its followers a sense of security in life . . . its beliefs are held by the community' (1992, p. 15). Thereby, the spiritual worldview of an individual is predetermined by the spiritual cosmology of their particular race, ethnic group, religion and gender. Scholars have found this to be also true in relation to Jamaican African/neo-African practices (Seaga, 1982; Lewin, 2000; Stewart, 2005). Mbiti goes further to contend that Africans and by extension neo-African people cannot disown their ethnic group or religion. Thus, within the Jamaican context, practices such as Jonkonnu Masquerade, Kumina, Revivalism, Bruckins, Dinkie Mini and Gerreh, amongst other African/neo-African forms repeatedly appear and re-appear within contemporary dancehall dance vocabulary. Importantly, they serve to secure dancehall by underscoring its Jamaican African/neo-African spiritual continuities. They further assist in facilitating the transference of religious coding, allowing African deities and masquerade characters to emerge and manifest through the interaction, engagement and unification that occurs during dancehall's coupling up section.

The fiery spirit of Shango and the flowing water spirit of Oya are explicitly clear in the hip-thrusting undulation and pulsation action of the daggering dance. Coupling, particularly 'exhibition dancing' (Orville 'Xpressionz' Hall, personal interview, 2010), as an extreme example of the daggering dance, frequently involves males or females jumping off speaker boxes, tables and/or chairs, landing on the genital/pelvic region of a member of the opposite sex, or on the buttocks of a female when performed by male dancers. Exhibition dancing is closely linked to the presence of the video camera, the video-light and the exposure it facilitates.

The 'video-light syndrome' as coined by Donna P. Hope (2006), signals the space within which dancers become illuminated as individuals, engaging a global audience as their skills, style and personas are streamed across the Internet and multiple social media platforms. The highly contested space within the video-light affects artistic standards as 'African retentions, creolized dance, and inner-city style merge with high technology . . . [and] encoded representations' (Hope, 2006, p. 137). As the performances and performative actions of individuals are streamed worldwide, the video-light heightens the possibility for individuals to 'buss' (achieve stardom and varying degrees of security), both temporarily and long-term.

Elsewhere (Patten, 2019), I replace the physical video-light with the ideological concept of the 'spot-light', which expands the dancehall space. The 'spot' signifies the physical place where individuals are recognised and seen, alongside the 'light', which represents illumination and visibility. Hence, the spot-light presents three core significations: 1) The theatrical stage light that demarcates the physical 'centre stage' and the audiences' focal point. Videographer, Jack Sowah rightly proclaims, 'you have girls wheh deh a England an America true my Videocassette' (Sowah in Hope, 2006, p. 73). Hence, most

Figure 6.4 Xpressionz Thursday – 'Coupling Up', 'Daggering' or 'Exhibition' dance. Video still, 2010

(Video still, 2010 by 'H' Patten)

serious dancers maintain 'camera-ready masks' (Stanley Niaah, 2010, p. 172) prepared for public exposure at any moment; 2) The 'centre stage' ideologically exists regardless of whether a physical light is present, as when artists assemble and start to dance or clash; a 'centre stage' manifests, attracting promoters and artistic scouts searching for performers, teachers and choreographers amongst the dancers who enter the spot-light; 3) The crossroads is an important 'spot-light' signification representing the liminal space (Turner, 1969) where place, space and time intersect to enable dancers to transcend between the physical and spiritual worlds both consciously and subconsciously.

Dancehall facilitates corporeal transcendence because it is the space, as Orville 'Xpressionz' Hall suitably asserts, 'where dance is the nucleus of what happen[s]' (personal interview 2010). The inextricable relationship between dance and music embodied in the dancers' corporeality secures dancehall as part of Jamaica's African/neo-African genealogical practices. Yet the video/spot-light highlights the in/security of dance as a career path, offering "outernational" profiles by capturing the dancer's movement, style, elegance and creativity, before streaming their corporeal dancing body to global audiences. The insecurity of this temporary success is all too apparent in the physical space, where at any moment another artist may rip away the spot-light mid-performance by performing either better or more daring movements than the previous dancer.

Female wining, particularly performed in dancehall's bare-as-you-dare dress code, often supersedes the strongest and most intricate of male dance bravado in commanding the spot-light. Moreover, the video footage streamed predominantly on social media sites, maintains in/security for dancehall dance artists. Whilst some may gain a degree of exposure, only a fortunate few secure real work, earning real money from their video appearances. The vast majority are unwittingly exploited daily, as their recorded and broadcasted dance movements are used by distant 'imagined communities' (Anderson, 1989) across social media sites. Consequently, far too many individuals learn, copy, teach and even make secure livings from insecure, underprivileged Jamaican dance originators. Hence, many independent dancers now more consciously represent themselves by fighting for personal recognition in an attempt to secure themselves and their cultural expressions. Thereby individuality, emotion, transformation and transcendence all enable marginalised individuals to both develop and negotiate in/secure identities, whilst remaining a committed part of their particular community.

Conclusion

As I have argued in this chapter, in/security is an integral part of the reggae/dancehall genre, but dance is attractive to its participants, not least due to its high-impact entertainment value. A large percentage of dancehall participants are obliged to negotiate the in/security of personhood, gender and identity alongside a whole range of other in/securities, including movement between garrison and home territories in attending the variety of dancehall events on offer each night of the week. A number of high-level negotiations occur between politicians, area dons, individuals, communities, the police, promoters, sound systems and artists, in addition to the various gang and posse members who all play an important role in the successful and secure functioning of any dancehall session (Charles, 2002; Stanley Niaah, 2010). The spot-light, whether physical, ideological, material or spiritual plays a crucial part in dancehall corporeal dancing bodies gaining varying degrees of security. Hence, in/security remains a key component of dancehall culture and is often a serious consideration in the decision as to whether the dancehall space warrants full engagement towards the performance of embodied in/security.

Notes

1 The term 'neo-African' is used to negate the negative connotations attached to the colonial terms, traditional or folk, usually attached to African cultural expression in the Jamaican context.
2 Cheryl Ryman (1984) has done an excellent job in charting dancehall's Jamaican African/neo-African precursors.
3 Rupert Lewis (in Henry, 2002, p. 9) recognises 'self-generated' words as speaking to and reflecting the lived experience of its originators.
4 See Stanley Niaah (2010; Patten 2019).
5 The word 'outernational' is a subversive term rejecting the European word 'international'. As coined by Rastafarians, 'outernational' better conveys the fact that travel is about moving/looking out from one's present location or perspective.

Dancehall dancing bodies 97

6 Grace Latoya Hamilton aka 'Spice', as a key recording artist, positions dance centrally within her performances, thus giving exposure and assisting to secure the careers of multiple Jamaican female dancers and DHQs.
7 The 'video-light' is developed upon and explored as the 'spot-light' concept below under the – Coupling and in/security section.
8 See Donna P. Hope (2010) for a deeper discussion of dancehall masculinity. See also Hyman (2012) for an alternative view towards daggering.
9 Dianne M. Stewart (2005) highlights the constant fear of the slave masters that celebratory gatherings by enslaved Africans could be used to plan uprisings against them.
10 Gerald 'Bogle' Levy has since been credited with creating a succession of popular dancehall dances including 'Urkel', 'World-a-Dance' and 'Row Like a Boat' (Stolzoff, 2000, p. 271.n.9; Stanley Niaah, 2010, p. 124).
11 The myal state occurs when the body becomes temporarily possessed or occupied by a spirit, usually an ancestor, for the purpose of instruction, teaching or guiding an individual. Myal is often referenced in relation to Obeah, with the former viewed as 'good' and the latter as 'evil', but Dianne M. Stewart (2005, pp. 61–65) rightly suggests the two are polar ends of one entity. Myal emerged in opposition to Obeah following the latter's moral criminalization by Euro-Christian theology in 1842.
12 *Adzogbo* is a ceremonial Ewe dance originating from Dahomey (Benin), which consists of the *Kadodo* dance (performed by the whole community) and the *Atsia* dance (performed by the young men) and is connected to the Vodou religious practice. (See Badu, 2002).
13 When individuals become successful, they are expected and often forced to donate money and/or resources to the 'area dons' (the mafia-style leaders) and their 'foot soldiers' (gang members) above and beyond their moral obligations to family and friends forming their community. (See Charles, 2002.)
14 Werner Zips (1998) and Deborah Gabriel both provide detailed accounts of Nanny of the Maroons as being both a queen and/or queen mother leader, whilst Cheryl Ryman (1984) and Olive Lewin (2000) outline the role and categories of the Kumina Queen. Although very little is written on the Bruckins queen (see Ryman, 1980), Edward Seaga (1982) furnishes details of the Revival Mother post.
15 The 'Lovers Rock' genre is spelt in multiple ways including 'Lovers' Rock' and 'Lover's Rock', but as clarified by the singer/songwriter Peter Hunnigale I will use 'Lovers Rock' as the statement that defines the genre.
16 The dancehall diaspora includes those countries where dancehall has been adopted, adapted and assimilated, regardless of race or colour (see Patten, 2016). Unusual locations include Japan, India and Russia (see Sterling, 2010; Koehlings and Lilly, 2012).
17 The term 'Black' is used here politically as in Jamaica's predominantly African society the term 'African/neo-African' is more appropriate and subsumes individuals who identify as Black but are resistant to the negativity embedded within concepts of being African from hegemonic/Western or Eurocentric perspectives.
18 Abrahams and Szwed (1983) reproduce many accounts of African cultural practices which are inadvertently recorded with overt and/or explicit sexual overtones by authors who misunderstood what they were witnessing.

References

Abrahams, R. D. and Szwed, J. F. (1983) *After Africa: Extracts from British Travel Accounts and Journals of the Seventeenth, Eighteenth and Nineteenth Centuries Concerning the Slaves, Their Manners and Customs in the British West Indies*. New Haven: Yale University Press.

Akinleye, A. (Ed.). (2018) *Narratives in Black British Dance*. Cham, Switzerland: Palgrave Macmillan.

Anderson, B. (1983, 1985–1987, 1989) *Imagined Communities: Reflections on the Origin and Spread of Nationalism*. London: Verso.

Badu, Z. C. M. (2002) *Ewe Culture as Expressed in Ghana West Africa Through Adzogbo Dance Ceremony: A Foundation for the Development of Interactive Multimedia Educational Materials*. PhD Dissertation. McGill University, Montreal.

Bakare-Yusuf, B. (2006) Fabricating Identities: Survival and the Imagination in Jamaican Dancehall Culture. *Fashion Theory* 10(3), pp. 1–24.

Beckford, R. (2006) *Jesus Dub: Theology, Music and Social Change*. Oxon and New York: Routledge.

Bhabha, H. K. (1994) *The Location of Culture*. London and New York: Routledge.

Bradley, L. (2000) *Bass Culture: When Reggae Was King*. London and New York: Viking, Penguin Books Ltd.

Brown, J. (1999) Masculinity and Dancehall. *Caribbean Quarterly* 45(1), pp. 1–16. www.jstor.org/stable/40793458.

Burt, R. (1995) *The Male Dancer: Bodies, Spectacle, Sexualities*. London: Routledge, Taylor & Francis e-Library.

Butler, J. (1988) Performative Acts and Gender Constitution: An Essay in Phenomenology and Feminist Theory. *Theatre Journal* 40(4), pp. 519–531, December.

Campbell, H. (2012) Lovers Rock: The Softer Side of Reggae. *Jamaica Observer Newspaper*. www.jamaicaobserver.com/entertainment/Lovers-rock-the-softer-side-of-reggae_11680583. /\....Last accessed: 3 May 2015.

Charles, C. A. D. (2002) Garrison Communities as Counter Societies and the 1998 Zeeks Riot in Jamaica. *Ideaz* 1(1).

Charles, C. A. D. (2013) *Saggy Pants and Exposed Underwear: The Politics of Fashion, Identity Transactions and the Navigation of Homophobia*. PhD Dissertation. Mona Campus, University of the West Indies. https://ssrn.com/abstract=2372208 or http://dx.doi.org/10.2139/ssrn.2372208.

Cooper, C. (1993) *Noises in the Blood: Gender and the 'Vulgar' Body of Jamaican Popular Culture*. Caribbean: Palgrave Macmillan.

Cooper, C. (2004) *Sound Clash: Jamaican Dancehall Culture at Large*. New York and Hampshire: Palgrave Macmillan.

Crenshaw, K. (1991) Mapping the Margins: Intersectionality, Identity Politics, and Violence Against Women of Color. *Stanford Law Review* 43(6), pp. 1241–1299. doi:10.2307/1229039.

De Saussure, F. (1959, 1966) *A Course in General Linguistics 1966*. Ed. C. Bally and A. Sechehaye. New York: McGraw-Hill.

Detweiler, C. and Taylor, B. (2003) *A Matrix of Meanings: Finding God in Pop Culture*. Grand Rapids: Baker Academic.

Du Bois, W. E. B. (1903, 1994) *The Souls of Black Folk*. Mineola, NY: Dover Publications, Inc.

Dyson, M. (2004) *The Michael Eric Dyson Reader*. New York: Basic Civitas Books, a Member of the Perseus Books Group.

Ellis, N. (2011) Out and Bad: Toward a Queer Performance Hermeneutic in Jamaican Dancehall. *Small Axe* 15(2), pp. 7–23.

Fuchs, T. (2003) The Phenomenology of Shame, Guilt and the Body in Body Dysmorphic Disorder and Depression. *Journal of Phenomenological Psychology* 33(2), pp. 223–243.

Fullerton, L. A. (2017) *Women in Jamaican Dancehall: Rethinking Jamaican Dancehall Through a Women-Centered Informal Economy Approach*. MA Thesis. Department of Social Justice Education, University of Toronto, Toronto.

Hall, S. (2001) Encoding, Decoding. In S. During (Ed.), *The Cultural Studies Reader*. New York: Routledge.

Henriques, J. F. (2011) *Sonic Bodies: Reggae Sound Systems, Performance Techniques and Ways of Knowing*. New York: Continuum. Goldsmiths Research Online. http://eprints.gold.ac.uk/4257/ Last accessed: 7 July 2011.

Henry, W. L. (2002) *Reggae/Dancehall Music: The 'Hidden Voice' of Black British Urban Expression*. PhD Dissertation. University of London, London.

Hickling, F. W. (2009) The Psychology of Stardom in Jamaican Popular Culture: 'We Never Know Wi Woulda Reach Dis Far'. *Wadabagei: A Journal of the Caribbean and Its Diasporas* 12(2), pp. 9–39.

Hope, D. P. (2006) *Inna Di Dancehall: Popular Culture and the Politics of Identity in Jamaica*. Jamaica: University of the West Indies Press.

Hope, D. P. (2010) *Man Vibes: Masculinities in the Jamaican Dancehall*. Jamaica: Ian Randle Publishers.

Howard, D. (2016) *The Creative Echo Chamber: Contemporary Music Production in Kingston Jamaica*. Jamaica: Ian Randle Publishers.

Hua, A. (2005) Diaspora and Cultural Memory. In V. Agnew (Ed.), *Diaspora, Memory and Identity: A Search for Home*. Toronto: University of Toronto Press, pp. 191–208.

Hyman, R-D. (2012) *Daggering Inna Di Dancehall: Kierkegaard's Conceptualization of Subjectivity and Nietzsche's Dionysus in Relation to Jamaican Dance*. PhD Dissertation. Simon Fraser University.

Idowu, E. B. (1973) *African Traditional Religion: A Definition*. London: SCM Press.

Johnson, L. C. (2012) *Selling Masculinity and Profiting from Marginality: Sex Work and Tourism in a Jamaican Resort Town*. PhD Dissertation. Department of Anthropology, College of Arts and Sciences, University of South Florida. http://scholarcommons.usf.edu/etd/4342.

Joseph, O. (2012) *Jamaican DanceHall: Misconceptions and Pedagogical Advantages*. Marston Gate: Amazon.co.uk, Ltd.

Koehlings, E. and Lilly, P. (2012) The Evolution of Reggae in Europe with a Focus on Germany. In C. Cooper (Ed.), *Global Reggae*. Jamaica, Barbados, Trinidad and Tobago: Canoe Press, pp. 69–94.

Laemmli, K. E. (2006) Culture as Commodity: Dancehall Queens and the Sale of Female Empowerment. *Journal of Criticism*, pp. 1–23. stonecenter.tulane.edu.

Lewin, O. (2000) *Rock It Come Over: The Folk Music of Jamaica*. Jamaica: The University of the West Indies Press.

Lynch, G. (2005) *Understanding Theology and Popular Culture*. Malden, Oxford and Victoria: Blackwell Publishing Ltd.

Mbiti, J. S. (1992) *Introduction to African Religion*. Nairobi, Kenya: East African Educational Publishers.

Mills, C. (1997) Smadditizin. *Caribbean Quarterly* 43(2), pp. 54–68.

Nettleford, R. (2003) *Caribbean Cultural Identity: The Case of Jamaica – an Essay in Cultural Dynamics*. Jamaica: Ian Randle Publishers, Markus Wiener Publishers.

Nii-Yartey, F. (2013) Dance Symbolism in Africa. In T. Manu and E. Sutherland (Eds.), *Africa in Contemporary Perspective: A Textbook for Undergraduate Students*. Legon: The Institute of African Studies, University of Ghana.

Norman, R. (2008) Jouissance, Generation and the Coming of God. *Theology & Sexuality* 14(2), pp. 153–180. http://tse.sagepub.com/content/14/2/153.

Palmer, L. A. (2011) 'Ladies a Your Time Now!' Erotic Politics, Lovers' Rock and Resistance in the UK, African and Black Diaspora. *International Journal* 4(2), pp. 177–192.

Patten, H. (2016) Feel de Riddim, Feel de Vibes: Dance as a Transcendent Act of Survival and Upliftment. In C. Adair and R. Burt (Eds.), *British Dance: Black Routes*. Oxon and New York: Routledge.

Patten, H. (2019) *The Spirituality of Reggae Dancehall Dance Vocabulary: A Spiritual, Corporeal Practice in Jamaican Dance*. PhD Thesis. Canterbury Christ Church University, Canterbury.

Philogene Heron, A. (2012) *An Aesthetics of Play: Dancehall Style and the Flamboyant Fashioning of Men in Jamaica*. Unpublished Master's Thesis. www.academia.edu/27205367/

An_Aesthetics_of_Play_Dancehall_Style_and_The_Flamboyant_Fashioning_of_Men_in_Jamaica. Last accessed: 20 April 2019.

Pinnock, A. M. N. (2007) 'A Ghetto Education Is Basic': (Jamaican) Dancehall Masculinities as Counter-Culture. *Journal of Pan African Studies* 1(9).

Ramdhanie, R. (2005) *African Dance in England: Spirituality and Continuity*. Vol. 2. PhD Dissertation. University of Warwick, Centre for British and Comparative Cultural Studies, Coventry.

Ryman, C. (1980) The Jamaican Heritage in Dance. *Jamaica Journal* 44, pp. 2–14.

Ryman, C. (1984) Kumina: Stability and Change. *ACIJ Research Review* 1, pp. 81–128.

Ryman, C. (2010) When Jamaican Dances: Context and Content. In S. Sloat (Ed.), *Making Caribbean Dance: Continuity and Creativity in Island Cultures*. Gainesville: University Press of Florida.

Seaga, E. (1969, 1982) *Revival Cults of Jamaica: Notes Towards a Sociology of Religion*. Kingston: The Institute of Jamaica Publications. Reprinted from *Jamaica Journal* 3(2).

Sklar, D. (1991) On Dance Ethnography. *Dance Research Journal* 23(1), pp. 6–10. Published by University of Illinois Press on behalf of Congress on Research in DanceStable. www.jstor.org/stable/1478692. Last accessed: 18 November 2010.

Stanley Niaah, S. (2010) *Dancehall: From Slave Ship to Ghetto*. Ottawa: University of Ottawa Press.

Sterling, M. D. (2010) *Babylon East: Performing Dancehall, Roots Reggae, and Rastafari in Japan*. Durham: Duke University Press.

Stewart, D. M. (2005) *Three Eyes for the Journey: African Dimensions of the Jamaican Religious Experience*. Oxford: Oxford University Press.

Stines, L. A. (2009) *Spirit Dancing (Daaancing) in Patois: L'antech as Contemporary Nation Dance Language*. PhD Thesis. University of the West Indies, Kingston.

Stolzoff, N. C. (2000, 2003) *Wake the Town and Tell the People: Dancehall Culture in Jamaica*. Durham: Duke University Press.

Tiérou, A. (1989, 1992) *Dooplé: The Eternal Law of African Dance*. Chur: Hardwood Academic Publishers.

Torres, L. D. D. (2010) Crossing the Border Between Secular and Religious-Dancehall's Spiritual Cleansing Rituals. *Queens, Kings and Swagga: Gender and the Will to Adorn in Jamaican Dancehall*. PhD Dissertation. UMI Proquest, Kean University, SUNY, Binghamton. Last accessed: 18 August 2016.

Turner, V. W. (1969) *The Ritual Process: Structure and Anti-Structure*. London: Routledge and Kegan Paul.

Walker, C. A. (2008) Dance Inna Dancehall: Roots of Jamaica's Popular Dance Expressions. In S. B. Shapiro (Ed.), *Dance in a World of Change: Reflections on Globalization and Cultural Difference*. Champaign, IL: Human Kinetics Publishers, pp. 41–67.

Wright, B. S. (2004) Speaking the Unspeakable: Politics of the Vagina in Dancehall Docu-Videos. *Discourses in Dance* 2(2), pp. 45–60.

Zips, W. (1998) Nanny: Nana of the Maroons? Some Comparative Thoughts on Queen Mothers in Akan and Jamaican Maroon Societies. In E. A. B. van Rouveroy Van Nieuwaal and R. V. Dijk (Eds.), *African Chieftaincy in a New Socio-Political Landscape*. Münster: Lit Verlag.

7 An in/secure life in dance; thoughts on dancehall's in/secure lives

Patsy Ricketts

My career as a dancer and teacher

My dance career started late – I was 18 when I started dancing.[1] I had wanted to dance from the start – I was born two feet first, breach. But I was from a religious family, Salvation Army, and dancing was not the thing to be done, so my parents sent me to learn the violin at six years old. My mother was a famous violinist in Jamaica, and I played until I was 15. My mother played for ballet schools. She would take me along to observe and took me to pantomimes. When I was about 15 years old, I watched a documentary. It was at the Carib Theatre in Kingston, and it was about classical ballet. It highlighted Margot Fonteyn. I remember seeing this fantastic ballet, and I knew I should have been doing this.

I wanted to dance. The funny thing about it, I did not go to learn ballet – I knew that if you are not in the middle class, you are not getting anywhere – but after that, I started dancing. An African ballet group came and performed live, Guinea Ballet (Les Ballets Africains): I remember seeing these people. I was caught now between classical ballet and the authentic African. Up until now, I am classically oriented, or I love original African dance. Modern, for me, is a child of both, but I am not that infatuated with contemporary dance. I saw those people dancing, and I said I have to start dancing.

At 18, I took my first dance class. Eddy Thomas, Rex Nettleford, and Neville Black worked with the National Dance Theatre Company of Jamaica (NDTC). I started with Eddy Thomas at a workshop, and Rex Nettleford came – we had a kind of open day – and if he saw potential dancers at that event, he invited them to do apprenticeships. I was selected to take dance training with the NDTC. In 1967 they had a tour to Canada Expo, and I got to go with them. When I was there, I spoke to Professor Nettleford and said that I would like to go to the US and attend a [dance] school. He arranged it, and I attended the Martha Graham School for Contemporary Dance.

I got a scholarship. When I was there, my friend Derek Williams was also studying at Martha Graham. He wanted to try something else. Arthur Mitchell was having auditions to form a company – he had just left the New York City Ballet Company, but as a Black dancer, he could not get the roles he wanted, so he formed his own company. I did the audition. He said, "Your feet are dreadful," but I had a dance spirit. I got into Harlem Dance Theatre. I was on a student visa – they would have to do something for me, or I had to go home, so they worked on my residency with a small stipend. They had a trip to Jamaica, but someone had stolen my passport, and my visa was in transit, so when they came on a tour to Jamaica, I had to stay back; that was horrible. I worked with them for about four years. During that time, they created a ballet that I performed. Very soon, I realized it was not my way of expressing myself. Starting that late dancing on points meant too much agony. I decided to return to Jamaica. Arthur was annoyed – he said I should stay, but I opted to leave.

During that time, I had gone on tour with them to Europe. I went to Italy and stayed there for a while, in Spoleto, and worked with a small school. I returned to Jamaica in 1972. I started working with the NDTC again. I worked with them for a few years and left in 1979 because I got pregnant with my first child. I had my children in rapid succession. I had five, but one passed away, Little Joe (he had an aneurysm). After six years of being absent from the stage, L'Antoinette [Stines, Artistic Director of L'Acadco] came and got me saying, "I'll bring you back." That was agony! I danced with her for about three years. *Satta Massagana*, I was the first to perform the lead in Jamaica, from music by Third World. I worked with her for about three years, freelancing, and came to England during that period.

A short while after, I got the chance to go to London, freelancing, but I wanted to get my kids to come. I was not particularly eager to travel without them. So we formed a group, and we toured England, performing together. The ensemble was called Jah Children. We returned to Jamaica and repeated the show to raved reviews. We did several shows in London, lecture demonstrations in schools, singing, and dancing – it was lovely. We performed for a few summers.

I never wanted to form my own dance company – that must be a stressful thing. Furthermore, I did not have the resources to get a studio and all of that. I have taught people that way and I could make a small living. Things are financially hard with dancing. In Jamaica, you have to have a teaching job to survive. Stella Maris Dance Ensemble is the only performing company I work with now. I do a little teaching for Edna Manley [College of the Performing and Visual Arts], L'Antoinette classes, and Excelsior High School. I taught in community college for 11 years. Orville 'Xpressionz' [Hall] learned his first tendu from me. Orville was a student and a teacher too.

My dance philosophy

I have written just for myself a few essential elements that are important in dance. The first is the breath. This is very important as it allows the blood to circulate better and relax and not hurt the body, thus creating a dancer who appears to be effortless on stage. You have to be breathing: if you are concentrating on the movement, you start to look stiff. When you are focused on breathing, the muscles stretch when you exhale. Eduardo Rivera was a Cuban, and an outstanding teacher. I learned through his technique the value of deep breathing while standing still. Because of the breathing, the body can do an undulation and a body roll effectively. He teaches it as a breath, so the breathing allows the body to look effortless, stretched, and relaxed while dancing. Without breathing, it looks stiff. That is bad for your muscles – it causes a lot of injuries. Breathing is the key to life. Second, the back is a crucial part of the dancer's body. Beginners should start by lying on the floor, pulling the back to the floor. The third is the chest. I teach the students how to open the chest because an open chest suggests confidence. It is the part of the body that catches the light – it gives the audience positive energy from the dancer. I teach my students to wear a sparkle on their chest. Then the neck. There are seven bones in the neck – on the dancer, all should be presented. Separating the neck from the rest of the body allows the dancer to look freer and more pulled up.

A strong technique is a means to an end – without it, the dancer's body does not last very long. The technique allows the dancer to do what the layperson cannot do, but this alone does not make a dancer. Contemporary dance is a fusion of African dance, Euro classical ballet, Indian and Asian dance. Martha Graham was able to fuse these techniques together and later became one of America's greatest choreographers. She showed that fusion should be like lemonade, one cannot see the lemon separate from the water. If you do not mix it well, you can still see the sugar. Some people mix ballet with dancehall, a wine, then an arabesque – how do I do the wine then get into the arabesque?

A movement must mean something – it cannot be for just movement alone. There must be a reason why the movement is executed. Emotion can drive action – that is what makes it dance: spirit, emotion, movement. In my notes, when I used to perform, it was like being in darkness – for people to see what I had to say, I had to carve my way out of that darkness. My limbs are my cutting tools. I have always been small, dancing with other tall people. I had to learn to move big to go with the tall girls – I had to carve my way out. Dancing in NDTC, people would come backstage, even critics. They would pick me out of the crowd. Your spirit takes over, but there is something in you that still remembers those steps, that is the weird thing, but you look different to everyone else. Something is carrying you.

Dancehall culture

Dancehall comes from the 1950s, from ska. Originally a dance hall was just a place that people went to in the 1950s and 1960s to listen to music and dance. A dance hall was a venue where people express themselves, feel happy, and get rid of problems. It was just a place at that time. To me, it has now become a culture – some people live with it, the dancehall has a language of its own, unique dress codes and movements. It has become a culture with certain people, not everyone, a lot in the ghetto areas, a culture of life. In the beginning, it was not – it is different than in the 1950s.

Even the language has changed – if you listen to somebody talking, there is a full direct link with the garrison. Dress is different for women and men. The walk is extra. To me, it has its positives and negatives. Positives first: everyone craves an identity, and for the people of the lower economic strata, though it is a pity to structure it like that, dancehall has given them an identity. That is a positive thing, but it has come with some negatives. Take, for instance, a youth going to school – I take my grandson to school early in the mornings; on returning, students are waiting to take particular buses to hear dancehall music. They have missed classes. When the bus arrives, the music starts playing. It has broken down a lot of the discipline – the discipline was already going, dancehall did not break it down, but many artists who sing certain kinds of songs on dancehall rhythms have helped. Dancehall gives the garrison man and woman identity, but many artists who sing on dancehall rhythms think they have to sing songs that are disrespectful to women and emulate the gun. That harms young people.

The lyrics of some of the dancehall artists talk about guns and the behavior of the gunman. Some people talk about poor people. Bounty Killer, for example,[2] speaks for the poor people in the ghetto. They use their voices for the more downpressed or disadvantaged – the artists become voices for these people. But because some are not as educated as they should be, they become a voice crying with violence but not showing them solutions in songs. Not because one is downpressed means you must lack discipline. Some lyrics inspire a lack of discipline with careless and reckless behavior. Reggae on the other hand was initially the voice of the downpressed. In the 1970s, Rasta coming through reggae was the voice of the downpressed. That was a different thing. Bob Marley was saying, "alright, don't worry, Jah will be there. Have patience". It was more a dignified voice – it was more a voice telling you things are bad but better will come, telling you to have faith. Even Bob would say, "I feel like bombing a church," but he never beat up on the point to say that it is right to bomb a church. Maybe the times got more challenging, so the voices got rougher. Reggae was about patience. I am not going to say everyone was goody two shoes, but still, in the songs, no matter what happens, Jah will be there. Have patience. Yes, dancehall is crying out, but it is not giving any solutions, so we are left with just the violent part but no solution. A lot of youths are depressed, with no jobs. They listen to music and watch cable TV. That is the problem – dancehall is an identity, and we have to be careful with that identity.

Still, my thing is not the dancehall culture. Some of the artists have given dancehall that stigma and helped create that kind of culture while there are others who sing on dancehall rhythms and are not singing disrespectfully. That is what I think. A rhythm is just a rhythm – it is what you do with it. I do not like to hear people say dancehall is terrible. It is not that dancehall is awful – it is some of the artists that are doing that. "Dutty Wine" was not a slack dance.[3] Maybe because I am a dancer, I saw the beauty in the movement of "Dutty Wine." African dancers do that head roll too. I did not find the action to be slack. The head is in circular motion; it makes a complete circle, which makes the neck look like there are no bones. The ribcage is rotating with a circular motion of the knees, ribcage, the pelvis, and the head. What they do now is that a girl will go in a split, and all manner of positions are going on while the head is wheeling. "Dutty Wine" was not a dirty dance but a dangerous dance. If you are not a dancer and do not know how to get your body warm, you can break your neck. But the initial movement, head rotating, I find that to be a beautiful movement.

Dancehall spirit

Dancehall has its roots in Africa. The dancehall rhythms are coming out of the traditional dance – Revival, Kumina, Dinkie Mini. The people making the rhythms do not realize they are doing this; for them, it is a blood memory. There is a dance named Higher Learning – when you look at that, it seems like Bruckins. When you look at some of the steps, you can identify some of the traditional dance steps. Up to the other day, they were doing Kumina, playing a rhythm with a natural Kumina feel, and shuffled their feet just like Kumina. They have memories of the traditional stuff – the bodies are the same, but the frame of mind is different.

I feel that there is a spirit that possesses the dancehall. I do not really go to dancehall, but I have seen a lot of videos. There has to be some spirit possession. Women would lie down on the ground, and a man would leap off of the housetop and land on her – a spirit would have to possess me to do that. I'd have to not be in my right mind, my conscious mind. I also believe that the music is coming out of the traditional form. The people doing the rhythms are mixing Revival and Kumina, but not doing it knowledgeably. They have a blood memory for these rhythms, but they do not know the origins. Maybe a myal spirit crosses over with some of the other stuff in the dancehall. Within the traditional rituals, rhythms are never mixed. Each one remains pure.[4] It is a crossover spirit. When the dancehall specialist musicians get into the studio and start making rhythms, the movement comes to them like water, everything mixes up, and you put things on top of it. Who is to say you are not attracting some spirit? For the spirit follows the rhythms!

The men do the dances, and the feeling is not the same – it is a different kind of spirit. Gully Creeper, Sweep, Nuh Linga, the men use their legs more because men do not wine. So the dance in the man is not sensual – it is in the women where the pelvis is moving that the dance becomes sensual. It is coming from our traditional culture saying to the spirit that you have taken us in death, but we can create. Coming from that, the pelvis in the dancehall is the dominant thing for the female. I look at the dancehall, and I know – I have never been to Africa, but I know – that this thing has its roots in Africa.

Dancehall's influence

Dancehall is still the expression of people. However, what does it say about these people, the fact that there is a lot of violence? The music might be reflecting the violence, but I think the violence is also coming from the music. Because the young people are so entrenched in the music, it must have something to do with how they think. It is a chicken or egg thing – it is hard to say. I am not going to say that dancehall causes the situation, but it reflects a very concerning problem. The living condition they [participants] endure might come out in the movement. A lot of it might be competition because you go into a space where people are dancing, and they are doing things that are "wow, look at that!" If somebody is doing a wine, head-top [an upside-down handstand], or foot up in the air, it will get more aggressive and sexual as the night progresses. A lot of it is competitive: "how do I stay on top? If you do something, I'm going to have to do something that makes that look foolish."

More men are dancing now, on TV, in film, in many of these dancehall spaces. You see the guys dancing, but the video-light is on women. There are crews of guys, and they have been gaining more prominent roles, but they are not overly dominant. Dominance remains on the women – the video-light is on women. The video man goes underneath the "tree" – these are very vivid images. Women sometimes live frustrated lives and going to dancehall and being in the video-light is vital for their self-esteem. Men are drawn to looking at the women, so the women have a slight edge. That is her moment. A lot of the time, she comes from a place where a man is not there supporting her. The only thing she can do is go to the dancehall – it is her moment.

When they play some dancehall tunes on the radio, they have to edit them, even though it is getting more blatant. In the dancehall, there is no editing. This is my problem, X-rated stuff. Dancehall has become an adult space. Yet still, through dancehall, more men now want to dance. First-time men did not want to dance or attend a dancing school or competition. Because of *Dancin' Dynamite* [a Television Competition], many males entered that. Some might go to Edna Manley and do a class or two or might pay a choreographer. Men are starting to come out more into the dance world, which will be good for the contemporary dance world. More men are coming out of the dancehall, getting scholarships at Edna Manley. They are studying modern dance but still in a dancehall frame. So there is not just one type of male dancer – there is more of a variety through the dancehall. It is a good thing for the dance because it provides opportunities.

Notes

1 This chapter has been compiled and edited from three interviews with Patsy Ricketts, by MoniKa Lawrence, 'H' Patten, and Patricia Noxolo, in recognition of the highly significant, but otherwise undocumented, influence that Patsy Ricketts has had on the dance practice of a number of dancers who have been key to dancehall, including Orville 'Xpressionz' Hall (see his chapter in this volume).
2 See for example https://genius.com/Bounty-killer-poor-people-lyrics
3 The dance was performed and made popular by the Tony Matterhorn "Dutty Wine" (2006) song which was a global hit.
4 See Ryman (1984).

References

Matterhorn, T. (2006) Dutty Wine. VP Records

Ryman, C. (1984) Kumina: Stability and Change. *ACIJ Research Review* 1, pp. 81–128.

8 The warrior wine – the rotation of Caribbean masculinity

Thomas "Talawa" Prestø

This chapter will be looking at the in/secure gendered negotiation of the male "winin'" hips, comparing various differences in praxis through the Caribbean and Africa. Offering perspectives both through secular and sacred lenses, the chapter looks at the male winin' hip from divine representations such as that of the warrior god and lover Shango to the modern male practitioners of Soca and dancehall. Interrogating the male winin' body through an African and international lens raises the question: Is dancehall's aggression toward any challenges of prescribed notions of masculinity and femininity a true representation of African-Caribbean traditions or a continuation of colonial attitudes toward the Black body?

Positioning the hip

I was trained by my grandfather, a father of 19, to me, the original "winaman". He passed on knowledge on how to vitalize the snake of life (the spine), Danballah, and invoke sacred power through my winin' and undulation. My view on the use of the hip and my point of departure is as such Caribbean deep culture and indigenous practices. It is through this lens and with this starting point that I have engaged with the in/securities of winin'. I have firsthand experience with the effects of geography on this practice, from being celebrated in Trinidad and Tobago for my winin' skill, to having started Scandinavia's first professional artistic dance company using the Caribbean and African practices (including winin) for high-end art production, to being beaten with a baseball bat in Jamaica for moving my hips.

Winin' has entered the discourse of Caribbean dance and dancehall. Usually, the written discourse is from a female perspective in negotiation with "slackness" discourse or respectability politics. The discourse has been on the potency of the wine and its link to Black and deviant sexuality, vulgarity, and the flip side of its capacity to display erotic power and reclaim the right to feminine pleasure as a means to empowerment. This discourse has shown that the hip provides a complex lens through which to decipher how Black/African sensuality, autonomy, reproductive power, and physio-spiritual power are met in today's racialized society. The action of winin' contends with discourses on

DOI: 10.4324/9781003205500-9

108 *Thomas "Talawa" Prestø*

race, gender, sexuality, trans-nationality, citizenship, and presence on the level of the body, in other words, corporeality.

As mentioned earlier, the wine (circular pulsating movements with the hips and pelvis), and especially masculinity and dancehall, has predominantly been written about by female scholars. The critical male voice within this discourse is underrepresented. The view of the winin' male I believe has been present on the scene, but not much on the page. The same could be said for the queer male voice within dancehall. The queer perspective is another "body" that is intrinsically present and in constant rebellion to the in/secure space that dancehall can be. Ironically many of the movements of dancehall, have been appropriated from the very hybrid (queer) bodies that many dancehall audiences verbally reject.

Before continuing, I must acknowledge some of the many voices of dancehall who champion a deeper understanding of the genre, winin', its expression, and the surrounding culture. Among these are Carolyn Cooper, Donna P. Hope, Sonja Dumas, Adanna Kai Jones, Sonjah N. Stanley Niaah, and L'Antoinette Stines. I acknowledge and pay respect to them here at the beginning of my chapter to invoke their presence and acknowledge them, as much as I will not reference them much in the remaining text. The predominant reason is that I am assuming the privilege given to the practitioner by writing from that perspective rather than assuming a pretense of having academia as a starting point. And, they do not write me and people like me "into existence", and I will not engage in the indignity of having to negotiate for such a presence. I will assume the centrality of our personhood, that of the winin' male. We can say I am stating that we are "smaddy"[1] and will not argue that case.

Winin' contexts

I seek to move beyond some of the existing readings of the dancehall genre. As an initiate and practitioner of African-Caribbean cosmological practice, I view most African-Caribbean practices in light of this. Through the teachings of my grandfather, I found Caribbean practices to be a continuation of our African worldviews, in my family that of very strong Ewe and Fon retentions, to the degree that we can still chant in Ewe.

I was born in Norway in an area 30 minutes outside of the capital, Oslo. The area is not multicultural and features a minimal Black presence. In my youth, I only knew of myself, my mother, and one adopted kid from Colombia. However, the place where I grew up is known as a neo-Nazi hub. For me, first through fourth grade, features repeated violent racism, including the burning of cigarette marks on my back, and sexual violence with beer bottles as well as neo-Nazi organs. This violence bears much resemblance to the colonial practices of "buck breaking". Johnson (2018, n.p.) has the following to say about Buck Breaking in Jamaica:

> This form of sexual abuse was very popular in the Caribbean and it involved white supremacist and slave owners as well as merchants raping a

male slave in front of the public to embarrass him and make him feel less of a man. Buck Breaking became very popular when slave rebellions had increased. Enslaved men were first stripped naked and flogged in front of a crowd after which they were raped by a white man to serve as a warning to other slaves.

I reveal this personal, and to some may be shocking, information in the spirit of honesty and transparency. I will not claim to have had a neutral engagement with Caribbean practices. Nor will I adopt a false academic distance. I offer this chapter and this honesty in order to break open how we view dancehall and other related practices in relation to racism, colonialism, masculinity, violence, agency, healing, and autonomy.

My Trinidadian grandfather came to Norway to visit and saw the marks of racism on my body. He took me to live with him in Barcelona, Spain. There he proceeded to reconstruct me after these experiences with racism, and its related violent torture. A central part of that reconstruction consisted of my grandfather introducing me to Kaiso,[2] Mento,[3] Voudun,[4] Kumina,[5] Shango baptism,[6] Obeah,[7] Calypso, SoCa, and Dancehall. This was done by studying these forms diligently. He introduced me to spiritual leaders: Hougans, Babalaos, Mambos from Voudun, and Ifé respectively. He had me write reports about the various musical genres, made me learn songs, and even write my own verses on known melodies. My grandfather is an old-school Caribbean who carved his success in life through diligence, hard work, and discipline, and he does not believe that the world has changed. The physics of matter being attracted to each other was explained to me through Erzulie, the goddess of love and the principle of attraction. Western science and deeply rooted African cosmology were seamlessly weaved together. I quickly moved from being far behind in school to coming home with only As, not that my traditional Trinidadian grandfather would accept anything less.

Similarly, SoCa and dancehall were contextualized by the spiritual practices of Voudun, Shango Baptism, and Kumina. I did not know then, but understand now, that my grandfather was laying out the foundation for me to navigate this world in a body that was full of contradictions, that defied context, and that circled identity, aka one that would "wine up de system". Caribbean deep cultural forms, old and new, were specifically used to give back ownership of my own corporeality, to re-center my agency as a Black male, and also to regain a healthy relationship with my own sexual being. They fused tradition and contemporaneity. They were made both concrete and liminal.

My grandfather's approach can be contextualized in that he is a strong cultural enthusiast, who was raised by a mother engaged in African-Caribbean spiritual practices and he himself is a western doctor and surgeon. He is as such wholly committed to healing and more specifically healing through culture. He is also, I might add, very much interested in the powers of regeneration and has himself 19 children, most of whom he himself delivered. Dancehall was passed to me as a continuation of ancestral practices in the context of trauma and healing. The mighty Sparrow, a calypsonian reputed to be the "ultimate winer man", and Yellow Man, a Jamaican pioneer of dancehall who also engaged the hip on stage, pre-homophobia craze dancehall, became my role models alongside my grandfather, who also introduced me to both these iconic men in person.

I do not want to leave the impression that my sole reference to dancehall is from the Caribbean Diaspora. As a practitioner, I have shared the stage with Sean Paul, Beenie Man, Elephant Man, Shaggy, T.O.K, Spice, Patra, Lady Saw, Destra, Alison Hinds, and Denise Soucywow Belfon and Machel Montano. I have watched the development of the international presence of dancehall since the 1997 *Dancehall Queen* movie catapulted dancehall into the European and American consciousness as a choreographed dance form. I do not claim the movie was dancehall's beginnings in Europe, but I simply point out that like *RISE* affected the presence of K.R.U.M.P and *Beat Street* affected how breakdance crews were established in Europe, *Dancehall Queen* had a similar effect and seems to be a catalyst for dancehall as a choreographed form outside of the Caribbean.

The cosmo-technical hip wine

My grandfather had what I call a cosmo-technical[8] approach to teaching. Cosmo-technical is a term I have coined in order to describe how African and Caribbean dance techniques can be based on spiritual and mythological and cosmologic functions and concepts. This might refer to the process of preparing the body to receive the spirit, but also to the simultaneous teaching of deep culture/mythology/history/knowledge, kinetic and anatomic approaches to the movement which is based in a specific world view or cosmology. Africana dance and Caribbean dance may differ from Euro-Western dance also in that they are based in a different cosmology. Most African retentive spiritual and religious practices in the Caribbean are danced spiritual practices or spiritual paths in which dance plays a major role.

My grandfather took particular pride in teaching me how to wine. He felt the wine, or rather the full control and codification of the hip, was particularly important to the flow of movement in the body, to grounding, to breathe, to balance, and to regain my agency in the world. He said that it is through the hip that you invoke the ancestral power. He taught me exercises with a bottle on my head. I have been teaching them for over 20 years. During the covid pandemic, several students who had attended my classes just some months prior started a challenge that went viral on Tik Tok and Instagram dancing with a bottle balancing on their heads. It was an interesting study in how quickly accreditation and citation were left out, and that it was based on Talawa technique exercises was quickly not visible to those not in the know. It was a first-hand view of how our movements are appropriated or rather *arrogated* through social media. I have coined the term *Cultural Arrogation* as I am not at ease with the unspecific way cultural appropriation is used as a term. Arrogation is to make claim or to take without justification. I feel this happens more often than appropriation. Appropriation requires a level of skill because you are copying an original. Most often the "appropriating" culture does not have the skillset to do this hence the rather imperfect rendition of movements, song styles, or others. They arrogate terminology such as, let's say, Jazz or Tap and give it to their own practices which are imperfect copies. Insisting that it is the same allows them to take and override the standards and criteria of the original. Hence, the process to me is that of arrogation, not appropriation. Seldom have I seen or heard appropriation if we are to be strict with the criteria of this term.

> It is through the hip that all new life is created. It is the power to manifest, the power to create. Every other part of your body can only take what is and reshape it, but the hip, the hip is where God enters and new life is created.
> Dr. Harold Charles-Harris ca.1997 (granddad)

I return to this statement and its potentiality. It is for this ability that he mentions that colonial patriarchy seeks to control women's hips and sexuality. It is for this power that Black men were castrated and sexually tortured. This very power is why sex is used for dominancy, oppression, and war. This is a power that can be both used and abused, and not one to take lightly, neither in ritual, in life, nor in our actions. The BaKongo[9] cosmogram was central in my grandfather's teaching of the wine. He initiated me in the Trinidadian version of Voudun, not practiced by many on the island. Shango baptism and Obeah are more prevalent spiritual directions on the island. However, Obeah is also a direction close to Voudun of Haiti. Christianity has done much to demonize these African retentions, and Obeah is often used as a term to denote Black magic. However, like Voudun these practices are all danced religions, embodying much knowledge about our past African and indigenous Caribbean experiences.

The cosmogram charts the path of the spirit from the spiritual realm to birth, adulthood, old age, and back into the spirit realm. This journey mirrors the path of the sun and would be seen as an anticlockwise circular journey. In relation to the body, the seated position would be the spiritual or the ancestral, also symbolized by the basic seated stance of many a West African dance. The hip then journeys circularly forward to the right, where you could say the wine is born. It reaches the height of its adulthood or physical power in the front center and wanes toward old age or end to the left only to regenerate in the seated position and start anew. The hip invokes the seasons, spirit, rebirth, and rejuvenation with every circular passing of the hip. An experienced winer also knows that additional life is given to the wine by pulsating or alternating the "height" or level of the wine. This spiritually also symbolizes the spiral of rebirth and the ebb and flow of time.

I am speaking of the spiritual symbolism of the wine. This also explains why winin' is often found in wake dances, and in celebrations of births. The wine, like the cycle of life, is ever-present. It is therefore alarming that winin', through homophobia, today might represent death to a male winer. By all

112 Thomas "Talawa" Prestø

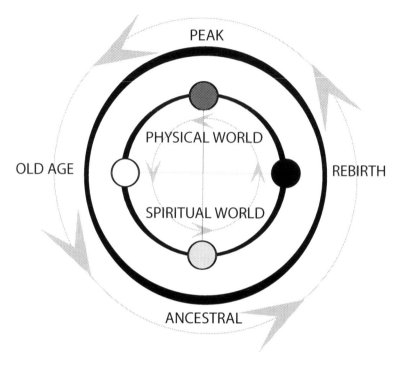

Figure 8.1 BaKongo Cosmogram by Thomas "Talawa" Prestø

accounts, this seems to be a recent development and a breach of tradition. It is further alarming that dancehall is representing similar conservativism and intolerance to that seen in totalitarian regimes and white extremist propaganda. An interesting difference might be that dancehall does not advocate piety and asceticism like these other directions often do.

Dancehall aesthetics and its role in nation-building is an interesting one. One might question the commercialism of it all. The Jamaican flag has been central in the branding of both Adidas and Puma, not to mention how the flag often features a ganja/weed leaf on clothing and paraphernalia found both on and off the island. Internationally, dancehall is closely linked with ganja, still in most countries considered illegal, and also to sexual behavior. This seems to both drive economy and tourism, by providing jobs and security, as well as represent many insecurities for the island, its people, and its image. Jamaica, like Black existence, is a space of extremes, juxtapositions, and contradictions. This is a context I believe we must always carry with us and realize that anything coming out of such a space cannot readily be interpreted by a white western gaze, theory, episteme, or philosophy. The differences are not only cultural but also foundational.

An astute studier of the wine would have noticed that most secular Caribbean winin' is done as a clockwise movement. However, much respect and credit are given to those who are able to "unwind", meaning those who have the ability to invoke an anticlockwise wine. Denise Soucy'wow Belfon, a Trinidadian SoCa celebrity, is perhaps the most famous "unwinder". Empress CC[10] is another commercial winer who is constantly getting viral videos and favors an anticlockwise wine like so many virtuosi winers.[11] Denise Belfon also features male winers in many of her music videos, maybe most notably in her hit "Winin'g Queen" from 2015.[12] However, I have gained permission (from my elders) to share that the anticlockwise wine is considered the spiritual wine. It moves with the rotation of the earth, invoking nature and the powers to generate life. The clockwise wine is spiritually considered a secular wine and also in actuality a less "potent" wine, as this would be a wine related to leisure or pleasure as opposed to a wine to create life. I also noted upon my first trip to the Congo and to Benin that much of the winin' in the traditional dances were anticlockwise like the Balubá dances especially those found in the Kasai area.[13]

Here I will add that there is a plethora of videos out on YouTube featuring the male wine, and even specific tutorials on how to engage the male wine. One notable instructor is Superibbean[14] with over 101,000 followers on his YouTube channel. He features the male anticlockwise wine and even stresses to his followers not to focus too much on the "sticking" part, showing how winin' and "daggering" are considered to be differing practices, so much so that it is not uncommon to come across videos where male artists from other islands and/or Guyana are poking fun at Jamaican men for not being able to engage with the male hip wine.[15] One such video is wrongfully tagged as "Guyana Soca Dance Competition"[16] and features two male singers demonstrating their hip skills to an enthusiastic female Caribbean audience, all the while negatively comparing what Jamaican men do to what they themselves are doing.

This shows that all Caribbeans do not share the dominant Jamaican perspective on the male wine and that Jamaican men have, to some degree, even become the butt of jokes coming from competing male performers from other islands. This is important to remember as it proves that the linking of hip winin' to homosexuality and then to violent homophobia is also a somewhat constructed hegemony. I have mentioned earlier the contradictory space that the dancehall can be. Winin', an ancestral practice not necessarily associated with queerness, is now strongly linked to this. However, the wearing of skin-tight pants, plucking eyebrows, full removal of body hair, coloring and relaxing hair, as well as skin bleaching, practices that in many other sites are linked to homosexuality or femininity, seem not to be in the current dancehall space. The Jamaican Gleaner states that male skin bleachers outnumber the females in

Jamaica.[17] These practices of skin bleaching very much have their counterparts on the African continent and especially in the Congo. However, in the Congo, practices of skin bleaching and trying to remove the Blackness of one's skin do not seem to have had any implications for the male winin' practice. On the contrary, many of the artists who actively engage the wine are also often active promoters of skin bleaching or, at the very least, active bleachers.

We have seen hyper-masculinity-appropriate female traits before. We see this readily in the portrayal of the *American Pimp*. This character simultaneously appropriates from the female body while subjugating, controlling, and oppressing the feminine. The pimp and the broader sex industry also adopt very similar rhetoric to that of the dancehall concerning women and femininity, and I hope that this line of questioning will be followed through by others in papers to come.

The divine wine

When I first questioned my grandfather about the male wine, and if it was somehow related to the feminine movement, he invoked Shango in order to explain it to me. I was at this point already familiar with the fact that female spirits could enter male bodies and vice versa during Voudun or Orisha rituals. However, I had yet to grasp the duality, or rather lack thereof, in African-based spirituality. Many of the spirits do not relate to gender the same as what we do in our binary understandings. You could say that they are non-binary or non-gendered to some degree. Elegua is an interesting example of this. The lore about the deities varies greatly from island to island and sometimes even within the same island. Common to most versions of Elegua is that this deity can be both young and old, and male and female. Elegua is a divine gender-bender. Elegua is also a great dancer who can mimic and mix the dance steps of all the other deities. In many ways, Elegua is the force of creativity and the liminal. Elegua is the guardian of the crossroads, the one who carries messages between the spirit and material worlds. Elegua is invoked in the dancehall. As much as I questioned the female aspects of the male dancehaller, I also posit here that it might be Elegua expressing duality and creativity in a highly creative space, such as the dancehall. In an in/secure space such as the dancehall, both theories might prove to be true. Such is the complexity and texture of Caribbean life. The dancehall reflects this corporeality.

Serena Williams has many similarities to the goddess Oya. Oya is a mother, protector, powerful athlete, and warrior. She is the goddess of change, storms, and tornadoes. She is equal to the male warrior gods if not even more than equal in that she can command their attention and enforce their good behavior. Storm in the X-men franchise is based on Oya. Oya is part of the Yoruba-based pantheon. Serene Williams invokes this force as the athlete mother that she is. Consider the world's best overall athlete, she has often borne the indignity of being likened to a man. It seems that white western spectators lack a way to contextualize her power without invoking a male image. However, to me,

Serena is extremely feminine. She reminds me of my mother, another highly athletic woman. I grew up with a mother who had a better six-pack than myself for years. Therefore, femininity and power were always one and the same in my mind. I was far into my teens before I realized that some assume that women are weaker. In dancehall, women used to be queens. A power and a force that dominated the floor. The title of queen is now more strongly associated with the gogo movement, video filming upskirts, and the dance floor is largely dominated by male dance crews or features men treating female bodies like rag dolls. Simultaneously, women such as Kimiko are claiming their space, showing their power, invoking Oya, and dominating the dancefloor with their presence. Both these impossibilities rotate and wine around each other, creating the liminal space that is dancehall.

Most people associate the goddess Oshun with beauty and softness. She is the goddess of fresh water and love according to Yoruba traditions, she too possesses a temper and can hold her own in any fight. Some people reacted when Beyonce invoked Oshun in her Lemonade music video: opening the doors, allowing fresh water to flow, as she wore the yellow flowing dress often associated with Oshun. The negative reactions were not related to the fact that Beyonce used Oshun aesthetics, but rather, from her using a baseball bat to break windows. Many limit Oshun representation to just soft beauty; however, this is not the case with this beautiful warrior goddess, Oshuns too has a temper and should not be provoked. She is not above retribution and many practitioners publicly supported Beyonce's rounded portrayal of Oshun.

Shango, a warrior god of thunder and lightning, sometimes married to both Oshun and Oya, is not as hypermasculine a god as he is often portrayed, nor does his origin mean that he must be tempered by a female and "cooled". More patriarchal portrayals of Shango often mention this in the defense of why men must wine with a woman. However, Shango is known to wine by himself and for himself. The ultimate warrior is also the ultimate lover. As an initiate, I came to learn of Shango as a god with both masculine and feminine qualities. He is as much a lover as he is a warrior, and he wars because he loves. His war is one of protection and nurturing, not one of destruction. Shango invokes the powers of birth and rebirth much like the cycle of the BaKongo cosmogram[18] and RA (the Egyptian sun god) through the hips, as well as portrays a very active use of the tongue, showing that he is willing and able to engage in lovemaking that does not center his own pleasure. This Shango, my grandfather spoke of and initiated as an important force in counteracting the commercial exploitation and genocide which was the transatlantic slave trade, the MAAFA (the afrocentric Swahili word used to describe the transatlantic genocide and its related suffering in its entirety).[19] and its continued after-effects. When I expressed concerns about the hip, and if anyone would perceive me as gay for moving it, his very forceful reply was:

"the stilling of the black man's hip is a genocide I refuse to take part in".
Dr. Harold Charles-Harris ca 2014

Charting the hip

I have used my grandfather's approach to answering questions about Caribbean practices by tracing some of these practices back to their roots. I am blessed to have been raised in Caribbean spiritual practices as these are indigenous knowledge bases which have much information about rhythm and dance. In relation to my research into dance techniques of the Circum-Caribbean and the African continent, I found it most logical to organize them similar to the polydiasporic system of Voudun, and thus be able to link rhythms, movements, roots, and routes to its origin in points of contact and the unique experiences which altered and or shaped them.

In table 8.1, I name Ewe peoples, Yoruba peoples, and the like as different Rhythm Nations acknowledging that they are nations in their own right, and also the centrality of rhythm as a marker of identity and as a carrier of culture. These again are organized under larger rhythm cultures. These are where I found the rhythms to be similar or the cultures of the distinct Rhythm Nations to be linked and or intertwined. Those organized under the same Rhythm Culture are also the ones I found to have most often merged in the Caribbean.

This form in itself warrants an entire book of analysis. In spite of the limitations of this chapter, I have decided to add this form to show the work, and because I know that it will be useful. It gives insight into how I think, and the process that has gone into making and structuring of the Talawa technique, of which I am known, and also the context under which I have studied the wine and the male wine especially. Hopefully, it is also a good starting point for continued research for those who are on a journey.

My knowledge of Indigenous Caribbean Knowledge Systems predominantly stems from initiation, practice, and apprenticeship, although I have later found some valuable sources to quote academically when needed. Yvonne Daniel writes beautifully and accessibly in her book *Dancing Wisdom* and I strongly advise reading this exceptional offering. One that also navigates the laborious task of the initiate to walk the line between sharing information and not touching too deeply on that which is not to be shared with the uninitiated.

In her book *Dancing Wisdom*, Yvonne Daniel (2005, p. 98) shows a similar, though less extensive, mapping of Brazil, Cuba, and Haiti. I was ecstatic to find that someone else had thought along similar paths as myself and that we had reached much the same conclusion. Yvonne Daniel (2005, pp. 141–146) also includes two charts showing which dances come from various origins. The following is an excerpt of my own chart:

This chart also serves to show which ethnic nations I have found to have been transported to the various Caribbean or circum-Caribbean geographical sites. It can, to some degree, provide a lens through which to look at roots and routes as well as to investigate possible cultural differences not only seen by the colonial lens of "who owned you" as in the effect of having francophone, anglophone, or hispanophone colonial masters, but also looking at which African cultures were in the mix. I have not been able to find any possible African

Table 8.1 Insecurities Selected African

AFRICAN RHYTHM NATIONS WITHIN CARIBBEAN POLY-DIASPORIC SITES

		AFRICAN POLY-DIASPORIC SITES				
	HAITI	CUBA	JAMAICA	TRINBAGO	BRAZIL	BELIZE
RHYTHM CULTURE	RHYTHM NATION					
FON, EWE, & DAHOMEY	Rada	Rada	Rada	Rada	Rada	
	Ewe	Ewe	Ewe	Ewe	Ewe	Ewe
	Mahi			Mahi	Mahi	Mahi
	Jéje		Jéje	Jéje	Jéje	Jéje
	Arárá	Arárá		Arárá		
YORUBA, NAGO, & GADE/GEDE	Yoruba	Yoruba	Yoruba	Yoruba	Yoruba	Yoruba
	Nago	Nago	Nago	Nago	Nago/Ketu	Nago
	Gade/Gede			Gade/Gede	Gade/Gede	Gade/Gede
	Iyesa	Iyesa	Iyesa	Iyesa	Iyesa	Iyesa
KONGO-ANGOLA	Bantu	Bantu	Bantu	Bantu	Bantu	Bantu
	BaKongo	BaKongo	BaKongo	BaKongo	BaKongo	BaKongo
	Bangala			Bangala	Bangala	Bangala
	Tshiluba/Luba		Tshiluba/Luba	Tshiluba/Luba	Tshiluba/Luba	
		Ovinbundu			Ovinbundu	
	Mbundu			Mbundu	Mbundu	Mbundu
	Lunda		Lunda	Lunda	Lunda	
SENEGAMBIA REGION	Wolof	Wolof	Wolof	Wolof	Wolof	Wolof
			Serer	Serer	Serer	
	Mandinka	Mandinka	Mandinka	Mandinka	Mandinka	Mandinka
	Fula	Fula	Fula	Fula	Fula	
	Jola		Jola		Jola	Jola
			Aku		Aku	
AKAN/ASHANTI & "KOROMANTI"	Ashanti	Ashanti	Ashanti	Ashanti	Ashanti	Ashanti
	Akyem		Akyem	Akyem	Akyem	Akyem
		Fante	Fante	Fante	Fante	
	Bono			Bono	Bono	Bono
IBIBIO & IGBO	Igbo	Igbo	Igbo	Igbo	Igbo	Igbo
			Annang	Annang	Annang	
	Efik		Efik	Efik	Efik	Efik
		Ekid	Ekid	Ekid	Ekid	
	Oron	Oron		Oron		Oron
	Ibeno	Ibeno		Ibeno	Ibeno	Ibeno
	Kalabari	Kalabari	Kalabari	Kalabari	Kalabari	Kalabari
	Awome		Awome	Awome	Awome	Awome

cultural explanation as to why the male wine is more featured in other sites than the Jamaican. To my knowledge and in my research, I have found all the African cultures that were transported to Jamaica to have examples of male winin' and some, like the roots of the Kumina practices, even dominantly so.

The chart proves relevant in mapping out the male wine. So far, I have found the male wine in danced practices of each one of the cultures/ethnic nations mentioned in the chart. Often in dances of fertility, funeral, preparation for war, agriculture, or leisure/celebration. An interesting observation is that, on the continent, the male wine rarely happens with a female partner in traditional dance. The Jamaican notion that the male wine negates masculinity unless it is performed with a woman does therefore not seem to be an African retention.

As I was looking to see if maybe other diasporan spaces had a similar treatment of the male wine as Jamaica, I quickly found the male wine even on bodies that also do K.R.U.M.P and found an amazing amount of videos featuring winin' or "hiprolling"[20] as it is readily called in America. In American hiproll battles, the participants can be same-gendered or a male and female battling each other. Some of the inter-gender battles have much similarity to what unfolds in the dancehall, although in a version that comes off as less aggressive and may I say more conducive or more easily translated to what could unfold in the bedroom without injury.

The European context of the black male wine

My context is also in part Europe and the other Caribbean islands, especially the Antillean. In France, dancehall has a very strong presence. It is often there referred to as Ragga. Why Them Faya[21] and Dem So Blazin[22] were two of the most established crews in France. The famous Les Twins[23] (Guadeloupean heritage) who are now known for their hip-hop, were active within the French dancehall scene. French dancehall is affected both by the dance practices of other Caribbean islands such as Guadeloupe, Martinique, and Trinidad as well as Ivory Coast, Congo, and Cameroonian dance practices. The first crew featured both male and female dancers. The French dancehall vocabulary then differed from Jamaica's significantly in that the males would also engage in dancehall acrobatics as well as jump into splits and stand on their heads. Most of these masculinities were straight. Of the male dancers who came up from these crews, Lil'GGB[24] is perhaps the most known. He tours giving classes regularly and has won several dancehall king competitions, a title that to my understanding was previously reserved for DJs and artists, while dancehall queen referred to female dancers. When I still competed, the competitions were then for best male dancers and dancehall queens.

In 2006, Nick Cannon made a movie where he frames himself as the king of the dancehall[25] and as a dancer. This movie and its framing of the dancehall scene, linking it to international drug cartels, and creating a picture of the dancehall being controlled by drug money, might warrant some attention. The dancehall feeling and framing of the movie invoked no nostalgia for me and did not reflect what I know, although it did feature many known dancers and communities.

These are some examples of how dancehall changes with its context. The male hip in dancehall is now often considered to communicate sexual orientation while, according to Yellowman, my grandfather, and older practitioners, this strong separation is a newer thing. They all reference that as much as winin' would usually happen with a woman, it would also happen as a solo act in order to display freedom or attract a woman. During carnival, winin' is an expression of joy and freedom and is, according to Sonja Dumas´ Doctorate, not necessarily linked to sex but rather to expressions of joy and freedom.[26]

Winin' is a circum-Caribbean activity, and as much as Trinidad and Tobago and Jamaica like to claim it, it is to be found on close to all the Caribbean islands as well as across the entire African diaspora, and to my knowledge most of the African continent as well, including the Islamic nations. Winin' should therefore maybe be seen as an Africanism on par with hair braiding, schuupsing (kissteeth), and other cultural expressions. Winin' usually comes with an acceptance of reproduction as an aspect of life but does not always communicate either sex or readiness for sex.

In the wider Caribbean diasporas such as European, African, and Caribbean diasporas interchange winin' practices, and dancehall music is considered to communicate both broader Caribbean citizenship and also a form of Black citizenship. The clubs featuring dancehall would often also feature other African and or Caribbean musical forms and have patrons with multiple cultural backgrounds. The European semiotics of dancehall therefore can differ much from the Jamaican form. European sites also seem to have rejected the Jamaican homophobic push of dancehall music, and many Jamaican artists have found their tours canceled or demonstrated against. Jamaican dancehall songs have long been considered hate lyrics and artists like Buju Banton have had to sign contracts promising not to perform songs like "Boom Bye Bye".[27] Jamaican dancehall got the unsavory tags of "murder music" and anti-gay or homophobic. This affected the industry and the possibilities for international tours for Jamaican artists, in particular. These hateful lyrics have both served to secure dancehall's international position in the same communities that favor American gangster rap and are highly popular among white middle-class males. Sixty percent of gangster rap consumers are white. The white male gaze must therefore be considered to be present even in dancehall, a piece of music and dance said to represent the Black youth of Jamaica.

The male gaze spectacularizing the female wine

As mentioned earlier, winin' is a practice found throughout the Caribbean. It features many names and takes on many forms. In most sites, it will in one way or another feature on both genders or even "all genders" including the more recent variations unfolded in gender discourse. A circular or active hip movement to Caribbean music is colloquially known as *winin'* in Trinbago, Guyana,

Grenada, Jamaica (and more), *wukkin'up* in Barbados, *sepelote* in Cuba, *perreando* in the Dominican Republic and Puerto Rico, *gouyad* in Haiti, and *punta* in Belize. This is just to name a few. There are multiple iterations, roots, and routes of the hip movements found in the African diaspora. The hip has no singular origin, nor does it have a singular function. In all these sites, the male hip also sometimes features. Usually, the hip does not feature as a singular movement but rather as a part of a larger dance complex. Therefore, the hip will move between being spectacularized or can feature as a subsidiary movement.

It is true that the hip wine is more often spectacularized on the female body and features as a subsidiary when portrayed on the masculine body. Commercialization, commodification, and the male gaze play a part in this. Experiencing a "real" daggering session is a hot commodity in Scandinavia where I reside. Rasmus Paulsen, a Norwegian documentarist and self-proclaimed reggae lover, traveled to Jamaica to make a documentary about the dance where women are "impaled". The title of the article translates to "Sex Dance: Daggering in Jamaica" and it featured footage that was cringeworthy: one is left wondering if all proper procedures were followed and whether the people involved were aware that they would be featured internationally. It will surprise me if all of them were. Unlike a lot of the material on Norsk Rikskringkastning (NRK), which is the Norwegian government-owned main channel, this documentary is no longer possible to view, though the article framing it is.[28]

The documentary was shared rampantly, and many young men talked in the Facebook threads about booking a trip to Jamaica to experience this. The way they wrote about the Black female body was at best objectifying. Dancehall videos filming up young ladies' skirts have had a similar effect for years, leaving the impression that this is what dancehall is really about and that the Caribbean is the capital of wild and uninhibited sex. Jamaica, like Cuba, Kenya, Senegal also features on Scandinavian women's sex trips.[29] Articles about this feature in Scandinavian media every two years or so. Dancehall has become a part of this industry, especially among the younger population. They travel to Jamaica and visit dancehall "Head Quarters", that is, where the studio's various dance groups have set up to rehearse with, or more importantly accommodate, traveling tourists and dance enthusiasts. It is not kept hidden upon return that the local dancing men also offer sex as part of the package, and some are quite open about this, as much as a love for dancehall, being the reason for traveling. In Scandinavia, the Caribbean is almost exclusively associated with holidays, sex, and easy living. We do not associate it with hardships, slavery, and oppression. This is particularly interesting considering that Scandinavian sailors were more than 10% of the cast on most slavers' boats as well as Scandinavia having considerable interest in the Caribbean slave trade.[30] It is clear that the historic pathologizing of African bodies in relation to the transatlantic slave trade still very much continues in Scandinavia and even in a broader European relation to the Caribbean, Black bodies and, as an extension of this, dancehall.

I did mention that the male gaze, or even more particularly the white male gaze, might have something to do with the spectacularizing of the Black female hip, even if their female counterparts seem to have been equally fascinated by the Black male physique and dance. This however was so taboo that it led to the death of many Black males, not negating the fact that white male or female fascination has killed many Black people over the years, as violence, sex, and enslavement are all parts of patriarchal colonialism and slave economy.

I will share some of my earlier findings on accounts of male and female winin' in the Caribbean. This is often through the eyes of white males. The findings acknowledge the presence of the white male gaze and how this could be the reason why so many texts reference the female hips. The male hip is largely ignored, other than documents from criminal court, linked to the disciplining of Black male bodies. The implications of this violence and sexual policing I will return to. For now, I am singling out the similarity between the rendition below and the story of the movie *Dancehall Queen*, where Marcia, a dark-skinned street vendor (higgler) from the lower classes, challenges a light-skinned Olivine, a more middle-class reigning dancehall queen, in a type of a dancehall Cinderella story. The following rendition might be referencing some of the first accounts of what evolved into the dancehall queen competitions.

Henrice Altink in "More than Producers and Reproducers: Jamaican Slave Women's Dance and Song in the 1770–1830" references the following:

> It seems that the best female dancers on an estate were held in high esteem by the rest of the slave community. When planter Monk Lewis wanted to see some slave girls dance, the slave community brought forward by 'general acclamation', a woman called Psyche. According to Lewis she was the best dancer because her performance was 'light, graceful, easy and spirited'. According to J. B. Moreton, a former bookkeeper, the criteria for best female dancer on an estate was the wriggling of the hips. It is difficult to say what criteria the slaves themselves applied. Monk Lewis' remark that 'there is a regular figure and that the least mistake or a single false step is immediately noticed by the rest' seems to suggest that 'skill' was their distinguishing criteria. Colour, however, was definitely not a criterium used by the slaves. Moreton mentions, for example, that 'flat-nosed damsels', by which he meant black women as opposed to coloured women, were also appointed as best female dancer.

The presence of the white male gaze and its patriarchy should be acknowledged even in dancehall spaces where there are no white males. The white male colonial power is insidious in its ability to infiltrate and mask as a norm. The overfocus on the female winin' body both historically and now and the accompanying negation of the male winin' body might be seen through the following historical lens as explained by calypsonian and historian Hollis Liverpool. He goes as far as to say that:

> it is a fact that when Whites and Elites tried desperately to ban the carnival in the 19th century, the fascination of the French Creoles for the winin'g, African women prevented the laws being passed for so doing.

The particular fascination that the white male gaze had with the winin' Black female body has shaped its representation and its corporeality over a very long period of time. Equally, we should contemplate what effect a white male gaze might have on the Black male body and its freedom to engage with winin'. My grandfather considers the locking of the Black male hip a continued genocide. He is directly linking it to the traumas of Black male emasculation. He is not the only one to do so. The previous referencing to "buck breaking" and other explanations that are common also brings into attention acts of sexual violence which the Jamaican male has had to endure. The question that remains unanswered is, Why has this sexual trauma stilled the male Jamaican dancehall hip but has had the opposite effect in other places like Trinidad and Tobago? It is hard to imagine a carnival without everyone winin' alone, together, on top of under or beside each other. It would not even be uncommon to see a policeman and a robber winin' up together.

Hips tell no lie – trauma and economy

In *Trinidad's Camboulay Street Dance Play and the Carnivalesque Placebo: A Neurological Interface Between Social Theatre and Post-Traumatic Slave Syndrome*, Braithwaite (2009) places the wine in the context of Jungian self-healing. He uses Jung's framework of uninhibited behavior to work through trauma. He argues that the trauma of enslavement led to certain behaviors that were, in effect, coping strategies. He links this theory to behaviors in the Trinidad and Tobago Carnival. Brathwaite posits that; "They [the formerly enslaved Africans] annually reproduced and reinstated the former Camboulay festival as an auto-therapeutic collective experience, a multi-faceted educational forum, and an anniversary symbol of mind/body/spirit liberation from the shackles of colonialism."

One could ask what is so different between the corporeality of the Jamaican and the other Caribbean islands that still celebrate the male wine. We know that the male hip at one point was a Jamaican export. The butterfly went viral around the world with Patra on live TV, showing Black American men how to do it.[31] Patra deserves special mention, both for the fact that she was a pioneering female dancehall artist who paved the way for many American female rappers and influenced the style Janet Jackson and other Caribbean female artists such as Salt'n'Peppa (who have Jamaican heritage) performed and styled themselves. Patra's song "Queen of the Pack" also features some of the earliest examples of dancehall choreography for the stage. She herself had taken classes with L'Antoinette Stines who had also done the choreography. Behind Patra I believe we started to see the beginnings of choreographed dancehall steeped in roots, a form quite different from the chopped and staccato representation so prevalent on the male dancehall body today.

The more staccato style is often referred to as "new school" dancehall. We must acknowledge that many of these movements were designed to go viral and cross over to other bodies. The very particular undulations, pulses, and curves invoked by the Caribbean body have proven difficult for others to adopt.

Simplifying the Black movement in order for them to "cross over" is a process we have witnessed time and time again.

Wine and function

This brings us over to purpose and function. Dancehall and SoCa have traveled quite differently in the world. One could say that dancehall seems to travel more easily out of the islands, but without always returning. SoCa however seems to be an experience more designed to bring people in the millions together in one place. Both traditions have aspects of bringing people to and exporting the music from the islands. Both traditions have the power to evoke citizenship and change the space it travels to. Some of the differences might simply be in that it is easier to recreate a dancehall in Russia than it is to create an entire Caribbean carnival. At this moment, it seems impossible to create a carnival that feels authentic without the participation of a large number of Caribbean people. Dancehall, Japan proves, can more successfully be copied without the presence of many Caribbean people. Or rather we can say that people have convinced themselves that they can recreate dancehall without involving Jamaicans. There is no place like Yaad, and the spirit of Yaad is essential to dancehall. The very aspect of dancehall's power to transform small spaces and unconventional spaces, and its ability to replace one body's centrality for another (privileged with the disenfranchised) might be the very source of dancehall's in/security.

Furthering this line of interrogation another difference might be in the direction that music has taken. Winin' is to the Trinidadian an assertive action. Winin' is considered a very real action of power. In dancehall, winin' on a male body seems to have been given the opposite connotation. An example of this is the lyrics in André Tanker's hit song "Ben Lion Bin Baad Man" from 2003, a play on Bin Laden and the chaos he caused in the West:

> Ben Lion U Bin Baad Man
> Why O Why suh Why yuh go wine in dese people place . . .
> Ben Ruude Boy, Ben Baaad Boy,
> Say you wine right down to de ground and mash up de place . . .
>
> De eagle was flying high
> Until you cause him to cry
> Now all all over de dance dey calling your name . . .
> Dey say you are wanted man
> And it is time dat you understan'
> De tings dat dey say you do dey coming for you . . .
>
> Now Bulldog looking for you
> India helping them too
> Monkey jump up and throw a net was master de fence
> Things not like they was before

> These grounds(?) are spreading(?) war
> And the party is who could wine who could go win this time
> So yuh best ask wine
> . . . .
>
> Bushman jump in de line
> He say what is yours is mine
> Bring Madonna to help him move was a waste of time
> So he sent for Jennifer
> (J-Lo!), a hip dancer
> So to get him to move in time but de man can't wine . . .
> (He jus can't wine)

In these lyrics, it is clear that winin' is considered an assertive action, a way to make the world around you liminal and affect the time you are in, even if it is just the square meters around you. Winin' skills are equated to victory. It seems the association of the wine' with resistance, assertiveness, power, and freedom might be the major contemporary cultural difference between Jamaica and some other Caribbean spaces. I say contemporary because I have only observed this not to be so in the more Americanized contemporary renditions of the culture. In traditional culture, such as in Kumina, and the folk dances, where the lyrics still very much retain this playfulness and ability to even ridicule self for laughter, it seems the wine' retains its power and its relevance even to males and their agency in the world much as it does in SoCa.

Winin' spirit

Many SoCa songs and riddims entered the Jamaican dancehall space, remixed as daggering songs. In this process, the same rhythms that used to feature rounded movements, designed for you to be able to last while constantly moving for three whole days, were recast as thrusting, aggressive movements, where you would usually be active for a limited space of time. The carnival rhythms draw from multiple sources. Often, they are taken from "Preparation for War" rhythms, which are rhythms designed to hype the body and prepare it for physical action, agricultural rhythms, designed to allow you to maintain a certain movement over time, and lastly fertility or social rhythms, designed to tantalize and draw the attention of a partner. The agricultural and fertility dances usually emphasize melo-rhythm (a rhythmical treatment of melody or vice versa) while preparation for war or war rhythms tend to feature the accents and strip away the softening and "cooling" factor of the melodic. In the dancehall, the daggering remixes tend to remove the melodic features and amplify the aggressive accent of the music. This translates into movement changing from circular and revolving (invoking the cosmogram and the cycle of life) to thrusting forward toward the zenith of power (forward). The power is channeled into the metaphysical or even physical penis, and in an action of dagger-like penetration, versus teasing and pleasure. In the songs, words like pleasure are replaced with agony and pain. I believe there to be both a physical and a metaphysical consequence to this. Multiple national and international newspapers have featured the rise of daggering-related injuries. The most common is that of a "fractured penis".[32] As an initiate, I believe there are very real spiritual consequences to taking deep cultural practices and rituals, which in a very real sense are spells designed for war and channeling them into the female body. I believe that the consequences of this can be felt in the rise of violence, killings, drugs, and aggression. I believe that not only our sisters, mothers, and aunties feel this but we all do, as we all possess the female energy. Furthermore, I believe nature and the spiritual world feels it too.

A note on the side: fertility ownership and hate

This chapter is about framing differently and encouraging a different line of inquiry. One such is to question history in relation to our practices. Jamaica does have a specific history when it comes to fertility and violence and genocide if you may. In the late 1800s and 1900s, Jamaican women's reproduction was significantly lower than that of many other comparable islands and compared to women in the US of African descendant. In the US, about 10% of the female enslaved population would remain childless, while in Jamaica and some of the British Caribbean islands this was usually around 50%. The enslavers did not deem it viable to "breed their own slave stock" and therefore calculated buying rather than encouraging reproduction. Trinidad, although anglophone now, has been owned by both France and Spain. It is noticeable that the island that has more of "French" and "Spanish" influences seems to also feature music with a higher emphasis on melo-rhythms and sensual partner dances such as zouk, salsa, mambo, and the like. As much as I hate to give the colonialists power, I believe further interrogation on how the enslavers' designs have affected and corrupted our rituals and practices should and must be given. Several practices that might have meant survival under such conditions might today be the cause of death and discomfort.

The pollinizing hip

> "*the stilling of the black mans hip is a genocide I refuse to take part in*".
> Dr. Harold Charles-Harris, ca. 2014

I repeat this quote as it bears repeating. As I have grown to become a man, and the more I have learned about the practices of racism and sexual violence against Black males, the more I have come to understand what he meant by this. The overfocus on the Black female buttocks and hips is part of the sexual violence that the Black female has encountered. As much as she was forced into a role of supposed sexual willingness and a reputed inborn "readiness", the Black male sexuality was policed differently by the white male. Any action which could make the Black man an object of white female desire was an action that could get a Black man castrated, beaten, lynched, tortured, flogged, and/or killed. He was portrayed as a brute, whose sexual activities were bestial, rape-like, and painful. A sophisticated and codified moving male hip does not fit the agenda of the patriarchal colonial enterprise. The only exception was when there was a need for a "stallion or buck" to breed "bitches and heifers". I use these violent terms in order to remind us of the violence we are tip-toeing around whenever describing Caribbean dance and their historical readings.

Sonja Dumas argues for winin' as an enactment of sexuality that does not require a partner. Winin' as a form of auto-sexuality. Here is an extract from her dissertation:

> What is enacted is essentially a sexuality which does not require men; it is not lesbianism but auto-sexuality. The women in Carnival, as they become involved in the dance, are not tremendously interested in who or what they are wining upon; they will wine on men, they will wine on each other, most often on no-one at all, but the object of winin' is in most cases really themselves. It is an expression of free sexuality not dependent upon men. The winin' is not a signifier of sex, but a signifier of freedom.

In my observations, the same is true of men and wining – they do not need to wine on anyone else to enter the state of personal bliss or freedom, although their tendency is to "wine on a bumsee" (local parlance for winin' on the buttocks of someone – usually a woman).

Only being able to wine in relation to a woman can, by the context provided by Dr. Dumas, be seen as the repression of Black male sexuality, where it cannot exist on its own. Also, that a man cannot do cunnilingus on a woman, that it is only the penis that should or can be used, is another way that the Black male sexuality is negated. It hints at the "only for reproduction" thinking of the colonial master who wanted you to create offspring that could be sold. It is neither for your own pleasure nor really for the pleasure of your partner. Your function is limited; your future foreshortened. It is an example of sexual violence toward Black men in the Caribbean. It is a masculinity opposite to that represented by Shango, with his active hips and tongue.

Caribbean culture is a culture full of subversive power; they are cultures of hidden and open messaging. This technology of hidden and unhidden messaging has been perfected in both its masking and its spreading. You know it as popular culture, blues, jazz, house, hip-hop, samba, rumba, bachata, merengue, dancehall, SoCa, zouk, reggae. Some of us know it as home. Let's flip the script, and let's say that the colonials, the abusers, usurpers, expropriators, and appropriators also are useful little worker bees, who have taken our homes and carried them across the world, giving us somewhere to live wherever we are. Flowers use bees to spread their pollen, and their seed, "pollinizing" the world around them. In our survival, in our homelessness, we created technologies, coded pockets of home, of soul, and planted them as flowers for the bees to pollinate. I am sure if you ask a bee that he feels he has conquered every flower he has landed on. I am sure the flower in return allows the bee his fancies, because in his believed conquest, he, the bee, has also carried with him the secret to the flower's continued survival. So do the appropriators, those who believe they have conquered Caribbean expression, Caribbean soul and made it their own. They have aided in spreading the secret, to be deciphered only by the few and worthy, but enjoyed by the many. The more they steal, the more it is clear who really owns the riches, and that what is taken can never serve as more than empty shells, to the thief. Therefore, the thief always returns to the scene of the crime, every time coming closer to the inevitable realization that one keeps stealing because one does not have, nor is able to create.

I define the process of "Pollinizing" as the creative spreading of survival to other parts than one's immediate surroundings or the fertilization of a barren or hostile space. I believe this to be the core and code of Caribbean expressive art together with the technology of revitalizing the exhausted body, soul, and mind. Anywhere Caribbean expression and Caribbean art is, there is a pocket of home, where any Caribbean youth or person may step in, for the duration of the rhythm, and completely belong and be restored. There are also lingering lessons of cool, stance, and belonging that one carries out of this space. Some heat keeps radiating and allows for social navigation. Those left out in the cold, feel the heat and want it. It is craved, the hot and cold, the paradox that is Caribbean survival in hostile environments.

Anansi, the spider spirit granted the gift of storytelling and communication from the sky gods in Western Africa and the Caribbean, this trickster god is the true radioactive spider biting Blacks all over the world, through art as communication, and granting superhuman powers. Every Black person you will ever meet who is thriving and alive is, to me, a superhero who has overcome tremendous odds.

The cast of *Black Panther* and the movie itself may be the least superhero-ish Black people we have had on the screen in some ways, because they have had the least to overcome and are risking less than those who came before them, but we love them, celebrate them, and they are valuable because they are our Superman, who no longer bothers to pretend to be Clark Kent, our Peter Parker out of costume casually climbing a wall and allowing his real job to be his only job. We love that because why should anyone need to fake bad eyesight, clumsiness, and social awkwardness, just to keep the jealous and mediocre people less self-conscious? No seriously . . . why? Like with racism and the multiple ways people of color are forced to accommodate the colonial gaze, which in truth has always been a jealous one, logic does not seem to apply and is as absent as decency, ethics, morale, and humane civilization.

Pollinizing also begs the question: who is truly being colonized and by whom? It is clear that this is not just a one-way street, and in the question of art, creativity, and expression, so-called Western domination is maybe as delusional as the aforementioned conquering bee. Delusional are also the males who believe his hip to be unnatural. Those who do not believe it to be part of his power, both his entry into this world and the road to survival. Pollinizing is **colonizing in reverse**, without the use of abuse, rape, murder, inhumanity, and indignity, but rather through creativity, ingenuity, soul, vibration, and survival. Colonizing in reverse is to *wine up de people place*, disrupting convention, and flipping everything. It is round and allows for the co-existence of multiple improbabilities and truths. It does not tip the scale the other way, it does not make it right, and it does not correct the effects of coloniality, as nothing can erase the past. What it does is make it clear that the "victim" is a clever spider that plays tricks, makes the best of things, and takes a wine in the corners of visibility. To flip the script, to reverse the scene, one must come full circle, one must wine and examine from every angle. This chapter has attempted to provoke you, challenge what you know, make you reflect on what you know, make you see dancehall and SoCa as a ritual, normalize the male hip, pollinize your mind with it, and make it the most natural thing in the world. As a matter of fact, there is a very high chance that if you have Caribbean heritage, a male wine is the reason you exist. You owe it to your ancestors to "leggo" the hip and not engage in the genocide of healthy Black male sensuality. Now and forever, as long as there are Black people brought to this earth through the ritual of love, the ritual of the cosmological wine vibrates in history, changes it, and makes what was impossible possible, for the first time for this generation, always for the next, and the last time for the past. So, you are welcome, and what an honor it has been to wine with you, knowingly or unknowingly, because who is to tell who at this moment is a flower, who is a bee, who the wina, and who the wine. Who but Anansi the trickster? Trust and believe, every trickster wines.

The male winin' is the center of much contention. Many false claims have been made in the defense of trying to kill the momentum of the male hip and its metaphysical and socio-political power. One such claim is that it is not what we (Caribbean men do). However, any SoCa party, any *Punta* session, any folk exhibition featuring Kumina, Dinki Mini, The Kongo, and more proves this wrong. It is what we do. It is also what Jamaican men do when engaging with their tradition. Disrupting the wine, to me, therefore needs to be interrogated along the lines of analyzing history, tradition, and culture, and what could be disrupting its flow, as well as the flow of the hip. The renewal of the wine is also a renewal of our ancestral practices. It is the return of the African, as much as it is the emergence of the Caribbean.

Notes

1 Patois word for "being somebody".
2 Trinidadian musical style considered the predecessor of Calypso.
3 Jamaican musical form, related to Kaiso, and said to strongly influence Ska and reggae.
4 Caribbean indigenous spiritual tradition deriving from Fon and Ewe peoples of Western Africa. Strongly associated with Haiti but present on other islands too.
5 Kumina, one of Jamaica's oldest African religious/spiritual practices.
6 An Ifé (Yoruba)-based spiritual path practiced in Trinidad and Tobago. Closely related to Santeria in Cuba.
7 Obeah is a spiritual healing practice indigenous to the Caribbean and derived from West African practices
8 *Black Dance: A Contemporary Voice*, Thomas Prestø, 2019. A cosmo-technical approach is an approach that acknowledges movement practices as both manifested in the seen and

unseen world. It draws from both science and cosmology. Many Indigenous Movement Systems are cosmo-technical. A modern example would be the folkloric Cuban technique. The movement of the Orisha deities are the sources of the technical information both de-and-re-constructed in the movement practice and performance modes. The term is coined by Thomas Talawa Prestø and first used in relation to his technique, The Talawa Technique.
9   https://en.wikipedia.org/wiki/Kongo_cosmogram and www.nps.gov/ethnography/aah/aaheritage/lowCountry_furthRdg4.htm.
10 www.facebook.com/EmpressCece/videos/429694530988434/.
11 www.facebook.com/EmpressCece/videos/722328991568018/?v=722328991568018.
12 www.youtube.com/watch?v=KEbYHan39AM.
13 www.youtube.com/watch?v=ug1giUVtamg.
14 www.youtube.com/watch?v=ug1giUVtamg.
15 www.youtube.com/watch?v=c06l1Twxlyk.
16 www.youtube.com/watch?v=OS4ywlpZfuo.
17 http://jamaica-gleaner.com/article/news/20181014/brown-men-wanted-male-bleachers-outnumber-females-jamaica.
18 https://en.wikipedia.org/wiki/Kongo_cosmogram and www.nps.gov/ethnography/aah/aaheritage/lowCountry_furthRdg4.htm
19 Afrocentric term for African Holocaust, Holocaust of Enslavement, or Black Holocaust
20 www.youtube.com/watch?v=yHK61Yi81R0
21 www.youtube.com/watch?v=JT2TE_Uif04 Why dem Faya
22 www.youtube.com/watch?v=1pXRIRjqxhQ Blazin Crew
23 Les Twins Dancehall: www.youtube.com/watch?v=Bt9Swx_cv80 and www.youtube.com/watch?v=DZMC5TK5E4k and www.youtube.com/watch?v=LIr6mJgMyfc
24 www.youtube.com/watch?v=sKs-XXSgjuM
25 https://en.wikipedia.org/wiki/King_of_the_Dancehall_(film)
26 THE HIP AS A WEAPON SONJA DUMAS: www.youtube.com/watch?v=NF0aaCyxQyg
27 www.independent.co.uk/news/uk/this-britain/reggae-stars-banned-after-breaking-gay-hate-pledge-6096191.html.
28 www.nrk.no/kultur/sex-dans_-_daggering_-pa-jamaica-1.6868281.
29 www.vg.no/nyheter/utenriks/i/VmrLd/kvinnelig-sexturisme-er-moderne-slaveri.
30 www.newsinenglish.no/2014/09/28/slave-trading-past-still-haunts-norway/.
31 www.youtube.com/watch?v=zHrritZr8Is.
32 www.jamaicaobserver.com/news/Penile-fractures-on-the-rise-urologist_18443383.

References

Braithwaite, T. W. (2009) Trinidad's Camboulay Street Dance Play and the Carnivalesque Placebo – a Neurological Interface Between Social Theatre and Post Traumatic Slave Syndrome. In S. Jennings (Ed.), *Dramatherapy and Social Theatre: Necessary Dialogues*. New York: Routledge.

Daniel, Y. (2005) *Dancing Wisdom: Embodied Knowledge in Haitian Vodou, Cuban Yoruba, and Bahian Candomblé*. Chicago: University of Illinois.

Johnson, E. O. (2018) 5 Horrifying Ways Enslaved African Men Were Sexually Exploited and Abused by Their White Masters. *Face2Face Africa*. https://face2faceafrica.com/article/5-horrifying-ways-enslaved-african-men-were-sexually-exploited-and-abused-by-their-white-masters/3. Last accessed: 24 February 2020.

Prestø, T. (2019) *Black Dance: A Contemporary Voice*. Lenablou.

9 'Sounding' out the system

Noise, in/security and the politics of citizenship[1]

Sonjah N. Stanley Niaah

Introduction

"It naa go really go so at all, at all
We a have wi likl fun and Babylon yu call
Dem come lock off the sound and the bashment done, done, done, jah know
Reggae help I through the hardest time
Prevent a lot of youths from turn to crime
Stop fighting the reggae"

(Anthony B 2018)

"Sound di big ting dem."

(Busy Signal)

Arguably, Kingston is the loudest city in the Anglophone Caribbean and Jamaica, whose national instrument is the sound system, is the noisiest country on the planet. This chapter seeks to analyse decades of observations regarding the historical problems around 'noise', entertainment, and work in Jamaica where the entertainment sector has been under siege and its promoters, proprietors and patrons have existed in an antagonistic relationship with the state and enforcers of the law charged with protecting lives. Indeed, the use of force by the Jamaica Constabulary Force (JCF) to regulate entertainment outweighs its use in any other sector or profit-making enterprise, except in where cases private security measures are arranged. Viewed as a case historically, the entertainment sector reveals a thriving culture of enforcement by security forces which has resulted in high degrees of in/security. Focused on the analysis of culture, in particular, popular culture, Caribbean culture, and cultural studies, a significant portion of my work on Jamaican popular culture, documented in the book *Dancehall: From Slave Ship to Ghetto* (2010), has engaged in historically grounded, geographically sensitive, and culturally comparative work. I extend that work here to examine the politics of noise and in/security around Jamaican music.

Located at the intersection of cultural history, cultural geography, and cultural studies more broadly, this chapter continues the exploration of Black Atlantic

DOI: 10.4324/9781003205500-10

performance of geography and history by placing entertainment practice in a wider comparative and analytical field along a historical trajectory where Africa as source and sensibility takes shape in a 'new world' of social and political challenges and opportunities. As I thought about my contribution to this collection of essays, I began more and more to ruminate on the hallmarks of Black life across the African diaspora which have been systematically suppressed or prostituted. I tried to document some of this in papers I presented over the last two years, namely, 'Africa on Stage', and 'Of Memory, Prisons, Crime and Profit' where I highlighted dimensions of Black life such as religion, recreation, and celebration, especially around music, which have been criminalized and ultimately suppressed. Following the arguments logically, there is a framework within which Africans in the diaspora can argue for reparatory justice based on systematic measures used for cultural erasure.

As I thought more about this chapter, artistes such as Busy Signal with his notable sound effect – 'sound di big ting' – entered my mind. He was referring simultaneously to the amplified sound of the sound system and to another sound which many have come to fear, and around which Jamaica has gained notoriety: the sound of the gun. Within dancehall, and for the artiste, Busy Signal gives a musical rendering of the gun, a tool of destruction which has caused much insecurity. But it is also the weight of sound, the sound system, the certain way that Jamaica has to sound itself to really be heard as the noisiest little place on the planet, because of its music. Arguably, Black life, and in particular entertainment, has been suppressed through various forms of oppression in Jamaica to the same degree that Jamaican music has grown correspondingly loud through the sound system, to signal agency and resistance. In many ways, the gun and the sound system have occupied a Janus-faced existence, but in this chapter I want to highlight the similarity in their habitus and operation. What roles has the sound system played for different stakeholders and the public? Can it be compared to the barking of guns? And who have been its real victims? What has been the impact of 'sounding the big ting' in true dancehall fashion, or the big sound system?

With the sound system as Jamaica's national instrument, I wish to zone in on the role of the sound system, sound practice, politics, and mechanisms of transgression. I also use sound deliberately in contradistinction from the pejorative 'noise' in order to engage in reparatory thinking, to reclaim sound, and to make redress to the extent that we have engaged in/enabled pejorative thinking about sound. This chapter is therefore an activist in its orientation, and I begin by locating Jamaica and the sound system in the cosmopolitan Caribbean, at the heart of modernity and globalization in the West. For, as Wardle (2001, pp. 1–2) concluded:

> People from the Caribbean – subject to slavery, the plantation economy, and labour migration – have one of the longest exposures to a global political and economic order of any social grouping. For centuries, Jamaicans have lived at a cross-roads of transnational economic, social and cultural

dynamics. A central argument here is that they are still living out the aesthetic and moral consequences and contradictions of the Enlightenment and modernity. . . . Jamaicans understand themselves as global citizens – as individuals who have the potential for making social and cultural connection with many parts of the world. This sense of self can be identified across multiple contexts – oral performance, music, kinship and friendship, economics and politics. It is also shaped by, and reacts against, manifest exclusionary practices in the countries that Jamaicans travel to and work in.
(Wardle, 2000, pp. 1–2)

With the foregoing as context, I do three things in this chapter. I say something about the work of entertainment by select citizenry historically, its location in a colonial past, and within contemporary Jamaica, and the Caribbean more broadly. I contextualize Jamaica's entertainment practice in a wider geographical, African diaspora sense, with a view to establishing the ground for a new vision for entertainment. Additionally, I use Jamaica as a case for putting the creative work around music first in activating creative industries for Caribbean development through analysis of sound as a form of labour, a certain form of practice for select citizenry. This chapter seeks to extend works by scholars such as Orlando Patterson, Tricia Rose, Julian Henriques, Jacques Attali, Walter Rodney, Barbara Browning, Carolyn Cooper, Louis Chude-Sokei, Frantz Fanon, among others, in centring the form of practice embodied in the work and politics of the sound system.

Re/defining noise, reinstating sound

This chapter that cultural studies grounded in the Caribbean must take account of sound as a reference for the power dynamics characteristic of the post-/colonial Caribbean in which people of African descent reside, and are consistently engaged in struggles to express, to identify, in space and place. Douglas Kahn in *Noise Water Meat* suggests "[w]e know they are noises in the first place because they exist where they shouldn't or they don't make sense where they should" (1999, p. 21). Among others, Marcel Cobussen (2017) highlights that noise, often defined based on volume, is not the only factor to be considered when trying to understand sound. He suggests that other factors such as context and environment are crucial. Cobussen (2017, p. 3) advanced a similar view to Kahn's out-of-place-ness, that:

> Sounds are thus not noisy in themselves but can become noise if they occur in a place where they are not supposed to be. Noisiness then becomes a label attached to them. If noise is indeed sound out of place, it implies that any sound occurring in its appropriate place is, by definition, not noise. "Out of place" then refers to disorder, instability, contravention of the expected, undermining the dominant organization, disharmony etc.

Cognitive dissonance was originally defined as a musical term denoting a clash of sounds or an unpleasant combination of notes, or simply noise. This terminology is being applied to the sounds being made by the descendants of Africans in the Caribbean, to be seen as noise, juxtaposed to the more Euro-centric construct of aesthetically pleasing acceptable sound. Notably, in the postcolonial world of sound, the acceptance of an audible expression, defined as sound or noise, is dependent not only on the environment but also on who is making the sound, and who has the power to define the sound. This results in the issues around sound being either subjective or moral or even aesthetic.

Against this background, noise in the Caribbean has been constructed to denote those sounds which are created in, or come from, spaces that are deemed immoral within a Euro-centric Christian ideology. This kind of subjective discrimination is often applied to the majority African enslaved (the masses), their descendants and their African influenced spiritual/performance practices, cultures, and memories. From slavery to an era of freedom, tensions over popular cultural expressions prevailed. Pickering and Rice (2017, p. 18) noted:

> This implies that labels such as "quiet" and "loud" can be mapped on to more overtly moral ones such as "harmonious" and "disharmonious" or "good" and "bad." And the general opinion is that . . . to be quiet is to be good, to agree to cherished classifications, to uphold the sonic and social order and to follow accepted ways of being. To be noisy is to be bad, to disregard convention, and to confuse or ignore classifications and have different and unacceptable ways of being. Noise, far more than just 'sound out of place,' is indicative of an entire moral system.

The task of re/defining the term 'noise', and understanding its politics, even its pejorative application, can further be traced in the writings of Attali (1985) and Rose (1994) among others. Taken in contradistinction to music, 'noise' can be seen as a representation of chaos, destruction, and disharmony in both nature and the violence of society. Attali offers four cultural stages in which to understand the structure, production, and dissemination moving from ritualized contexts to that of commodity and recorded artefact for reproduction by the start of the 20th century. Rose positions Black music such as hip hop and rap as social movements in their political uses against the 'system' – racial, sexual, cultural, and aesthetic. While this chapter does not seek to account for the history of use or definition in relation to 'noise' and sound, the adoption of terms such as noise without understanding their intellectual genealogy or history of usage is part of the awareness this work offers. It is cognizant that the question of musical value cannot be subsumed in terms such as noise and that one person's rhythmic purity is another's disharmony, or even another's standard of excellence. My argument is that, counterposed with the essentially subjective 'noise', the term 'sound' inserts rudimentary physical characteristics which are more objectively isolated and engaged.

Sound and the politics of citizenship: a Caribbean cultural studies perspective

The politics of Caribbean citizenship, indeed Jamaican citizenship, is bound up in experiences and discourses around the post/colonial enterprise. This politics around Jamaican citizenship, invokes questions such as – Who is the citizen? How do they live in the everyday and have their being? What securities do they enjoy? What are the spaces and habitus of their creativity? What are the symbols, fantasies, and products of their imaginings? Who has rights to the nation and its privileges? The citizenry at the heart of this chapter are those involved in the creation and consumption of Jamaican popular music, in particular, amplified music inside the dance hall and around the sound system. Such a citizenry has been produced through particular forms of 'smadditizin'[2] vis-à-vis sound, and the politics of citizenship has to be seen through an interdisciplinary lens based on the degrees of disenfranchisement and exclusion.

The instruments of the colony and later of the nation, their creators, and enforcers (the *system*) in the colonial era and the postcolonial present have never been favourable in their intentions towards the way the masses have lived and had their being. Arguably, this amounts to somewhat of a departure from the vision of nation builders, but if this statement is too naïve, then at least a departure from what can be interpreted from their writings. Leighton Jackson (2014, p. 4) explained the following:

> The people are in reality the centre of the institutional universe which comprises the State. The objective of laws which are the mechanism to officially order relationships within the state is to bring its institutions in alignment with this truth. Norman Washington Manley echoed this sentiment when he declared that the mission of his generation in creating a new "self-governed" state is "to win political power for the black masses of my country." There is no win if this state does not reflect the people's insight and values, which are in turn reflected in their language and *culture*.[3]

The extent of the struggle to re-engineer self and society, for even nation builders as they departed from a colonial era, can be explained by the creole term "smadditizin'". A development from the word "somebody," "smadditizin'" is an active Jamaicanism explaining the process of becoming somebody. Added to this are the factors of class and hierarchy that dominate the process of becoming somebody, especially for those who are at the bottom of the class and race ladders, or not on the ladders at all. Charles Mills asserts (1997, p. 55) that smadditizin' should be understood as a "struggle for, the insistence on, personhood . . . in a world where, primarily because of race, it is denied," and thus, essentially, smadditizin' is a political, cultural, moral, epistemological, and ontological (metaphysical) struggle that is not yet complete, as the structures against which it struggles are "in many ways intact." For those who have been creators and consumers of amplified Jamaican reggae and dancehall sounds, it is correct to assert that the creative process has been their proverbial 'road to Zion', their means of becoming and of struggle, where a reprieve from the making and remaking of the everyday self and identity collides with a world that privileges the colour and class of the colonial and metropolitan ideal, compounded by the competition inherent in the urbanscape.

The complexity of the urbanscape notwithstanding, Orlando Patterson (1973), through research he conducted in five inner-city Kingston communities, reported to the Office of the Prime Minister in 1974 that every community should have its own sound system. His recommendation was based on the collective bond he observed based on economic and social gains for the communities where music was consumed using sound systems. As sugar and bauxite lost their appeal and financial sustainability, there was something else emerging as bars and street corners with sound systems became the enterprise of choice for many who found alternative pathways in musical expression. Patterson's recommendation was ignored by the government, but the people advanced it on their own terms. The Jamaican case is hardly unique and reflects an ethos across the postcolonial African diaspora. Evidence suggests that in various sectors of life and through time, not least of which is the sector of entertainment, little or no space was made available through a *system* that included legislative suppression.

'Sounding' and 'grounding' the reasoning

A historically grounded analysis of sound in the African diaspora and the wider Caribbean reveals a high degree of creativity as much as attempts at suppression. Wrapped in the creativity is that underexplored dimension of transgression, of action through sound, sounding like grounding (Rodney, 1969), which insists on an orientation to action, activism, pushing at the limits of expression and selfhood, the absolute necessity of expression, and celebration. While 'grounding' is a form of practice intended to raise consciousness through reasoning, honed in discourse, sounding as in through the sound system is intended to be heard, amplified audibility, countering disenfranchisement and erasure. The sound system became the voice which was not to be silenced by the 'system', the same 'Babylon system' that Peter Tosh referred to as the 'shitsem' (cited in Chang and Chen, 1998, p. 114). The only good system after all is a sound system. DJs were 'sounding' off on the system through improvised and carefully orchestrated lyrical virtuoso, both live and recorded. 'Sounding the big ting' became a pastime favoured by the Jamaican masses which gathered weekly to celebrate various dimensions of life.

It is the sound system, like the body as an instrument, a kingdom of memory, a landscape of power, which ultimately gains attention in this chapter. I extend Julian Henriques' thinking about the African body, the African diasporic, its acts of memory across time, and on 'stage'. Henriques pointed to the inextricable link between the body, earth, and sound, at once democratizing the access to memory, movement, and corporeal power. Whether it was in the work songs, the blues, the studio, or dance floors around the sound system, *the body* in these spaces aimed to find and maintain a primal connection (see Henriques, 2008, p. 231). This is the body that historically has sought refuge from the days of being forced to dance on the slave ships to the insistence that it reduces gyration of the hip girdle (see Pesto, this volume). Examining the history provides important insights into how this history can function to serve popular culture scholarship in the re/representation of the legacies of slavery.

The culture of celebration, indeed the will to celebrate, the culture of entertainment born in a mostly African experience with cross-fertilization from European and other experiences, has been characterized by an ethos of containment, force, and eradication. Barbara Browning's (1995) comments on Brazil shows clearly that African-derived performance practices, such as Samba, are considered infectious rhythms, considered in terms of diseases, such as the AIDS pandemic, and are seen as in need of elimination. Evidence of such elimination is found across the spectrum of African aesthetics, whether in the form of dance, drumming, or spirituality, which were banned and regulated in deadly ways. Notably, the politics of noise within the African diaspora, from jazz and the blues to calypso, passinho, grime, and dancehall, has been documented by writers beyond Browning such as Rose (1994), Martis (2016), and Scruggs (2014), among others. As various states over time have sought to cement the words 'negro' and 'noise/black' and 'boisterous' together in pathological ways, various populations have remained steadfast in their imperative to live, celebrate, and affirm their being. There is an imperative to celebrate even as states have been militant in their attempts to stem the prevailing tide. Martis (2016, n.p.) documented the following in an article:

> I've watched as black people have been silenced, arrested, and even killed for the noise they make. Black people aren't more or less loud than anyone else, and yet the noise we make is feared, scrutinized, and made public. Understanding why there's such a sensitivity – and fear – of black noise is a complex and intricate question that doesn't supply a simple answer.

Closer to home, "[t]he debate in Kingston," according to Scruggs (2014, n.p.), "is similar to those that have ... erupted in New York and New Orleans over the rights of street musicians and dancers to perform in public space." However, less recently, with a focus on the period of the 1960s, it can be noticed the same kind of animosity between those entertainers and the broader populations and, in particular, the State. Killing music in the city can be said to have been a sort of aim for some time which continues today inside more contemporary musical populations such as the Grime generation (Rawcliffe, 2017). An African diasporic perspective therefore reveals common genetic ties around 'noise', sound, and suppression.

Historicizing entertainment and crimes of the state

While the likes of Bournemouth Club, Silver Slipper, Myrtle Bank Hotel and other prestigious clubs in Kingston around the 1960s were not seen as a threat but rather popular spaces hosting several performers from across the world, there were other ways in which entertainment was being regulated in

Table 9.1 Caribbean Laws Implicating 'Noise'

Name of Legislation	Year	Location
Customs of the Islands Prohibition on Drums and Horns	1688 *amended in 1717	Jamaica
Acts Passed in the Island of Barbados – law against drums and horns	1699	Barbados
Antigua Act	1702	Antigua
Law banning communication by horns and drums	1711 *amended in 1722	St. Kitts
An Act to Remedy the Evils Arising from Irregular Assemblies of Slaves	1760	Jamaica
Act for the Encouragement, Protection and Better Government of Slaves	1788	Dominica
An Act for the Punishment of Such Slaves as Shall Be Found Practicing Obeah	1806	Barbados
Act for the Punishment of Obeah	1819	Montserrat
Grenada Consolidated Slave Act	1825	Grenada
Summary Convictions Ordinance	1868 *the anti-obeah clauses were removed from the law in 2000.	Trinidad
Ban of Calinda Bands	1883	Trinidad
The Obeah Law	1898 *still in effect today	Jamaica
The Leeward Islands Obeah Act	1904 *remains the basis of the law in several of these countries.	Anguilla, Antigua, Barbuda, Montserrat, St. Kitts, Nevis, British Virgin Islands
The Medical Law	1908 *while not explicitly aimed at obeah practitioners, they were punished under this act for unlawfully practising medicine.	Jamaica
Shakerism Prohibition Ordinance	1912	St. Vincent
Shouters Prohibition Ordinance	1917 *repealed in 1951	Trinidad and Tobago
Noise Abatement Act	1997	Jamaica

disadvantageous ways. There had been the enactment and enforcement of the law by apparatuses of the State which operated in opposition to the people. A close examination of the history of entertainment revealed that no space was made, and temporary "shrubs" were used for the slave dances in the early and mid-19th century. They were sometimes constructed with bamboo and as often as they were erected, they were demolished after the event.

Waddell reported (2010, pp. 17–18, 147, 161–162) that slaves in Jamaica had three holidays at Christmas, which lasted one week among the town slaves. His report of the character of slave entertainment, and the physical and philosophical spaces it occupied, was revealing. There was "unbounded revelry" in the "shrub made for the occasion", with crowds dancing "Johnny Canoe," singing and drumming, and set girls. There were "rude and demoralizing 'balls and suppers,'" as well as "the soiree," of which the first one, in the schoolhouse, an official space, was introduced "to promote the great cause of temperance and of social improvement." Waddell recounted "revelling and rioting" in the negro yards by "ill-disposed, disorderly people . . . pervert[ing] their freedom" with singing, drumming, and dancing in "the booth" constructed in a certain yard, which the powers of the plantation society were not able to prevent. One resident of the yard was later arrested and jailed for staging the ball and threatening the life of a constable, and Waddell and other "quiet good people rejoiced" that this person would no longer be able to "disturb all their neighbours" with revelry into the morning.

In the same era and across time, sanctions have not been proportionately applied to Euro-centric gatherings and activities of the established Church, until recently – long after Noise Abatement Acts concerning 'night noises', which sought only to regulate the entertainment economies in cities such as Kingston, were passed. Table 9.1 shows several legislations that were passed in the anglophone Caribbean, following from the inherited frameworks for 'noise' abatement.

The Noise legislation from the 1600s to the 1900s seemed to be largely preoccupied with regulating African sound and expression specifically the drum and obeah. The fact of being defenceless against physical and verbal abuse, gatherings were the most effective weaponry possessed by the enslaved. Although drumming, as a central part of these gatherings, disturbed the peace of the colonizers, it was not the main intention. Although it was a rebellious act and was not allowed, drumming was more for communal healing purposes. In a Fanonion sense (1963, p. 226), the 'crystallizing of souls' that have been dismantled from the day's whipping and abuse, is covertly at work/play. It is the putting back together of self, or the putting together of a new self, which is the power of the communal gathering. However, ironically the drum symbolizes a foreign sound, from a foreign land, from foreigners – causing it to be defined as noise, and unconnected to citizenship.

What the Noise Abatement Act inadvertently suggests is that only some people make sound while others make noise. In order to make a distinction, the state security apparatus has been employed to ensure that no noise crime is committed or that any noise crime committed must be punished. Since the state in any society is there to prevent violence and maintain peace, the noise is then perceived not just as disturbing the peace but as violent and has the need to be punished. Since noise disturbs the 'peace', the 'peace' in this sense has to be the law-abiding non-violent citizenry. This can only also mean that the noisemakers are not a part of the citizenship and are being othered as lawbreakers, bad, immoral, and violent people.

Correspondingly, the State sees dance gatherings as a safe den for criminals. Evidence of the State being in conflict with the masses can be highlighted in the issue of police raids on dancehall events. Venues could be perceived as being under siege. Dance venues throughout the 1960s and 1970s till the present have been raided with such considerable frequency that 'locking down the dance' became a feature of dancehall life, and film crews could request re-enactment. Several dancehall artistes have made mention of these lock-offs in their music. In a 1994 para-military operation of the JCF Anti-Crime Division, eighty persons were detained and one arrested for murder and shooting at the House of Leo Venue (Jamaica Broadcasting Corporation, Entertainment Report, 1994). This particular raid was thought to be staged for a British film crew. These ideas were immortalized by Buju Banton who recorded 'Operation Ardent' which details the DJ's experience of a raid in the early 1990s. Opening with blaring sirens, Buju asked:

> What's di motive? Why dem keep meddling around the poor people dem business? . . . What more? What oonu want di massive fi do? Every dance wey wi keep oonu mek dem get curfew.
>
> (Buju Banton, 1993)

The DJ was asking: what does the State want the poor, who have no adequate space in which to live, recreate and recreate self, to do when every attempt at entertainment, especially through the dance, is curfewed? From the 1960s to the present day, many more raids than those receiving media coverage have occurred, all causing varying degrees of damage to the community and to the people, sometimes the artists themselves such as DJ U-Roy. For U-Roy and his team, having a reputation of being 'rude boys' or 'bad men', raids, beatings, locking down the sound, and arrests were common around them. U-Roy himself was once beaten by the police and subsequently imprisoned and his turntable confiscated because he was creating "night noise".

If the reason for raiding street dances is because criminals frequent them, this assumes that criminals are only found downtown and in inner cities, while clubs and parties uptown are filled with law-abiding citizens. For night noise associated with entertainment, police raids take on a different nature and comparatively little enforcement is carried out for Christian evangelical crusades, Church services, and 'Nine Nights' or Dead Yaads. This haphazard enforcement of the law is ultimately discriminatory and serves to violate the effort of creators of entertainment products for decades.

Additionally, since geographical space helps to determine the definition of 'noise', it becomes critical to note that successive governments in Jamaica, just as in the colonial period, have not supported an enabling environment for the production and consumption of entertainment. As such, much of the sound from dancehalls and night noises exist on the margins, in lanes, on gully sides, parking lots, open lots, and the like, that are converted to accommodate dance activity. However, the contradiction is that the state in Jamaica seems to protect carnival processions that are more expansively on the streets of Jamaica, publicly paraded to disrupt traffic and pedestrians alike. There is hypocrisy regarding noise, as carnival takes control of daylight hours even on business days, for parades involving the middle- and upper-class traditions imported with roots from a Catholic European Christian philosophy. Instead of sanctions, there are tangible ways in which the State through practice supports carnival as an active policy to expand its potential as a tourism product. Furthermore, when naked brown bodies exposed in carnival parade the streets of Kingston, they are fully accepted as this 'carne' of the mostly brown flesh that can afford the skimpy costumes at a premium cost. However, when Black bodies from the inner cities are on display or exposed, the argument becomes discriminatory, condemnatory, shameful, and judgemental.

Here, shame is embedded in the use of terms such as 'loud' or vulgar. The loud and vulgar bodies, and the sounds they gyrate to, are also transferable to and describe the fashion worn by some dancehall patrons: bright or colourful clothing, wigs, nails and accessories are also classed as 'vulgar' especially for fashion that is too revealing. In this sense, the appearance of the person is making too much noise, disrupting the moral silence that Black bodies should be subjected to, as a kind of under-class and/or second-class citizen (see also Lawrence and Stines, this volume). Additionally, political rallies used for campaigning activities exist outside the scope of the Noise Abatement legislation. Political motorcades often take the shape of a merger between a carnival and a dancehall event by virtue of the taking over of the streets to obstruct regular traffic and business activities, as well as the plethora of dancehall and reggae songs that litter the soundtrack of political rallies.

Due to the class-stratified status of Jamaica, citizenship is tied up with the politics inherited from enslavement: it becomes attached to persons from the middle- and upper-classes who are largely the business class of owners with means to generate wealth and influence policies and laws that work in their favour. As such, access to the privileges of 'citizenship' is denoted by their values and morals. It is therefore clear who the real citizens are and how their roles and privileges are reinforced or diminished.

Venues politicized

Focusing on the idea of 'entertainment geographies', an analysis of spaces such as venues reveals that they have retained their character, use, and meaning over many decades. They could be considered nomadic, occupying marginal domains, but the well-spring of venues never dries: these spaces are constantly being created or re-fashioned. Even though they may be seen outside of the sensibilities and aesthetics of Jamaicans of 'quality' in the Nettlefordian sense, they are central to the articulation of a sense of community and cultural identity among the lower class and those abroad, some in spaces of exile.

The police have been an extremely problematic symbol of the tensions between dance patrons and promoters and the State. Up until today, the police continue to be accused of provocation, profiling persons, and exerting excessive force of their authority. Police have been said to profile persons at this time into the stereotypical notion of what a 'rude boy' or 'bad man' looked like in the 1960s. Markers used to identify these persons was typically their attire of khaki style clothing and Clarks brand of shoes. Police officers were also incensed by the playing of certain tunes. Of these, Max Ruby's song with the line, "Babylon likkie likkie and beggie beggie" was sure to be a dance stopper. The police would immediately appear to end the dance by ordering the selector to turn off the sound system. An interviewee, one of the collaborators in my early research, recalled:

> Police look for wanted man in the dance. I used to think Bablyon don't want man enjoy themselves back then . . . 'Sound system waan turn down' was the constant warning at midnight. If they [had to] come back it's trouble. Sometimes police mash up the dance. Sometimes the Black Maria van was there with the police, and after they line up everybody and search them they would load the Black Maria. Some of this was just harassment."
> (personal interview, Harry, April 24, 2002)

Foundation DJ King Stitt, in an interview, expounded on police harassment by saying that, for the police, the vocation of being a DJ was tantamount to a criminal offence, such as smoking marijuana. The fact that these activities were often found in the same space – DJs would often be users of marijuana, some of them even Rastafari in their cultural and religious convictions – it was harder to separate the police from dance activity. Raids have also been tainted by the suggestion that police officers demand money from dance promoters in exchange for allowing the event to continue. A classic example of this going wrong was the incident at the La Roose venue in St. Catherine on January 27, 2003. This ended in a conflict as persons at the dance allegedly resisted police bribery, and a shooting incident ensued leaving at least five persons injured (see Stanley Niaah, 2010, p. 9).

The State, including but not limited to the police, is not the only entity to blame. According to U-Roy, politics did not play such an important role in the raids on dances. Intervention by the police was common and their authority was particularly invoked when 'society people' (middle and upper classes) complained about the noise as sound systems played in venues that were above crossroads. In a report on Television Jamaica's Prime Time News (August 11, 2003), it was acknowledged that 'uptown' venues – Constant Spring Golf Club, Priscilla's, Weekenz, and Villa Ronai, utilized at the commercial end of dancehall for stage shows in particular – were disturbing nearby residents but not always subject to stipulations. The authorities instead were appealing to these entities while reminding them of stipulations under the Noise Abatement Act (1997) to seek permits ten days prior to the event and to end events by 2:00 a.m., and 'promising' its enforcement.

The accusations of party raiding and locking down have increased since the passing and subsequent re-enforcement of the Noise Abatement Act (1997) and the Places of Amusement (1999) regulations. The Noise Abatement Act regulates both public and private spaces and events and is designed to control the noise around a number of public activities, from political and public meetings to dance events. It states that no person in a private or public setting shall sing, play or sound noise-making or musical instruments, use any loudspeaker, microphone, or other means of amplifying sound to a level 'reasonably capable' of annoying individuals, particularly residents, visitors, and the infirm, beyond a range of 100 metres from the origin. The regulations further stipulate that loudspeakers should not be operated at levels capable of annoyance beyond 11:00 p.m. in the case of public meetings, or midnight for political meetings held during political campaigns, or between the hours of 2:00 a.m. and 6:00 a.m. on a Saturday or Sunday, and between midnight and 6:00 a.m. on Sunday, Monday, Tuesday, Wednesday, or Thursday. Where the commission of an offence is proven, sanctions apply in the form of fines not exceeding JA$20,000 or imprisonment up to six months. The act requires that persons intending to stage events capable of disturbing nearby residents must seek permission from the police up to ten days prior to the event (The Noise Abatement Act, 1997).

As a policing apparatus, the Noise Abatement Act is closely associated with the Places of Amusement Regulations under the Parish Councils Act (1999). Close scrutiny of the Kingston and St. Andrew Corporation (Places of Amusement) Regulations (1999) further outlines the nature and context of regulating events. 'Places of amusement' is defined as any public place freely accessed by patrons paying a fee or not, including a cinema, club, dance hall, open-air dance venue, festival, discotheque, roller disco, skating rink, or amusement arcade. Operators of such places are granted licenses upon paying fees ranging from JA$2,000 to JA$10,000. While the definition of amusement activities is not limited to the staging of dance events, it is safe to say that a large number of these permits were issued for dancehall events.

Since 2018 there has been an increase in calls to revise the Noise Abatement Act because it serves the needs of the State but not always the citizen, night economy entrepreneur, music promoter, or the community. Due to combined efforts on the part of the Ministry of Culture, Gender, Entertainment and Sport, the Ministry of National Security, the Ministry of Local Government, and the Ministry of Tourism, it was announced in 2019[4] that party hours would be extended until 4:00 am, allowing two additional hours for entertainers and patrons in Jamaica over the limited Christmas and New Year holiday periods. While this extension brought criticism from residents and parliamentarians representing citizens, it highlighted that a critical mass of persons were now convinced of the need to relax historically problematic legislative platforms that were never assessed in light of Jamaica's status as an entertainment capital in the Caribbean. Minister of National Security Dr Horace Chang asserted that the government "must create the balance between the continued growth of our music and entertainment industries, and maintaining public order, safety and well-being of the general public" (see Peru, 2020, n.p.).

'New world' sound landscapes: the 'unbounded' red bull culture clash

Ironically, as Jamaica faltered on structuring its night economy and finalizing frameworks to grow its creative economy, entities far and wide were busy exploiting Jamaica's musical capital. In this section I analyse the fragile context of luminosity, using Jamaican dancehall's and in particular sound system's relationship with the transnational corporation Red Bull. Not only is Jamaica's place on the music video production scene secure, but Jamaican aesthetic practices have populated the commercial performance and video production landscapes around sound clashes staged for global appeal. A popular dancehall performance mode, the sound system clash, which became prominent after the 1960s, has been the source of heightened engagement with indigenous Jamaican music and has resulted in symbolic as well as real violence. By the 1980s and 1990s, sound systems such as Stone Love, Kilimanjaro, and Bass Odyssey, among many others, ruled the Jamaican nightscape and sound system clashes became popular beyond Jamaica to occupy 'outernational' terrains. Violent clashes produced a damper on the sound system scene in Jamaica, but they gained popularity abroad in the 1990s when the World Clash events organized by 'Irish and Chin' began in New York. Even though there have been attempts to revive the practice through the Jamaica Sound System Festival,[5] clashes remain a rare aspect of Jamaica's dancehall scene. However, as the sound system clashes at home subsided, they increased on a global scale, especially in metropolitan centres such as New York, Atlanta, London, Lisbon and further afield in Johannesburg.

Most importantly, for those who are not resident in such cities, the spotlight has been cast on sound system clashes within the global videoscape inside primary visual repositories such as YouTube, where Jamaican dancehall aesthetics are paraded in such events as the Red Bull Culture Clash. Red Bull has been explicit about its transnational commercialization of the dancehall performance mode usually staged in indoor venues (a departure from the typical Jamaican scene where events are usually outdoors). Originating in 2010, the Red Bull Culture Clash series is hailed as "the world's biggest musical battle" and has featured artistes/disc jocks/MCs/rappers/sound systems such as Metalheadz, Skream & Benga, Channel One, Major Lazer, Federation Sound, Wiz Khalifa, Stone Love Movement, Disturbing London, David Rodigan, Unruly (featuring Popcaan), African Storm, Durban Massacre, and Tinie Tempah, among many others. The modus operandum is similar to the typical Jamaican sound clash with four sounds (sometimes referred to as crews) competing in a series of four or five clash rounds, and success in each round is determined by crowd response. The events have seen up to 25,000 persons in attendance, making them some of the most successful one-night events staged around sound system culture globally.

Following the first Red Bull Culture Clash in 2010, the England Riots of 2011 spotlighted Jamaica, as accusations circulated about the role Jamaicans, and more specifically, the Jamaican language[6] played in the successful spread of the riots. Beyond these years, I argue that the consumption of Jamaica as a product and personality reached a high point in 2013, a saturation point in a sort of boundaryless hegemonic dissolution, and Louise 'Miss Lou' Bennett's poem 'Colonization in Reverse' captures this idea well.[7] The sound system and the dancehall culture that it produced depending on your vantage point has become productive work for many beyond Jamaica's shores.

As Red Bull Culture Clashes sought to cement Jamaican aesthetic practices in specific sites, by 2013 we saw a critical increase in the consumption of Jamaica as a brand, made visible through a different sort of 'videolight' in a global landscape. Highlights of 2013 as a year of critical consumption contained the following representations of Jamaica occupying various forms of visual media, and their spotlight: the Volkswagen commercial at the Super Bowl Sunday featured a Caucasian male speaking Jamaican and cajoling his co-workers to be happy[8]; Beyoncé performed her hit song featuring Grammy-winning act Sean Paul to millions at the same Super Bowl; the BET Awards featured dancehall performances from Beenie Man and Elephant Man, among others; the Saturn Ad, which featured the highest symbolic representation of hegemonic dissolution, with burning of the Jamaican flag, earned the ire of Jamaicans at home and abroad so much so the AD was pulled in short order; Jamaican songster Tessanne Chin won *The Voice* competition; the 'No Woman Nuh Drive' video, remixing Bob Marley's 'No Woman Nuh Cry' bringing attention to advocacy for Saudi women to be allowed to drive, circulated around the globe; and Major Lazer's release of dancehall productions has contributed to him becoming one of the top paid DJs globally, featuring acts such as Sean Paul, Busy Signal, Chronixx, and Protojé.

By way of context, the preceding outline regarding the explicit consumption of Jamaican popular culture highlights the 'cool factor' which Jamaica embodies. I use cool here, arcing back to Farris Thompson's (1973) articulations, and subsequent analyses, on 'an aesthetic of the cool' to engage with the translation of self-conscious confidence seen in attitude, determination, pleasure in the self, bodily carriage, dress and performance which manifests not only from a *certain* mental state but also in a performance aesthetic as 'cool as water', linked to ancestral histories. Moreover, the clash, mobilizing the seriousness of competition and pleasure of play around music, is one of the cool aspects of Jamaican performance which has gained new visibility. What is arguable, however, is that this visibility is muted by virtue of Red Bull's marketing in an arena of unbounded global media consumption that can easily occlude sites of origin and make way for interpretations of cultural appropriation.

The consumers of the sound clash content transmitted through Red Bull's site, among others, can be gleaned from online comments. They are youth music lovers generally, Red Bull Academy/Culture Clash fans, and music aficionados of all ages beyond the jurisdiction of the clash. Specifically, the online video teasers[9] for the culture clash engaged viewers in the international spread of sound clashes with videos advertising the culture clash event featuring the competitors – 'The enigma and career of patoranking', South African music – 'The oral history of durban kwaito music', and the art and culture around dubs.

The politics of noise here, or in fact silence in this case, is about a particular absence in mention of Jamaica; the mention of Jamaica's centrality as a nation state to the emergence and proliferation of dubs was only sparse (it was mentioned only once in the article on dub previously mentioned). However, there was no doubt that Jamaica's solid musical innovations received global visibility in spite of Red Bull's crafty marketing strategies, at the intersection between authentic dancehall culture and the corporate power brokering, in ownership of the mega-successful music events featuring local music in multiple locations that have often gained new notoriety because of cross-fertilization with Jamaican musical aesthetics. In pushing its brand, Red Bull used Jamaica contradictorily as a 'backdrop' with cursory mention as site of origin and producer of its 'cool factor'. However onstage, in the midst of dubs being hurled in musical battle, Jamaica was central, inside the 'videolight' of an infectious musical landscape seeing a revival through such sound clashes. Jamaican sound system clashes have transcended national borders to occupy transnational soundscapes, with Red Bull sound clashes at the contemporary centre, providing another dimension for the analysis of dancehall culture in the context of boundarylessness beyond the visions of dancehall creators and perpetrators who do not own the means of production in a visual economy.

The value of sound as work and building sound capital

Speculations are that there are over 1,400 live events per day on average in Jamaica. The total number of licenses issued for places of amusements in the year 2015 was 26,687 according to the Planning Institute of Jamaica's (PIOJ) Economic and Social Survey for that year. This figure is a 9.6% increase from the figures shown in 2014 and a 28% increase from 2012 (PIOJ, 2002–2007, 2012–2015). These figures are much higher, being in the 20,000 range, when compared to figures shown of licenses issued in 2008 which was a total of 15,700. The data suggests that events would be taking place within 3.5 miles of each other across the island's length, reflecting registered parties, bar openings, and stage shows, but excluding the many illegal or informal dances held without permits.

The formal industry is growing despite the 'zero tolerance' of the JCF in respect to enforcement of the Noise Abatement Act. All the licenses have shown fluctuations in the number of requests between the period of 2012–2018; however, by 2015 the numbers levelled. The parishes seen with the highest number of licenses issued were Kingston and St. Andrew and Clarendon having 9,413 and 3,575, respectively, for the year of 2015.

Data from the Ministry of Culture, Gender, Entertainment and Sport and the JCF Operations Branch shown in **Table 9.2** confirms the health of the entertainment sector, as far as events gaining permits and extensions for time limits beyond the stipulations of the Noise Abatement Act.

The Kingston and St. Andrew Municipal Corporation (KSAMC) reported revenues of J$28 million from entertainment permits alone in 2017 and 2018

Table 9.2 Entertainment Permits and Extensions Issued in Jamaica (2012–2018)

	Year	Permits	ENT Capex	# of Extensions	Total Value $JA
	2012	18,956			
	2013	24,790	207,237,300	300	17,124,708,890.00
	2014	18,917	380,755,808	518	13,904,937,490.22
	2015	19,297	365,597,448	348	20,272,798,718.55
	2016	19,146	169,314,000	87	37,260,756,827.59
	2017	19,158	448,643,020	264	32,557,208,246.82
	2018	19,765	423,120,000	342	24,453,119,298.25
Total Avg Event Figure over (7 yrs)		20,004	1,994,667,576		145,573,529,471.43

showed a 13% increase in revenue with J$33 million collected from entertainment permits. The KSAMC is the highest-grossing municipality in relation to entertainment events (Economic and Social Survey of Jamaica data, 2019). While there has been a crackdown from the Noise Abatement Act, the ministry with responsibility for entertainment provides the possibility for persons to request a time extension for their events to be able to go on beyond 12 and 2 a.m. during the week and on the weekend, respectively. This is in correspondence with permission from the JCF. Table 9.2 shows the number of extensions approved for the period 2013–2018.

Having a healthy culture of amusement and a significant portion of the country's population, Kingston presents an urgent case for the examination of policies that are sensitive to the history and form of the entertainment practices. Suggestions regarding zoning of entertainment as well as the provision of proper venues for staging events can be seriously explored to shift the popular stance of policing to policymaking. In October 2017, Fort Rocky in Port Royal was announced as the first entertainment zone in Jamaica, a space that will be used particularly for entertainment. However, with these relevant steps happening, it is still up to policymakers to seriously look at the dilemma of raids and police clashes that often ensue from them, in order to cultivate healthy entertainment practices around dancehall in particular. Entertainment promoters continue to complain about the double-edged sword which characterizes the production and consumption of dancehall and its relationship with the State and its apparatuses. Due to the 'zero tolerance' approach, promoters feel dance events have been increasingly policed as a method of minimizing criminality. However, at the same time that the authorities are increasing surveillance, such as through Zones of Special Operations (ZOSO) introduced in 2018, there is an increase in the number of events, the revenue they earn, and the means by which they serve as a release valve for the many who are frustrated with daily 'sufferation'.

All that has been discussed is significant because it has implications for the development of Kingston, especially as an entertainment and creative industries capital. This history of music and creation has been instrumental in the naming of Kingston as a UNESCO Creative City of Music. The KSAMC working with the ministry with responsibility for entertainment (Ministry of Tourism and Entertainment at the time) through the Entertainment Advisory Board initiated the campaign to designate Kingston as a UNESCO Creative City of Music which it officially earned on December 15, 2015. This is a very important initiative, not only in solidifying the history and achievements of Kingston as an entertainment scene but also as an important guide towards continued development as a creative city and music capital of the world. This allows Kingston to not only work alongside and network with other creative cities of music, but it also provides Kingston with guidelines on what is needed to be done in order to maintain the designation. It is a good point for the marketing of the city and creation of entertainment life around this title.

The sound economy: towards a culture of regulated sound

In seeking to solidify security for the citizenry at the heart of Jamaica's entertainment and celebratory practices, so they may fulfil the mandate of contributing to the development of Jamaica as a small island state, it is therefore crucial that entertainment is seen as fulfilling both economic and well-being imperatives. In all these nomenclature matters, work must continue around not just relaxation of stipulations in the Noise Abatement Act but ultimately replacement of said act by a more appropriate Sound Regulation Act with use of sound meters to measure sound both within and outside designated entertainment zones. While the social gains from music/entertainment have been under-researched and under-acknowledged, it is critical that we grapple with the postcolonial problem of inheriting philosophical, moral, and economic models which have not been able to sufficiently evoke and make visible, as well as quantify, the value of creativity to the articulation of the self, the maintenance of cohesive citizenry, in national budgets, leaving a huge disconnect between what we do as work to create income and the creativity we use for pleasure after work, that is after the 'real income work' has been done. In conclusion, what I place on the table is the fact that there is a disconnect in what we do for play, work, income and therefore what is seen as viable for development. While we have come a long way, there is still much further to go in solidifying security and well-being of citizens as they navigate the daily imperatives to celebrate.

Notes

1 This is a revised version of the paper "Shifting the Philosophy and Geography of Entertainment Reason – A Jamaican Music Culture of Sound Regulation versus Noise Abatement in a New Regulated Era" first presented at the Inaugural Law Faculty Symposium, April 25, 2015, then the York University Workshop on Expressive Cultures, UWI,

August 2016, at the Dancehall In/Securities Symposium, UWI, February 3, 2017, and at as a guest lecture at the Western Jamaica Campus on February 28, 2017. A version of this paper was also presented under the title 'Sound and the Politics of Citizenship: A Caribbean Cultural Studies Perspective', Universidad de Los Andes, Colombia in April 2019, and as 'Sounding Out the System: Noise, and the Politics of Citizenship' at the 5th Sound System Outernational Conference, Naples, Italy, in April 2019.
2 I use 'smaddification' here after Mills (1997).
3 Italicized for author's emphasis.
4 See for example Jamaica Observer (2019) and Peru (2020).
5 It is important to note that attempts at reviving the sound system landscape in Jamaica have resulted in the staging of the Sound System Festival or SoundFest initiated by Bass Odyssey which converted its annual anniversary event (2017 saw the 28th anniversary) into a major festival event now in its 3rd staging. Similarly, Sumfest incorporated the Heavyweight Sound System clash in the 2017 staging of the long-standing festival.
6 The fusion between British street lingua franca and Jamaican is sometimes referred to as London Metropolitan English.
7 See the text of Louise Bennett's poem here http://louisebennett.com/colonization-in-reverse/ (accessed October 19, 2017).
8 See more on the Get Happy Volkswagen commercial 2013 here www.youtube.com/watch?v=09JTtVxztv4 (accessed October 20, 2017).
9 See teasers for Red Bull Culture Clash – South Africa, in particular Red Bull's tweet of the culture clash 101 teaser which https://twitter.com/RBMA/status/911167962257678336 which I commented on here https://twitter.com/SonjahStanley/status/911185704075 612161 (accessed October 20, 2017).

References

Attali, J. (1985) *Noise: The Political Economy of Music*. English Trans. B. Massumi. Minnesota: University of Minnesota Press.

Banton, B. (1993) Operation Ardent. *Voice of Jamaica*. Universal Music LLC. https://en.wikipedia.org/wiki/Voice_of_Jamaica.

Browning, B. (1995) *Samba: Resistance in Motion*. Bloomington: Indiana University Press.

Chang, K. O. and Chen, W. (1998) *Reggae Routes: The Story of Jamaican Music*. Philadelphia: Temple University Press.

Cobussen, M. A. (2017) *Noise, Sounding Art, and Urban Ecology*, INTER-NOISE 2017, the 46th International Congress and Exposition on Noise Control Engineering, Hong Kong.

Fanon, F. (1963) On National Culture. In *The Wretched of the Earth*. London: Penguin.

Harry. (2002) Personal Interview, 24 April.

Henriques, J. (2008) Sonic Diaspora, Vibrations, and Rhythm: Thinking Through the Sounding of the Jamaican Dancehall Session. *African and Black Diaspora: An International Journal* 1(2), pp. 215–236. https://doi.org/10.1080/17528630802224163

Jackson, L. (2014) *Language, Culture and the Law: A Theoretical Framework for Paradigmatic Change in Institutional Governance in the Commonwealth Caribbean*, paper presented at the Inaugural Law Faculty Symposium, p. 4, 25 April.

Jamaica Broadcasting Corporation. (1994) *Jamaica Broadcasting Corporation Entertainment Report 1994*. Kingston: Jamaica Broadcasting Corporation.

Jamaica Observer. (2019) Chang Optimistic After Meeting on Entertainment Issues. *Jamaica Observer*. www.jamaicaobserver.com/latestnews/Grange,_Chang_optimistic_after_meeting_on_entertainment_issues. Last accessed: 26 April 2019.

Kahn, D. (1999) *Noise Water Meat: A History of Sound in the Arts*. Cambridge, MA: MIT Press.

Martis, E. (2016) The Politics of Being Black and Loud: Black People Have Been Profiled, Policed and Even Killed for the Noise They Make. But What if You Listen to What They Are Actually Saying? Culture/Politics. *The Fader*, 28 June. www.thefader.com/2016/06/28/the-politics-of-being-black-and-loud.

Mills, C. (1997) Smadditizin. *Caribbean Quarterly* 43(2), pp. 54–68.

Ministry of Justice, Jamaica. (1997) *The Noise Abatement Act*. Jamaica: Ministry of Justice, 26 March.

Ministry of Justice, Jamaica. (1999) *Kingston and St. Andrew Corporation Act*. Jamaica: Places of Amusement Regulations.

Patterson, O. (1973) *The Condition of the Low Income Population in the Kingston Metropolitan Area*. Kingston: Office of the Prime Minister.

Pickering, H. and Rice, T. (2017) Noise as 'Sound Out of Place': Investigating the Links Between Mary Douglas' Work on Dirt and Sound Studies Research. *Journal of Sonic Studies* 14.

Peru, Y. (2020) *Extended Party Hours Big Boost to Business – No Word Yet on Consideration for Further Extension of Noise Abatement Act*. http://jamaica-gleaner.com/article/entertainment/20200129/extended-party-hours-big-boost-business-no-word-yet-consideration. Last accessed: 29 January 2020.

Planning Institute of Jamaica. (2002–2007, 2012–2015) *Economic and Social Survey Jamaica*. Kingston: Planning Institute of Jamaica.

Rawcliffe, S. (2017) *State of Play: Grime*. The Grime Report. http://blog.ticketmaster.co.uk/stateofplay/grime.pdf. Last accessed: 1 April 2019.

Rodney, W. (1969) *The Groundings with My Brothers*. London: Bogle-L'Ouverture Books.

Rose, T. (1994) *Black Noise: Rap Music and Black Culture in Contemporary America*. Middletown, CT: Wesleyan University Press.

Scruggs, G. (2014) A War on Jamaican Dancehall Is Threatening Kingston's Street Life. *Public, Next City*, 18 December. https://nextcity.org/daily/entry/a-war-on-jamaican-dancehall-is-threatening-kingstons-street-life.

Stanley Niaah, S. (2010) *DanceHall: From Slave Ship to Ghetto*. Ottawa: University of Ottawa Press.

Television Jamaica. (2003) *Prime Time News Report*, 11 August.

Thompson, R. F. (1973) An Aesthetic of the Cool. *African Arts* 7(1), pp. 40–43, 64–67, 89–91 (11 pages).

Waddell, H. M. (2010) *Twenty-Nine Years in the West Indies and Central Africa: A Review of Missionary Work and Adventure, 1829–1858*. Cambridge: Cambridge University Press, pp. 17–162.

Wardle, H. (2001). An Ethnography of Cosmopolitanism in Kingston, Jamaica. NY: Edwin Mellen.

Index

Note: Page numbers followed by 'n' indicate a note on the corresponding page.

Abrahams, R. D. 97n18
acid attacks 91
Adidas 112
Admiral Bailey (Della Move) 88
Adzogbo dance 87, 97n12
African/neo-African people: communities 90; corporeal dancing bodies 85; cultural expressions 86, 92; Eurocentric perceptions of 93; genealogical practices 79, 80, 95; spiritual practices 5, 11, 79, 85, 87, 90, 91, 94
African Religions and Philosophy (Mbiti) 70
African Storm 143
AIDS pandemic 136
Altink, H. 121
America's Top Dance Crew 33
Anansi 127, 128
ancestral data/knowledge 80
Anderson, B. 21–2, 25n5
appropriation 30–2, 110–11
Arts and Humanities Research Council 2
As Raw as Ever (Ranks) 35
Atsia dance 87, 97n12
Attali, J. 132, 133
attitude 3, 41, 43, 45, 51, 69, 81, 144

Babalaos 109
bachata 126
Bakare-Yusuf, B. 67, 72, 91
BaKongo cosmogram 111, 112, 115, 129n9, 129n18
ballet 30, 32, 48, 50, 52n9, 101–2, 103
Balubá dance 113
Bamba Amblique, La 64n2
bammy 52n2
Banton, B. 21, 34, 35, 46, 85, 119, 139
Baptists 90, 97n14

bashment gal 7, 19, 20
Bass Odyssey 143, 148n5
Beatles 63
Beat Street (film) 27, 110
Beckford, W. 50
Beenie Man 2–3, 110, 144
Belfon, D. S. 110, 113, 129n12
Ben Lion Bin Baad Man 123
Bennett, L. 64n1, 144, 148n7
Bettelheim, J. 68
bhangra 56
Bieber, J. 57
Big and Nasty and Tender Touch (Dance Xpressionz) 89
Bimbo *see* Silk, G.
Binghi 50, 53n33
Bin Laden 123–4
Black, N. 101
Black, S. 10
Black bodies 15–16, 17, 18, 80, 92, 97n17
Black Dance: A Contemporary Voice (Prestø) 128–9n8
black male wine, European context of 118–19
Black Panther movie 127
Black Roses Crew, The 86
Blackwell, C. 58, 59
bling (jewellery) 51
blues 126
Bogle 32–3, 46, 60, 88, 97n10; aesthetic dress sense 86; arm movements of 87; dance 11, 85, 86–7; dancehall language, development 28–9; movements 38, 52n10
Bolt, U. 46
Boom Bye Bye 119, 129n27
Bounty Killer 104, 106n2

Bourdieu, P. 64n7
Braithwaite, T. W. 122
break (dance movement) 49, 54n45
breakdance 27, 28
breathing 102–3
bridging light 44, 53n27
British Link-Up 18–19
Brodber, E. 9, 49
Brown, F. 45
Brown, H. 57
Brown, J. 85
Browning, B. 132, 136
Bruckins 8, 33, 49, 50, 54n44, 90, 105; *Bogle's* 87; movement in 54n45; practices 94; queen 97n14
bubble (dance step) 46, 53n34
Buck Breaking 108–9
Budder, M. 67
Buffalo Soldier 2
Buster, P. 2
Busy Signal 130, 144

Callum, S. 47
Calypso 109
Campbell, Y. 24n2
Canada Expo 101
Candomble 53n41
Cannon, N. 118–19, 129n25
canon system, Caribbean 47–9
Caribbean In/Securities and Creativity (CARISCC) 2, 4, 14, 24n1
Caribbean slave trade 120, 129n30
carnival 119, 121, 122, 123, 124, 126, 139–40
carnivalesque, the 42, 47, 50
Catch a Fire 59
Chaka-Chaka and Sweep (Ding Dong and Ravers Clavers) 88
Chaka Demus 62, 63, 642n2
Chang, H., Dr 142
Channel One 143
Charles-Harris, H. 7, 111, 115, 125
Chevannes, B. 49, 54n52, 72
Chin, T. 144
Chronixx 46, 144
Chude-Sokei, L. 132
citizenship politics of Caribbean 134–5; *see also* sound system in dancehall, legislative context
Cliff, J. 46
Cobussen, M. 132
co-culture daaance'all, shifting in/securities within: code-switching 43; definition of daaance'all 37; overview 36–41;

plantation ritualistic spirit daaance*s* 50–1; securities/insecurities in 42; underground faaambily 41–3; warrior wo/men 43–7, 53n17; zight 47–9
cognitive dissonance, defined 133
Cole, A. "Skill" 59
colonizing in reverse 127–8, 144
community(ies): crime in 35; economic and social gains for 135; garrison 24n2, 38, 42, 46, 59; tourism 35
confrontational space 72–6
contemporary dance 5, 32, 49, 52n9, 92, 94, 101, 103, 106
Cool Herc, DJ 32
Cooper, C. 4, 18, 21, 24n4, 41, 80, 89, 90, 91, 108, 132
corporeal in/securities in dancehall space: affect and livelihood in/securities 21–2; corporeal dancing body 79–80, 81, 84, 85–6, 89, 92; dancehall contexts 17–19; negotiation 15–17, 19; overview 14–15; sonic forces and existential in/securities 19–21; visual performance and in/securities of meaning, effects of 22–4
cosmo-technical hip wine 110–14, 128–9n8
coupling up and in/security 92–6
Cow Foot (Shelly Belly) 89
Crab 38, 52n11, 53n35
Creative Approaches to Race and In/Security in Caribbean and UK (CARICUK) 2, 11n1, 14, 24n1
creativity/creative: labour in/securities 60–1; risk in genre labelling in/securities 56–9; understanding of 14–15
Crenshaw, K. 89–90
crimes 35, 136–40
crossfire 91
Csikszentmihalyi, M. 56, 63
culture/cultural: arrogation 110; clash 143–5, 148n9; dancehall 2–3, 79, 80–1, 103–4; knowledge 80; memory 80; reggae 2–3, 78, 79, 91; of regulated sound 147; resource, dancehall as insecure 30–2; security in dancehall space, re-creating 32–4; sound system 3
Cumfa (Guyana) 50

daaance 37, 41–2, 52n8
daaance'all, in/securities within co-culture *see* co-culture daaance'all, shifting in/securities within
Daaancing Crystals 38
Dance Expressionz 68, 71, 83, 88, 89

dancehall: contexts 17–19; culture 2–3, 79, 80–1, 103–4; globalization 28–30; impact of US dancehall parties and European dancehall tourism 28–9; influence 105–6; as insecure cultural resource 30–2; and in/security 3–4, 6–11; in Kingston (1980s and 1990s) 27–8; in Kingston and livelihoods 34–5; masquerade in 67–72; participants 3, 4; spatio-temporalities of 17; spirit 105
Dancehall: From Slave Ship to Ghetto (Niaah) 130
Dancehall Queen (movie) 110, 121
dancehall queens (DHQ) 3; advent of 90; Carlene 5, 7, 28, 47, 67–8, 72; Danger 82–3, 92; dress code 28; Tall Up 82–3, 92
dancehall space(s) 81–4; construction of 17; corporeal negotiations in 19; cultural security in, re-creating 32–4; in/securities in 10, 15, 19; *see also* corporeal in/securities in dancehall space
dancers 3, 90; choreographic choices by 16; social media/internet 33
Dancin' Dynamites (dance competition) 88, 106
Dancing Rebel 46
Dancing Wisdom (Daniel) 116
Daniel, Y. 116
Danielle, D. I. 5, 68, 75, 76
daunce 37, 52n9
Day Rave 41
deejays (DJs) 2–3, 23, 57; Cool Herc 32; King Stitt 141; Pan Head 60; Patra 45; URoy 54n53, 139
deep breathing technique 102–3
Della Move (Admiral Bailey) 88
Dem So Blazin 118, 129n22
dengue fever 3
Destra 110
diaspora, glocal 92, 97n16
Ding Dong Ottey, K. 46, 82, 88
Dinkie Mini 50, 86, 94, 105
Dirts Man 60
Disturbing London 143
divas 3, 11n3, 90
divine wine 114–15
DJs *see* deejays (DJs)
drug(s) 29, 118, 125
dub 93
Dumas, S. 108, 126
Durban Massacre 143
Dutty Wine 104, 106n1
Dyson, M. E. 85

Economic and Social Survey 145, 146
EDH (electronic dancehall) 57
Elegua 114
Elephant Man 110, 144
Ellis, N. 24
Empress CC 113, 129n10, 129n11
England Riots of 2011 143, 148n6
enslavement 109, 138, 140; Africans 2, 6, 43, 70, 71, 85, 97n9, 133; era 9, 66; European 6; female enslaved population 125; fertility ownership and hate 125; history of 36; masquerade 66; oiled skins of enslaved people 24; on plantations in Jamaica 42, 45, 66; racialisation of post-enslavement 15; trauma of 122
entertainment: history and form of 146; of state, historicizing 136–40
Entourage 23
environmental in/security 59, 64n4
Etana 45
Etu 50
Eurocentric canons 47, 48, 49
European context of black male wine 118–19
evo-revo 36, 41, 52n4, 52n14
Excelsior Community College 30
exhibition dancing 94, 95
existential in/securities and sonic forces 19–21
Exodus 58

faaambily, underground 41–3, 52n13
Facebook 29, 120
Fanon, F. 132
fashion 3, 5, 7; daaance'all 36, 41, 43, 45, 46, 47, 50, 51, 52; of dancehall participants 18, 36, 41, 42, 43; temporal mapping of 8
fearlessness 91
Federation Sound 143
fertility ownership and hate 125
flexing 60, 64n10
Florida, R. 59
flossers 3, 11n3
Fonteyn, M. 101
Fowl, F. 60
fractured penis 125, 129n32
Frazier, S. A. 46
Fuchs, T. 80
Fyah, S. 47

Index 153

Gabriel, D. 97n14
ganja 112
garrison community 24n2, 38, 42, 46, 59
gender: -based violence 9–10; differences 92–6
genre: blending 57; labelling in/securities, creative risk in 56–9
Gerreh 94
Gleaner 113–14
Gordon, R. 45
gouyad in Haiti 119–20
Graham, M. 101, 103
Grammy Award 3
Griffith, M. 46
grounding 135–6
Guinea Ballet (Les Ballets Africains) 101
Gully Creeper (David 'ICE' Alexander Smith) 88
gun Bogle 11
Guyana Soca Dance Competition 113, 129n16

Half Way Tree (Kingston) 81
Hall, M *see* Lady Saw
Hall, O. 'Xpressionz' 4, 5, 8, 10, 11, 23, 68, 70, 71, 75, 81, 88, 95, 102, 106n1; dancehall as an insecure cultural resource 30–2; dancehall secures livelihoods in Kingston 34–5; dancehalls in Kingston (1980s and 1990s) 27–8; dancehall space, re-creating cultural security in the 32–4; global impact 28–30
Hall, S. 16, 22, 74, 80
Hamilton, G. L. 47, 83, 97n6
Happy Feet 46
Hardy, M. 'Ovamars' 89
Harlem Dance Theatre 101–2
Harris, W. 16–17
hate and fertility ownership 125
Havendale and Fairfax Drive 27
head-top bubble 46, 53n35
hegemony: counter-hegemonic potential 73; cultures of consumption 19, 22; dissolution 144; form of 47; issues 43; male insecurity in relation to 85; marketing and performance 9; masculinity 86, 90; reverse 48; society 3; structures 4, 90; value systems 2, 19, 84
Henriques, J. 4, 15, 19, 20, 22, 23, 81, 132, 135
hierarchical ocular regime 23
Higher Learning 105
Hinds, A. 110

hip: hiprolling 118, 129n20; pollinizing 125–8; positioning 107–8; wining 6, 7, 11n4; *see also* in/security of the hip wine and male body
hip-hop 30, 32, 43, 46, 58, 118, 126, 133
historicizing entertainment and crimes of state 136–40
homophobia 113
homosexuality 6, 86, 113
Hope, D. 4, 11n3, 18–19, 22, 23, 42, 86, 94, 97n8, 108
Hougans 109
house (popular culture) 126
House of Leo Venue, murder and shooting at 139
Howard, D. O. 5, 8, 9, 10, 24n3, 55–64
How the World a Run 21
Hunnigale, P. 97n15
Hurston, Z. N. 69–70
Hutton, C. 2
Hyman, R-D. 97n8
Hype, C. 29

identity 58, 72
Ifé 109
Inaugural Law Faculty Symposium 147n1
insecure cultural resource, dancehall as 30–2
in/securities in dancehall: affect and livelihood 21–2; concept of 1–2, 14; corporeal dancing body 89; and coupling up 92–6; and dancehall 3–4, 6–11; environmental 59, 64n4; existential, and sonic forces 19–21; of meaning 22–4; in streets 59–60; and women 89–92
in/securities in recording studios of Kingston: creative labour in/securities 60–1, 60–1; creative practice 55–6; creative risk in genre labelling in/securities 56–9; in/security in streets 59–60; making of sound recordings 61–2; overview 55
in/security of the hip wine and male body: cosmo-technical 110–14; European context of black male wine 118–19; female wine 119–22; and function 123–4; hip positioning 107–8; mapping out male wine 116–18; positioning 107–8; *see also* masculinity and Caribbean traditions
in/security within reggae/dancehall culture, levels of: bone, muscle and flesh 16; corporeal 79–80, 81, 84,

85–6, 89, 92; dancehall and in/security 78–9; dancehall space 81–4; female perspectives 89–92; gender differences and in/security 92–6; male warrior perspectives 84–9; perceptions of dancehall culture 80–1; reggae/dancehall culture 79
Instagram 110
intellectual property rights 61
internet dancers 33
intersectionality 89–90
Irish and Chin 143
Isley Brothers 63
Is this love 59
It Hurts to Be Alone 59

Jack Radics 62–3
Jackson, J. 122
Jackson, L. 134
Jackson, M. 27, 28
Jamaica Constabulary Force (JCF) 130, 139, 145, 146
Jamaica Cultural Development Commission, The 37
Jamaica Labour Party (JLP) 27
Jamaican language 143, 148n6
Jamaica Sound System Festival 143, 148n5
jazz 30, 32, 46, 53n33, 111, 126, 136
Jemunja 43, 53n21
Johnson, E. O. 108
Jones, A. K. 108
Jonkonnu Masquerade 50, 79, 94
'jouissance,' conceptualisation of 93

Kadodo dance 97n12
Kahn, D. 132
Kaiso 109, 128n2
kalypso 57
Kartel, V. 70–1
Kartoon 89
Kasai area 113, 129n13
Kaya 58, 59
Kelly, D. 62
kidnapping 60
Kilimanjaro 143
King, D. 45
Kingston: dancehall secures livelihoods in 34–5; dancehall spaces in 1980s and 1990s 27–8; 1980s and 1990s 27–8
Kingston and St. Andrew Municipal Corporation (KSAMC) 145–6, 147
knowledge 80
Koffee 3

Kumina 8, 33, 37, 48, 49, 54n52, 124, 128; inching of 50; matriarchal structure of 90; movement in 54n45; practices 28, 79, 86, 94, 109, 118, 128n5; Queen 90, 97n14; and Revival 105; traditional music 28
Kwasa Kwasa (Congo) 8, 91

Lacan, J. 93
Lady Saw 41, 46, 53n15, 53n37, 110
Landry, C. 59–60
Lawrence, M. 5, 7, 8, 35n1, 106n1
legato 58
Leverhulme 2
Levy, G. 'Bogle.' *see* Bogle
Lewin, O. 91, 97n14
Lewis, M. 121
Lewis, R. 82, 96n3
Lewis, S. 'Shelly Belly' 87, 88
Life and Debt (film) 10
Lil´GGB 118, 129n24
Limbo 8, 33, 50
livelihood in/securities 21–2
Liverpool, H. 121
Livingston, R. 62
Lizombe (Tanzania) 8, 91
Lovers Rock 91, 93, 97n15
Lovey Dovey 38
Lynch, G. 81

MAAFA 115, 129n19
Machuki, C. 2–3
Magnum Wednesdays 41
Mains, S. P. 10
Major Lazer 143, 144
Major Worries 60
Makishi (Zambia) 91
Mambos 109
Manley, E. 102, 106
Manley, N. W. 134
mannish water 52n1
marijuana 141
Marley, B. 2, 24n4, 35, 45, 46, 53n33, 58–9, 104, 144
Marley, D. 46
Marley, S. 46
Marley, Z. 46
maroons 49
Martha Graham School for Contemporary Dance 101
Martis, E. 136
masculinity and Caribbean traditions: cosmo-technical hip wine 110–14,

128–9n8; divine wine 114–15; European context of black male wine 118–19; female wine 119–22; fertility ownership and hate 125; hip pollinizing 125–8; hip positioning 107–8; mapping out male wine 116–18; overview 107; wine and function 123–4; winin' 107–10; winin' spirit 124–5
masquerade in dancehall: impact of image in dancehall 67–72; introduction 66–7; Jonkonnu 50, 79, 94; and the middle class 72–6
massas 43
Matterhorn, T. 106n2
Mattie 44, 53n26
Maxfield Avenue (Kingston) 59
Mbiti, J. S. 70, 71, 94
McIntyre, P. 56
McKenzie, E. 71
melisma 58
melo-rhythm 124
men/male: dancehall style 28; gaze, spectacularizing female wine 119–22; warrior perspectives 84–9; *see also* masculinity and Caribbean traditions
mento 53n33, 56, 57, 109, 128n3
merengue 126
Metalheadz 143
middle-class masquerade 72–6
Miller, K. 38, 46, 115
Mills, C. W. 15–16, 66–7, 134
Minott, S. 57
Missa 49
Mitchell, A. 101
M.O.B (Men of Business) 29
modellers 3, 11n3, 90
Mojito Mondays 38, 41
Moncrieffe, F *see* Tippa
Montano, M. 110
Moreton, J. B. 121
Morgan, V. 47
Mowatt, J. 46
Murder She Wrote 63, 64n2
myal state 87, 97n11

Nanny of Marroons 47
narrative of loss phrase 74
National Dance Theatre Company (NDTC) 85–6, 87, 101, 102, 103
Natty Dread 59
NDTC (National Dance Theatre Company) 85–6, 87, 101, 102, 103

negotiation: corporeal 15–17, 19; creative 56; of in/security 11
Nelson, C. 46
neo-African (new African) music 79, 96n1, 96n2
Nettleford, R. 15–16, 43, 53n16, 66, 74, 85, 101
New York City Ballet Company 101
Niaah, S. S. N. 4, 6, 8, 9, 11n3, 17, 21, 22, 42, 81, 108, 130–48
Nipples and Boasy Tuesdays 41
Nitty Gritty 60
noise 130; Caribbean laws implicating 137, 138; re/defining 132–3131; *see also* sound system in dancehall, legislative context
Noise Abatement Act 6, 138, 140, 141–2, 145, 146, 147
Noise Water Meat 132
Norman, R. 93
Norsk Rikskringkastning (NRK) 120
No Woman Nuh Cry 144
No Woman Nuh Drive video 144
Noxolo, P. 9, 10, 55–6, 60, 106n1
Nuh Linga (Marlon 'Ovamars' Hardy) 89
Nyahbingi 49

Obeah 109, 111, 128n7
Ogun 43, 53n24
Olympic Gardens (Kingston) 59
O'Meally, T. G. 46
One Love Concert 58–9
One Two Three Four 33
Oniel Voicemail 60
On Stage 67–8
Orishas 43, 49, 53n19, 53n41, 114, 129n8
Oshun 43, 53n20, 115
outernational regions 82, 87, 96n5
out of place, defined 132
outsider 44, 53n25
Oya 43, 53n22, 94, 114, 115

Palmer, L. A. 93
Palo (Cuba) 50, 53n41
Pan Head 60
Parish Councils Act 142
patois 128n1; *see also* Jamaican language
Patra 45, 110, 122
Patten, H. 5, 7, 11, 35n1, 106n1
Patterson, E. 23, 24
Patterson, O. 132, 135
Paul, S. 45, 46, 110, 144
Paulsen, R. 120

pelvis 7, 69, 93; articulating 83; bubbling 92; circling or rotating 91; limbo dance 33; moving 105; ribcage 104; tumbling 92; undulating motion with 86–7; wining 83–4, 91, 92
penis 124, 125, 126, 129n32
Penn, D. 46
Pentecostalism 90, 97n14
People's National Party (PNP) 27
perceptions of dancehall culture 80–1
perreando, in Dominican Republic and Puerto Rico 119–20
Pickering, H. 133
Pitchy Patchy 66
Places of Amusement (1999) regulations 142
Planning Institute of Jamaica (PIOJ) 145
pleasure 107, 113, 115, 124–5, 126, 144
Pliers 62, 63, 64n2, 64n13
politics of Caribbean citizenship 134–5; *see also* sound system in dancehall, legislative context
pollinizing hip 125–8
Poor People Fed Bounty Killa 64n2
Popcaan 143
posses, daaance'all 51, 54n49
poverty 1, 4, 22, 47
Pressure Dem 87, 88
Prestø, T. 'Talawa' 6, 7, 10, 11, 107–29
Protojé 144
provocation 68, 72, 76, 140
Puma 112
punta in Belize 119–20

Queen Ifrica 47

racism 15, 17, 23, 107, 108, 109, 125, 127, 133
Ragga 118
Ramdhanie, R. 85
Ranks, S. 35, 45, 53n30
rap 133
rape 6, 91, 108–9, 126, 127
Rastafari 52n5
Rastaman Vibration 59
Ravers Clavers 46, 82, 88
R&B 53n33
reasoning, sounding and grounding 135–6
recording studios of Kingston, in/securities in *see* in/securities in recording studios of Kingston
record producer 60
Red Bull Culture Clash 9, 143–5, 148n9

Red Rose, A. 62–3
reggae 92, 93, 126; bangara and la trengue 56; blends 53n33; blues/rock aesthetics in 59; corporeal dancing body 80; culture 1, 2–3, 78, 79, 91; lyrics, Ricketts 10, 104; Marley, Bob 2, 24n4, 35, 45, 46, 53n33, 58–9, 104; Paul, Sean 45, 46; Ranks, Shabba 35, 45, 53n30; riddims 57; rocksteady to 81; Shaggy 46, 62; Stevens 32, 56–7; voice of downpress 104
regimentation, absence of 74
religion(s): African/neo-African 93, 94, 110, 128n5; of ancestral worship 48; Christian 90; music 36; Rastafarian religious doctrine 86; ritual 16; spirit daaances 50; transference of religious coding 94; Vodou religious practice 97n12; Yoruba 43
Revival 28, 48, 50, 53n40, 87, 97n14, 105, 105
Revivalism 79, 86, 90, 94
Rhythm Culture 116, 117
Rhythm Nations 116, 117
Rice, T. 133
Rich, R. 29
Ricketts, P. 5, 8, 10, 31; career as a dancer and teacher 101–2; dancehall culture 103–4; dancehall's influence 105–6; dancehall spirit 105; dance philosophy 102–3
riddim(s): riding 63; set of 57–8; Sleng Teng 11n2; and SoCa songs 124
Rietvald, H. 22–3
Rihanna 32, 57
Riley, W. 60
Rivera, E. 102
Roache 60
robbery 60
Robbie 56, 62
Rodigan, D. 143
Rodney, W. 132
Rollington Town (Kingston, Jamaica) 52n6, 59
Roose, La, incident at 141
Rose, T. 132, 133, 136
royalties, music 60, 61, 64n11
rub 93
Rugs, B. 53n33
rumba 126
Rum bar 69
Rumbar, S. 92
Runkus 38

running boat 44, 53n28
Ryman, C. 93, 96n2, 97n14, 106n3

Sagittarius 58
salsa 56, 125
Salt'n'Peppa 122
Salvation Army 101
samba 126, 136
Sanctified Church, The 69
Santeria 53n41
Satta Massagana 102
Saussure, F. de 86
Savannah Plaza (Kingston) 92
Scandinavia, women's sex trips 120, 129n29
Scott, T. 44, 53n29
Scotty 64n1
scrub 93
Scruggs, G. 136
Seaga, E. 73, 74, 97n14
security 1–2, 3, 6; creating 84–9; livelihoods in Kingston 34–5; *see also* in/securities in dancehall
selectors 3
self-definition 67, 72
sensuality 6, 28, 34, 69, 107, 128
sepelote in Cuba 119–20
Sex Dance: Daggering in Jamaica 120, 129n28
sexuality 19, 28, 67, 69, 72, 81; auto-sexuality 126; black 85, 107–8, 125–6; enactment of 126
sexual violence 90, 108–9, 122, 125, 125, 126
Shaggy 46, 62, 110
Shango 43, 53n23, 53n41, 94, 114, 115; baptism 109, 111, 128n6
Shelly Belly (Cow Foot) 89
shitsem 135
Signal Di Plane and Pon Di River (Jonathan 'John Hype' Prendergast) 88–9
Silk, G. 9, 60, 64n8, 64n9
Simpson, P. 47
singjaying 57, 58, 60
Sizzla 46
Skanking in Bed 64n1
ska tech 56–7
skin bleaching 113–14
Sklar, D. 80
Skream & Benga 143
slave/slavery 72, 131, 133, 136; community 121; dances 121, 137; economy 121; entertainment 138; fertility ownership and hate 125; owners 54n44, 97n9, 108–9; rape 108–9; ships 2, 136; trade 115, 120; *see also* enslavement
Sleng Teng (1985) 11n2
Sly Dunbar 56, 62–3, 64n12
Sly Dunbar & Friends 62
smadditization 67, 72, 84, 88, 134, 148n2
Small Axe 9
Smith, C. (Carlene) 5, 7, 28, 34, 47, 67–8, 69, 72, 73, 74
Smith, D. 'ICE' A. 88
Smith, W. 11n2
SoCa 109, 113, 123, 124, 126, 128
social media 8, 33, 36, 95, 96
sonic forces and existential in/securities 19–21
sound as work and building sound capital 145–7
Sound Clash 18, 143–5
Sound Regulation Act 147
sound system in dancehall, legislative context: culture clash 143–5, 148n9; historicizing entertainment and crimes of state 136–40; operator/selector 61; overview 130–2; politics of Caribbean citizenship 134–5; recordings, making of 61–2; Red Bull Culture Clash 143–5, 148n9; re/defining noise, reinstating sound 132–3; sound economy 147; sounding and grounding 135–6; soundmen/women 3; value of sound as work and building sound capital 145–7; venues politicized 140–2
Sowah, J. 94
So You Think You Can Dance? 33
Spear, B. 46
Spice 46, 83, 97n6, 110
spirit: daaances 50–1, 52n8; dancehall 105; winin' 124–5
spirituality 7, 94, 111; African/ neo-African 5, 11; dancehall space 28
'spot-light' concept 94, 95, 96, 97n7
spousal abuse 91
Squad One 52n6
St. Andrew Corporation 142
Stella Maris Dance Ensemble 30, 102
Stephens, M. 23
Stephens, T. 46
Step Up 33
Stevens, R. 32, 56–7
Stewart, D. M. 97n9, 97n11
Stines, L'A. 4–5, 7–8, 10, 11, 16, 17, 37, 38, 80, 91, 102, 108, 122; code-switching 43; definition of daaance'all

37–8, 41; in-depth examination of dancehall 41–3; plantation spirit daaances and daaance'all 50–1; warrior wo/men 43–7; zight 47–9
Sting 62
Stitt, K. 141
Stolzoff, N. 11n2, 41–2, 72–3
Stone Love Movement 143
street(s): dances 53n35, 54n49, 139; in/security in 59–60
Style, L. 46
Super Bowl Sunday 144
Superman 127
Supreme Promotions 56–7
switching codes 43
syncretism 57
synerbridging 16, 17, 46, 53n36
Szwed, J. F. 97n18

Talawa technique 116
Tambu 50
Tanker, A. 123
Tap 111
Taxi Gang 62
teaching dancehall to foreigners 30–2
Temper Wine dance 89
Tenor Saw 60
Them Faya 118, 129n21
Thomas, E. 101
Thompson, F. 144
tick tack 50
Tierou, A. 69
Tik Tok 110
Tinie Tempah 143
Tippa 37, 38, 52n6, 84
T.O.K 110
Torres, M. D. De 90
Tosh, P. 53n33, 135
tourism, community 35
Toxic 32
trauma and economy 122–3
Trinidad's Camboulay Street Dance Play and the Carnivalesque Placebo (Braithwaite) 122
trump 49
Turner, V. 85
Twins, Les 118, 129n23
Twist & Shout 62, 63

UNESCO Creative City of Music 147
United Caribbean Dance Force 2018 Season of Dance 38
Unruly 143

Uptown Mondays 38, 92
URoy 54n53, 139, 141

venues, politicization of 140–2
video light: dancehall parties 28; development 97n7; syndrome 18, 22–3, 94; on women 106
violence 1, 2, 3, 10; in community 35; gender-based 9–10; high incidence of 59; into party 27; political 4; -prone areas 59–60; racism 108; real and ideological 4; of 1980s 9, 10; sexual 90, 108, 122, 125, 125, 126; and slackness 81; of society 133; urban, kind of 18, 24n2
visual effects, of dance performance 22–4
Vodou religious practice 97n12
Vodun 53n41
Voice, The 144
Voice of the Jamaican Ghetto 70–1
Voice of the People 2
Volkswagen commercial 144, 148n8
Voudun 109, 111, 114, 128n4
vulgarity 66, 92, 107, 140

Waddell, H. M. 138
Wailers 2, 53n33
Wake the Town and Tell the People (Stolzoff) 72
Walker, C. 81, 87
Wardle, H. 131–2
warrior wo/men 43–7, 53n17
Waterhouse 59
Weddy Weddy Wednesdays 41
weed leaf 112
Williams, D. 101
Williams, S. 114–15
Williams, W. 67–8
winding the waist 11n4
winin', Caribbean 107–10, 111, 113–14, 119–20, 122–5, 126
Winti (Suriname) 50
Wiz Khalifa 143
women: dancehall style 28; enslaved population 125; female wine 119–22; in/securities 89–92; perspectives 89–92; video light on 106, 106; warrior wo/men 43–7, 53n17; wine 119–22
'Work Work' song 32
World Clash events 143
World Dance (Bogle) 88

World Reggae Dancehall Competition 37, 38
Wright, B.-S. 91, 93
wukkin'up in Barbados 119–20

Xpressionz, S. 92
Xpressionz Thursday 95

Yanvalou (Haiti) 50
Yellowman 119
Yeng Yeng on Fridays 41
Yoruba Orishas 43, 53n19

Yoruba religion 43, 114, 115
You Got Served 33
YouTube 29, 30, 47, 113, 143

zero tolerance approach 145, 146
zight 43, 47–9, 53n18
Zika virus 3
Zips, W. 97n14
Zones of Special Operations (ZOSO) 146–7
zouk 126

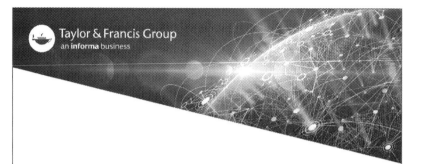

Printed in the United States
by Baker & Taylor Publisher Services